Human Dignity, Human Rights, and Social Justice

Zhibin Xie · Pauline Kollontai ·
Sebastian Kim
Editors

Human Dignity, Human Rights, and Social Justice

A Chinese Interdisciplinary Dialogue with Global Perspective

Springer

Editors
Zhibin Xie
Shanghai, China

Pauline Kollontai
York, UK

Sebastian Kim
Pasadena, CA, USA

ISBN 978-981-15-5080-5 ISBN 978-981-15-5081-2 (eBook)
https://doi.org/10.1007/978-981-15-5081-2

This Springer imprint is published by the registered company Springer Nature Singapore Pte Ltd.
The registered company address is: 152 Beach Road, #21-01/04 Gateway East, Singapore 189721, Singapore

Acknowledgements

The Editors wish to acknowledge those who contributed to the symposium series on human rights and social justice: one is the "International Symposium on Religion and Social Justice" in Shanghai 2015, organized by the Institute of Christian Culture, Academy of European Cultures, Tongji University (Shanghai, P. R. China), the Institute of Sino-Christian Studies (Hong Kong, P. R. China) and the Center for Religion in Society, York St. John University (United Kingdom) and the other is the "International Symposium on Dignity, Morality and Rights: Christian Theology, Interdisciplinary Studies and Inter-cultural Dialogue" in Hong Kong in 2017, organized by the Institute of Sino-Christian Studies, the Center for Christian Studies at The Chinese University of Hong Kong, the Center for Religion in Society at York St. John University, the Public and Contextual Theology Research Center at Charles Sturt University (Australia), the Center for Theology and Public Issues at University of Otago (New Zealand), and MF Norwegian School of Theology (Norway). The chapters included in this volume are selected and developed from the papers from these two symposiums.

In particular, we wish to thank Prof. Kjetil Fretheim, Prof. Clive Pearson, Prof. Zhouxing Sun, Prof. David Tombs, Prof. Francis Yip, and Mr. Daniel Yueng for their support to the symposiums. We also would like to recognize the involvement of those scholars in the symposiums: Prof. Honglin Chen, Prof. Jason Lam, Prof. Xin Leng, Prof. Quan Li, Prof. Monghong Lin, Prof. Robin Lovin, Dr. Joshua Mauldin, Prof. Michelle Miao, Prof. Diane Obenchain, Prof. Jiajun Qiu, Prof. Milton Wan, and Prof. Chuanxing Wang. We would like to thank Dr. Lasma Latsone for her efficient and skilled assistance with editing and proofreading. Thanks are also due to the staff of Springer for their support for the publication of the volume.

Introduction

Themes: Human Dignity, Human Rights, and Social Justice

In the Chinese and other global contexts today, social justice has been a significant topic among many disciplines and we believe it is an appropriate topic for philosophers, theologians, legal scholars, and social scientists to sit together, discuss, enrich each other, and then deepen our understanding of the topic. On the one hand, there are traditional religious teachings about justice concerning the poor, slaves, and the oppressed. On the other hand, more recent approaches to social justice come from the perspectives of moral philosophy, political philosophy, law, sociology, etc., highlighting the themes of distribution, procedures, equality, rights, pluralism, culture, community, etc. The aim of promoting social justice in practice is one area which the United Nations (UN) continues to work on. Its "World Day of Social Justice" (February 20) is one of the ways the UN continues to promote development and human dignity in face of serious challenges including insecurity, poverty, exclusion, and inequality within and among societies. As its document states, "social development and social justice are indispensable for the achievement and maintenance of peace and security within and among nations and that, in turn, social development and social justice cannot be attained in the absence of peace and security or in the absence of respect for all human rights and fundamental freedoms."[1]

In academia, there are a lot of discourses on the conjuncture between social justice, human rights, and human dignity. The questions this book asks are: what's the place of human rights in social justice? How is human dignity important in the discourse on human rights? And, through these inquiries, we ask further: how is possible to achieve humanist justice?

A crucial issue arising from social justice is human rights, even though there are debates about the connection between justice and human rights. This volume is sympathetic with Nicholas Wolterstorff's idea of "justice as grounded ultimately on

[1]See https://undocs.org/A/RES/62/10 [accessed December 19, 2019].

inherent rights."[2] His main concern is "to speak for the wronged of the world….to see the faces and hear the voices of those who are wronged."[3] To this end, his ideal is distinctive from distributive and communicative justice.[4] While this volume examines various issues of social justice in different contexts, it concentrates on the problem of human right and its "human" aspect.

We then come to the central question of the morality of human rights, as Michael J. Perry states, "[a]lthough it is only one morality among many, the morality of human rights has become the dominant morality of our time."[5] The idea and practice of human rights demands our understanding of humanity herself. The morality of human rights, particularly the theme of human dignity is crucial in the rights talk. We recognize the role of human dignity in human rights discourse is indispensable but also rather controversial.

According to Michael Freeman's summary, there is some consensus on the characteristic of human rights, i. e., "(1) they are universal: everyone has human rights; (2) everyone has them equally; and (3) they are the rights of individuals."[6] Still, there is partial consensus on the relevance of human dignity to human rights, "Human rights may be grounded in the value of human dignity, but the justification of human rights must provide arguments that lead us from human dignity to human rights."[7] As "human rights may have various justifications,"[8] other reasons such as moral actions, human sympathy, and human flourishing also support human rights in their own ways. Despite these, it is recognized that "we would give human dignity a very fundamental role in the understanding of human rights"[9] even though we need to give careful clarification of the meaning of human dignity itself.[10] Marcus Düwell further proposes that human dignity as categorical demand for ordering legal and political institutions, "To see human rights as based on or derived from respect for human dignity would here be the recognition that it is morally required to respect human dignity, to ensure the legal provisions of the human rights would be an institutionalized answer to this moral requirement."[11]

In this regard, while we see human dignity has its own constitutional value and constitutional right,[12] a lot of efforts have been made to connect human rights,

[2]Wolterstorff [1].

[3]Ibid., ix.

[4]Ibid.

[5]Perry [2].

[6]Freeman [3].

[7]Ibid., p. 69.

[8]Ibid., 87.

[9]Düwell [4].

[10]Marcus Düwell clarifies human dignity in three senses: as a right, as a norm, and as a principle. It is in the third sense which provides "unique status as the primary source of moral and legal obligations" and "guiding for the interpretations of the entire set of human rights." Ibid., p. 30.

[11]Ibid., p. 32.

[12]See Aharon Barak, trans., Kayros [5]. This volume explores the sources of human dignity as a legal concept and its role in constitutional documents in different locations.

human dignity, and human nature,[13] to affirm the value of human dignity for common humanity and the justification for various forms of human rights,[14] and to endorse that "The notion of human dignity is intimately connected to the cornerstones of modern human rights thinking."[15] In particular, Perry expounds the twofold meaning of human dignity for human rights, "…to say that (1) every human being has inherent dignity and we should live our lives accordingly (that is, in a way that respect our dignity) is to say that (2) every human being has inherent dignity is inviolable: not-to-be violated, in the sense of 'violate' just indicated."[16]

While we explore the connections between human dignity, human rights, and social justice, we have to acknowledge this investigation should be conducted from various disciplinary and cultural perspectives. As John Witte suggests, "The task of defining the appropriate ambit of human dignity and human rights must be a multi-disciplinary, multi-religious, and multi-cultural exercise."[17] Freeman also expresses the idea of human rights as a topic which different disciplines engage in and should work together for by saying "the concept of human rights lies in the domain in which normative philosophy, law and social science meet" and "human-rights law is inadequate without support from the social sciences; and the social sciences are inadequate without from philosophy."[18]

From cultural and religious perspectives, the issues of social justice and human rights are studied by different religions and through inter-religious dialogue. In the case of Christianity, the topic of social justice has been considered one that public theology has to address. Nicholas Sagovsky claims, "Since the end of the Second World War, one crucial task for public theology has been to support the institutions and political practice of democratic states publicly committed to social justice. A key task for public theology today is to articulate in a secular public sphere the fundamental Christian commitment to the struggle for social justice."[19] This public theological commitment is also to include the issue of human rights. John Witte highlights the contribution of Christianity to the public discourse on the scope and

[13]Mieth [6].

[14]See Gilabert [7].

[15]Roger Brownsword, "Human Dignity from a Legal Perspective," in Düwell, et al. eds., *The Cambridge Handbook of Human Dignity*, p. 1.

[16]Perry, *Towards a Theory of Human Rights,* p. 6.

[17]Witte [8].

[18]Freeman, *Human Rights: An Interdisciplinary Approach*, pp. 117–118.

[19]Sagovsky [9]. Also see Forrester [10]. Of course, we need to be aware of the relation of various religions to social justice, see Palmer [11].

substance of human rights protections[20] while he simultaneously attempts to discover the engagement with human rights by different religious resources.[21] Among these resources, and in the Chinese context, Confucianism provides its own understanding of social justice and human rights.[22] We believe this multi-disciplinary, multi-cultural, and multi-religious method will contribute to the understanding of the complex, the richness, and challenge regarding social justice and human rights and its inherent problem of human dignity.

Rationale for the Volume

This volume addresses the questions raised above through philosophical, theological, sociological, political, and legal perspectives and these are placed in dialogue between the Chinese and other global settings. We are concerned with the norms regarding human dignity, human rights, and social justice while we take seriously into account their practice. This volume presents the significance, challenges, and constraints of human dignity in human rights and social justice, rather than simply support or undermine their affinity. In this way, we aim to further the discourse.

This volume consists of two main sections. The first section examines Chinese perspectives on human rights and social justice, in which both from Confucianism and Christianity are considered and the issues such as patriotism, religious freedom, petition, social protest, the rights of marginalized people, and sexual violence are studied. Several questions regarding the theory and practice of human rights and social justice in the Chinese context are raised: What's the role of social justice in Confucianism? What's the Confucian contribution to human rights and human dignity in light of human nature and virtues? What's the contribution and limitations of Christian theology on humanity and love, in particular, in understanding the problem of human rights and social justice in China? What's the role of political authority and governance in the protection of human rights (including religious rights)? What kind of state-society relations can advance social justice and human rights in China? These studies demonstrate the significance of such ideas as the communal aspect of social justice, benevolent rule, virtue approach to human rights, affective care in governance, and a loving, forgiving, and dignified manner in pursuing justice and human rights in the Chinese context.

---

[20]Witte and Latterell [12]. Also see Witte and Alexander [13].

[21]See Witte and Green [14].

[22]On social justice, see Joseph Chan, "Confucianism: Historical Settings," in Palmer, ed., *The Wiley-Blackwell Companion to Religion and Social Justice*, pp. 77–92 and Stephen C. Angel, "Confucianism: Contemporary Expression," in Palmer, ed., *The Wiley-Blackwell Companion to Religion and Social Justice,* pp. 93–109. On human rights, see de Bary and Weiming [15]. One example of comparative study on human rights between Confucianism and Christianity is Lai [16]. On human dignity, a good example is Zhang [17].

Many of the authors of the second section are Christian public theologians. They examine the influence of Christian thought and practice in the issues of human rights and social justice descriptively and prescriptively and address issues such as religious laws and rights, diaconia, majoritarianism, general equality, social-economic disparities, and climate justice from global perspectives including in the contexts of America, Australia, Israel, and Europe. Several points are addressed here: common good, human responsibilities, Christian responsibility, social diversity, etc.

The contributors to this volume are from mainland China, Hong Kong, South Korea, Australia, New Zealand, United Kingdom, Norway, and the United States, etc. Their various academic disciplines and contextual geographical locations provide important cross-cultural and interdisciplinary insights and perspectives on the challenges and opportunities of human dignity, human rights, and social justice in theory and practice. Many points of common concerns regarding the topic draw these essays together such as the human aspect of human rights, Christian identity, the problem of minority or marginalized people, the relation between individual, community, and state, all of which contribute to our thinking and efforts toward a responsible and humanistic social justice in our world today. It is our hope that this volume will open up a conversation on the public, social, and moral issues in global settings from Christian, Confucian, and different disciplines' perspectives while engaging the ideas developed in the West from special Chinese context and issues. We look forward to further engagement from those scholars who are interested in the roles of religions in the public sphere, the interface, and inter-relationship of religion, politics, and society, and Chinese culture, religion, and society.

References

1. Nicholas, W. (2008). *Justice: Rights and wrongs* (p. 21). Princeton and Oxford: Princeton University Press.
2. Michael, J. P. (2007). *Towards a theory of human rights: Religion, law, courts* (p. 4). Cambridge University Press.
3. Michael, F. (2011). *Human rights: An interdisciplinary approach* (p. 68). Cambridge: Polity Press.
4. Marcus, D. (2014). Human dignity: Concepts, discussions, philosophical perspectives. In D. Marcus, B. Jens, B. Roger, & M. Dietmar (Eds.), *The Cambridge handbook of human dignity: Interdisciplinary perspectives* (p. 30). Cambridge, UK: Cambridge University Press.
5. Aharon, B., trans. D. Kayros. (2015). *Human dignity: The constitutional value and the constitutional right.* Cambridge: Cambridge University Press.

6. Corinna, M. (2014). The double foundation of human rights in human nature. In A. Marion, H. Thomas, & R. Jörn (Eds.), *Human rights and human nature* (pp. 11–22). Springer.
7. Pablo, G. (2018). *Human dignity and human rights* (p. 119). Oxford: Oxford University Press.
8. John, W. (1999). Rights in the Western tradition. In F. Erwin et al. (Eds.), *The Encyclopedia of Christianity* (vol. 4, p. 708), Grand Rapids, MI: Wm. B. Eerdmans; Leiden, Netherlands: Brill.
9. Sagovsky, N. (2015). Public theology, the public sphere and the struggle for social justice. In S. Kim, & K. Day (Eds.), *A companion to public theology* (p. 251). Leiden and Boston: Brill.
10. Forrester, D. B. (1997). *Christian justice and public policy*. Cambridge: Cambridge University Press.
11. Palmer, M. D. (Ed.). (2012). *The Wiley-Blackwell companion to religion and social justice*. Hoboken: John Wiley & Sons.
12. Witte Jr., J., & Latterell, J. J. (2015). Christianity and human rights: Past contributions and future challenges. *Journal of Law and Religion*, *3*(30), 353–385.
13. Witte Jr., J., & Alexander, F. S. (Eds.). (2010). *Christianity and human rights: An introduction*. Cambridge University Press.
14. Witte Jr., J., & Green, M. C. (Eds.). (2012). *Religion and human rights*. Oxford and New York: Oxford University Press.
15. De Bary, Wm. T., & Weiming, T. (Eds.). (1998). *Confucianism and human rights*. New York: Columbia University Press.
16. Lai, P.-C. (2013). Human rights and confucian—christian dialogue. *Studies in Interreligious Dialogue*, *2*(23), 133–149.
17. Zhang, Q. (2016). *Human dignity in classical chinese philosophy*. New York: Palgrave Macmillan.

Contents

Editors and Contributors

About the Editors

Zhibin Xie received his doctorate from The University of Hong Kong and is Professor of Philosophy at Tongji University, Shanghai, P.R. China. He is a Research Fellow of the Institute of Sino-Christian Studies (Hong Kong) and a member of the Center of Theological Inquiry in Princeton. His research interests include Christian philosophy and ethics, public theology, religion and politics in China. His major publications include *Religious Diversity and Public Religion in China* (in English, 2006), *Public Theology and Globalization: A Study in Max Stackhouse's Christian Ethics* (in Chinese, 2008), and *Why Public? How Theological? A Retrospect and Prospect for Sino-Christian Public Theology* (in Chinese, 2016). He has also published articles in a number of journals including *Asian Journal of Theology*, *International Journal of Public Theology*, *Political Theology*, and *Journal of Church and State*.

Pauline Kollontai is Professor of Higher Education in Theology and Religious Studies in the School of Humanities at York St. John University, UK. She has published in journals and been invited to contribute chapters for several edited books. She has co-edited a number of books, which include *Peace and Reconciliation: In Search of a Shared Identity* (Ashgate, 2008); *Religion Creating Cultures of Peace*, Vols. II & III (Nanumsa, 2012); *Mediating Peace: Reconciliation through Visual Art, Music and Film* (Cambridge Scholars Press, 2015); and *The Role of Religion in Peacebuilding: Crossing the Boundaries of Prejudice and Distrust* (Jessica Kingsley Publishers 2018). She is one of three series editors for a new book series published by Routledge: *Religion Matters: On the Significance of Religion in Global Issues*. In 2019, she was appointed as a resident member of the 2019 International Spring Seminar on Religion and Violence at the Centre of Theological Inquiry, Princeton, USA.

Sebastian Kim is Professor of Theology and Public Life and Assistant Provost at Fuller Theological Seminary. He is a Fellow of the Royal Asiatic Society and former Editor of the *International Journal of Public Theology*. His research interests include public theology, world Christianity, Asian theologies, and peace building. He has authored and co-authored four books: *A History of Korean Christianity* (CUP, 2015), *Theology in the Public Sphere* (SCM, 2011), *In Search of Identity: Debates on Religious Conversion in India* (OUP, 2005), and *Christianity as a World Religion* (2008 & 2016). Books he has edited include *A Companion to Public Theology* (Brill, 2017), *Cosmopolitanism, Religion, and the Public Sphere* (Routledge, 2014), and *Christian Theology in Asia* (CUP, 2008).

Contributors

Jingyang Fei School of International Relations & Public Affairs, Fudan University, Shanghai, China

Kjetil Fretheim MF Norwegian School of Theology, Religion and Society, Majorstuen, Oslo, Norway

Jieren Hu Institute of advanced Studies in Humanities and Social Sciences, Beijing Normal University, Zhuhai, Guangdong, China

Sebastian Kim Fuller Theological Seminary, Pasadena, USA

Pauline Kollontai School of Humanities, York St John University, York, UK

Lap Yan Kung Department of Cultural and Religious Studies, The Chinese University of Hong Kong, Shatin, Hong Kong, China

Pan-chiu Lai Department of Cultural & Religious Studies, The Chinese University of Hong Kong, Shatin, Hong Kong, China

Yong Li School of Philosophy, Wuhan University, Wuhan, Hubei, China

Clive Pearson Public and Contextual Theology Research Centre, Charles Sturt University, North Parramatta, NSW, Australia

James W. Skillen Center for Public Justice, Birmingham, AL, USA

R. Drew Smith Pittsburgh Theological Seminary, Pittsburgh, PA, USA

David Tombs Center for Theology and Public Issues, University of Otago, Dunedin, New Zealand

Yunping Wang School of Public Affairs, Xiamen University, Xiamen, China

Tong Wu School of Social Development, East China Normal University, Shanghai, China

Zhibin Xie School of Humanities, Tongji University, Shanghai, China

Zhifeng Zhong School of Philosophy, Renmin University of China, Beijing, China

Part I
Human Dignity, Human Rights, and Social Justice: Chinese Perspectives on Theory and Practice

Chapter 1
Individual Rights or Community? A Confucian Perspective of Social Justice

Yunping Wang

Abstract A close reading of early Confucian texts does impress us that Confucians fully appreciate the significance of livelihood of the people and distribution of economic resources, usually as the manifestation of benevolent rule. It does not mean, however, that Confucians try to figure out a framework of social justice, as what western contemporary political philosophers do with social justice. Instead, the value of emphasizing material goods and their allocation there is actually located in a specific framework in which political community is a moral community and the relation between kings and the people is the kind of care. What Confucians present us is a different picture of social justice with its underlying assumption of human nature and community, which may not be familiar in modern times but also be relevant.

Introduction

Justice is a celebrated concept in contemporary political philosophy. It seems also the only value, which is endorsed by people with different worldviews. It is well known, nonetheless, that justice has a long history.[1] It is only in contemporary political philosophy that the concern of justice is focused on distribution. John Rawls, the philosopher who dedicated his life to the philosophical argumentation of justice, takes these three terms—"justice", "distributive justice" and "social justice" as exchangeable. It follows that social justice must be in some way related to distribution. As Rawls states, his aim in *A Theory of Justice* 'is to present a conception of justice which [...] free and rational persons [...] would accept'.[2] However, the ancient

---

[1] Acknowledgement: I am indebted to Tin Ka Ping Foundation in HK for inviting me for a short-term research visit in Department of Religion and Philosophy in HKBU in 2015. I am grateful for Prof. Kuan Kai Man, Prof. Lo Ping Cheung, Dr. Ellen Ying Zhang, Dr. Ng Yau-nang and Dr. Kwok Wai Luen for their hospitality and helpful comments on the earlier draft of this article.

[2] Rawls [15, p. 11].

Y. Wang (✉)
School of Public Affairs, Xiamen University, 422 South Siming Road, Xiamen 361005, P. R. China
e-mail: wyunping@xmu.edu.cn

Z. Xie et al. (eds.), *Human Dignity, Human Rights, and Social Justice*,
https://doi.org/10.1007/978-981-15-5081-2_1

Confucian ethics do not share the assumptions with modern philosophers such as 'free and rational persons', which have strong implication of individual rights. Then, one may be curious about what Confucians would have said about "social justice" which is so topical a issue today? What would be the image of social justice from the Confucian perspective? Will that image have any modern relevance? This paper aims to provide some exploration showing that the Confucian understanding of social justice carries with it a communal characteristic, which is closely related to its pursuit of a good life with its underlying assumption of a holistic human nature.

A Literature Review: Confucian Idea of Social Justice

In recent years, some scholars with Confucian expertise try to make a connection between Confucian ethics and social justice, more exactly to figure out a Confucian understanding of social justice, among whom Joseph Chan is a leading one. Chan argues that in contemporary discussion on Confucianism, the theme of distributive justice has been seriously ignored. The reason is that Confucian politics is often taken as the extension of Confucian ethics, and that the state is believed to be the extension of the family. Chan argues that this is not true. According to Chan, Confucianism also consists of some essential political principles and strategies, including those of distribution. Moreover, proper distribution of economic resources is central to a benevolent rule. Based on the above understanding, Chan insists both that a framework of Confucian social justice could be reconstructed and that the reconstruction could be done without presupposing the liberal concept of person and community as Rawls holds, or assuming the fewest philosophical presuppositions about human nature, personhood, and community.[3] In his newly published book *Confucian Perfectionism*, Chan brings the Confucian idea of social justice into his more comprehensive project of Confucian perfectionism. He argues that due to the fact that the idea of benevolent rule occurred earlier than Mencius, taking care of people's livelihood is not merely a natural display of a ruler's virtue, but rather the objective requirement of legitimate authority. Therefore, benevolent rule is the prescribed duty of all rulers and the essential foundation of political authority. It is a political obligation ordained by Heaven. And what lies in the centre of benevolent rule is the distribution of economic resources.[4] Through interpretation of some relevant passages in *Mencius* and *Xunzi*, Chan summarizes the main principles of a rudimentary Confucian perspective on social justice:

1. Sufficiency for all: Each household should have an amount of resources sufficient to live a materially secured and ethical life.
2. Priority to the badly off: People who fall below the threshold of sufficiency—those who have special needs and are badly off—should have priority in being taken care of.

[3]Chan [2, p. 262].

[4]Ibid., [3].

3. Merit and contribution: Offices and emolument should be distributed according to an individual's merits and contributions; any subsequent inequality of income is not illegitimate.[5]

Moreover, these principles, according to Chan, fit perfectly with Confucian perfectionist conception of the good life in the sense that good life requires material resources. It is exactly right here that we identify the importance of distribution. Further, Chan argues, Mencius' ideal of society combines justice and care in which government, family and community work together as a multi-layer system for the purpose of distribution.

Chan's reconstruction of Confucian social justice is vigorous and reasonable. Nonetheless, it is not without doubt. First, he says that the Confucian principles of social justice are not about equality but about "sufficiency". Then the problem comes whether sufficiency can serve as an alternative of equality?[6] Second, and more important, if there is a concept of social justice in Confucianism, then what the justification for that concept will be? In other words, what is the role of the so-called social justice in the Confucian perfectionist framework? The answer to the latter question may give us clue to the former one.

For the latter question, we can refer to the Mainland scholar Tian Chenshan. Tian tries to grasp the difference between Chinese "rightness, righteousness" (*zheng, yi*) and the western "social justice" through the lens of world outlook, epistemology and value system. According to his understanding, the basis of western social justice is the assumption of equality, which sees persons as separate individuals with rather conflicting than inter-dependent and inseparable interests. He writes, 'Chinese 'justice' is always understood in the sense of inter-relations and therefore always appeals to returning to propriety, rather than to get something from outside'.[7] In a word, in Tian's conceptual framework, western concept of social justice, taken as a whole, is attached to a special world outlook which is dual, transcendental and one-directed, advocating equality and getting from the outside, while the Chinese sense of justice is attached to a world outlook which is not dual but inter-related, with the value focusing on the inseparableness of individuals and the derived equality and mutual offering.

The relevance of Tian's view is that, on the one hand, when we try to interpret or reconstruct Confucian understanding of social justice, we should keep in our mind the Confucian context or conceptual framework; on the other hand, we have to consider the extent to which that understanding could be granted its independent status. How should we interpret the Confucian understanding systematically having a dialogue with the modern social justice? This is not an easy question. Although Chan's effort in digging into Confucianism and figuring out Confucian sense of social justice is really appreciable, it is also controversial.

Along the way of questioning Chan's effort, there are some equally distinguished Confucian scholars, among them Ruiping Fan is well-known. For many years Fan

---

[5]Ibid., pp. 175–176, Chan [3, pp. 175–176].

[6]I will return to this point later in the third section.

[7]Tian [18, p. 76].

has been concentrating not only on uncovering but whole-heartedly practicing Confucian values. His interpretation of Confucian bio-ethics, for example, has strong explanatory power and practicability.[8] According to Fan, Confucian ethics cannot be interpreted in modern conceptual framework. Concerning the theme of social justice, Fan's basic idea is that even if Confucians are concerned about justice, this concern is not a primary one:

> Procrusteanly put, for Rawls social justice primarily concerns the way of society in which to distribute instrumental goods; for Confucians it primarily concerns the manner of society in which to pursue intrinsic goods. As both need principles to explicate their theories, Confucius set forth the general principle of *ren*,[9] whereas Rawls proceeds to elaborate upon his two principles of distribution.'[10]

Therefore, he argues that we cannot fully understand Confucianism without mentioning its presupposition about human nature. In his recently published book, Fan strengthens his persistent standpoint that the particular Confucian understanding of human nature and its implications for human society does not allow a focus on distribution of social goods, although the distribution of some goods may be important and must be involved in Confucian view of social justice.[11] Fan insists that Confucian view of general justice is not primarily about the distribution of some instrumental goods. Rather, its focus is on internal goods, which constitute the good of humans in a fundamental sense. Among the list of such goods, we may identify individual rights and liberties, but not economic values such as money and income.[12]

This obviously puts to use the terms popular in contemporary political philosophy, especially those of Alasdair MacIntyre's interpretation of Aristotelian virtue ethics. We may doubt why the list of Confucian internal goods may include "individual rights and liberties" but not "money and income". Does Fan imply that individual rights and liberties are compatible with Confucian value system? If that is the case, then how? However, the real point is that in Fan's eyes, the Confucian concept of justice is a comprehensive rather than a distributive one. And the present-day sense of distributive justice or social justice cannot become a major concern of Confucians. This view seems to contradict Chan's interpretation project, although he does not try to isolate his Confucian understanding of social justice from the Confucian context. This pulls us back to the Confucian context to see what Confucians say about social justice.

---

[8]Fan [8].

[9]*Ren* is the key virtue of Confucian ethics, usually translated as benevolence.

[10]Fan [6, p. 434].

[11]Ibid., [7, p. 47].

[12]Fan [7, p. 48].

An Exploration of Confucian Texts

Two notes need to be added here. First of all, to avoid complicity, I confine Confucian texts to pre-Qin classics, meaning early Confucian texts. Secondly, my interpretation will not be limited to certain terms of original Confucian texts but rather I will take the whole Confucian conceptual framework as the background. Scholars often like to appeal to some terms like 'righteousness (*yi*义)' to figure out Confucian idea of justice. The problem is that at least in *Mencius*, *yi* does not contain a unitary meaning, even harder it can be directly translated to justice. As Sor-hoon Tan says, it is not appropriate to translate *yi* to social justice as what *yi* deals with is personal relationship.[13] Similarly, Shen Shunfu maintains that *yi* in Mencius is merely a moral concept instead of justice. Mencius' *yi* is an incomplete duty. It is a prior rather than empirical personal virtue.[14] The Taiwan scholar Chen Ruoshui did a comprehensive examination of the concepts of *gong* (public) and *yi* throughout Chinese history but did not find a similar connotation between these two words and social justice.[15]

Reading Confucian classics easily impresses us that wealth is one of the most important concerns of early Confucians, who often make connection between wealth and virtue, just as the old saying tells: 'with adequate food and clothing, people will naturally know the honour or disgrace'. Confucius says, 'Riches and honours are what men desire […] Poverty and meanness are what men dislike'.[16] It means that wealth has a positive value. Nevertheless, 'Riches and honours acquired by unrighteousness are to me as a floating cloud'.[17] Therefore, the attitude towards wealth and the way of approaching it could be a criterion to testify one's virtue, saying, 'The mind of the superior man is conversant with righteousness; the mind of the mean man is conversant with gain'.[18] However, for the common people material goods are necessary. They cannot be expected to be like the superior man whose objective is truth rather than food.[19] Seeing people are numerous, Confucius urges to enrich them and teach them.[20]

[13]Tan [17, p. 489].

[14]Shen [16, p. 168].

[15]Chen [4, p. 158].

[16]*The Analects* 4:5.

[17]Ibid., 7:16.

[18]Ibid., 4:16.

[19]Ibid., 15:32.

[20]Ibid., 13:9.

Confucians Fully Appreciate the Importance of Wealth (and its Distribution)

Mencius realizes that:

> The way of the people is this—If they have a certain livelihood, they will have a fixed heart. If they have not a certain livelihood, they have not a fixed heart. And if they have not a fixed heart, there is nothing which they will not do in the way of self-abandonment, of moral deflection, of depravity, and of wild license.[21]

Certain livelihood is directly related to people's heart and therefore indispensable. We can elaborate the Confucian emphasis on the importance of wealth in two ways.

Negative Way

Mencius takes rulers as 'people's parent' with the expectation that they can take care of the people just as parents taking care of their children. However, in numerous situations, Mencius expresses his disappointment and blames his contemporary rulers by lamenting 'Where is his parental relation to the people?' Here are some examples:

> When the parent of the people causes the people to wear looks of distress, and, after the whole year's toil, yet not to be able to nourish their parents, so that they proceed to borrowing to increase their means, till the old people and children are found lying in the ditches and water channels: – where, in such a case, is his parental relation to the people?[22]
>
> King Hui of Liang said: 'I wish quietly to receive your instruction'. Mencius replied, 'Is there any difference between killing a man with a stick and with a sword?' The King said: 'There is no difference'. 'Is there any difference between doing it with a sword and with the style of government?' The king's reply was: 'There is no difference'. Mencius said: 'In your kitchen there is fat meat; in your stables there are fat horses. But your people have the look of hunger, on the wilds there are those who have died of famine. This is leading on beasts to devour men. Beasts devour one another, and men hat them for doing so. When a prince, being the parent of his people, administers his government so as to be chargeable with leading on beasts to devour men…[23]

Once when there had been a brush between Zou and Lu, the prince Mu of Zou did not understand why none of the people would die in defence of his thirty-three officers who were killed in the field and asked Mencius how to deal with this hard situation—to punish the people or not. Mencius replied that,

> In calamitous years and years of famine, the old and weak of your people, who have been found lying in the ditches and water-channels, and the able-bodied who have been scattered about to the four quarters, have amounted to several thousands. All the while, your granaries, O prince, have been stored with grain, and your treasuries and arsenals have been full, and not one of your officers have told you of the distress…[24]

---

[21] *Mencius* 5:3.

[22] Ibid., 5:3.

[23] Ibid., 1:4.

[24] Ibid., 2:12.

It is often through accusing his contemporary rulers who abandoned their people for the sake of enlarging their territory and so on, that Mencius expresses his expectation of benevolent rule in which rulers serve as ‘parent of the people’, especially in the sense that they will take good care of their people’s material life. Mencius often appeals to the ancient-present contrast to highlight his present day’s situation in which the latter rulers are violent and selfish.[25] He writes,

> When contentions about territory are the ground on which they fight, they slaughter men, till the fields are filled with them. When some struggle for a city is the ground on which they fight, they slaughter men till the city is filled with them. This is what is called ‘leading on the land to devour human flesh.’ Death is not enough for such a crime. Therefore, those who are skilful to fight should suffer the highest punishment…[26]

Positive Way

Confucius comments with appreciation of Zi Chan, a politician in Spring and Autumn Period explicitly, ‘that he had four of the characteristics of a superior man’, one of which is ‘in his nourishing the people’.[27] He admires a man who ‘extensively confers benefits on the people, and able to assist all […] has qualities of a sage’.[28] In a word, for Confucians, the basic idea is to nourish people just as the nature nourishes trees. For the ways of nourishing, we can see that Mencius and Xuanzi put forward different measures, including conferring people land, reducing taxes and taking care of the weak.

Mencius suggests the proper scale of livelihood a ruler with wisdom and virtue should formulate for the people. The scale is proper in that age in the sense that if farming season is not interfered then a family will have enough to feed the family members, including the aged and the kids, escaping death even in a famine year, and then involving in education of virtues. In Mencius’ own words,

> An intelligent ruler will regulate the livelihood of the people, so as to make sure that, above, they shall have sufficient wherewith to serve their parents, and, below, sufficient wherewith to support their wives and children; that in good years they shall always be abundantly satisfied, and that in bad years they shall escape the danger of perishing. After this he may urge them, and the will proceed to what is good, for in this case the people will follow after that with ease.[29]

Other than regulating the livelihood of the people, an intelligent ruler also needs to pay attention to taxation, whose principle is light rather than heavy in order to make people rich.[30] Generally speaking, if a ruler can put into practice a benevolent

[25] See *Mencius* 14:8.

[26] Ibid., 7:14.

[27] *The Analects* 5:16.

[28] Ibid., 6:30.

[29] *Mencius* 1:7.

[30] Ibid., 13:23.

rule, loving people, sparing in the use of punishments and fines, making the taxes and levies light, then he will not have any enemy and has no need to go to war.[31] Mencius emphasizes this point by referring to the ancient King Wen's governance which 'more importantly [...] takes care of four kinds of people: widows, widowers, solitaries and orphans, being among the weakest people'.[32]

Xunzi writes more realistic and calmer. But Xunzi shows the similar concern with people's livelihood. He writes, 'Heaven covers and Earth bears everything, among which nothing cannot be fully explored and their utility exhausted, thus the abundance obtained for decorating the intelligent people in the upper while feeding the people and making them happily ease. This is called the great order'.[33] If a ruler could make a good use of the material, then an ideal situation could occur. Xunzi also proposes to enrich the country and the people by making the agricultural taxes light and customs and market tax rate decreasing, reducing requisition manpower, no interference to farming season.[34] To the above scheme, he adds, as Mencius does, some further ways such as to bring up orphans and the solitary and subsidize the poor.[35]

A Confucian Justification for the Importance of Wealth and its Distribution

As the statements above show, Confucians lay stress on the importance of the people's livelihood and more generally on economic goods and their assignment. What is the reason for that emphasis? This requires more careful and deeper observation. It is true that, just as Chan points out, benevolent rule and loving the people is not merely a natural manifestation of the ruler's virtue but an ordained command of *tian* (Heaven). Confucian *tian* is not personalized Heaven or God. 'Heaven does not speak. [...] Heaven sees according as my people see; Heaven hears according as my people hear'.[36] If we want to know Heaven's will, we should turn to see the living condition of the people. If it is the case that the people have the look of hunger, on in the wilds there are those who have died of famine, then we can infer that Heaven is not happy with this and will not confer the throne to the ruler. Then, does Heaven here in Confucian context have a deontological connotation? It seems not. The Confucian Heaven is rather an ethicized but not an independent and transcendental existence like God in the Bible. Another thing is that, if it is like what Chan says, that the benevolence rule and loving the people is the ruler's political obligation, then there should be accordingly the political duty of the people.

---

[31] Ibid., 1:5.

[32] Ibid., 2:5.

[33] *Xunzi* 9:17. All translations of *Xunzi* are mine.

[34] Ibid., 10:4.

[35] Ibid., 9:4.

[36] *Mencius* 9:5.

However, Mencius seldom talks about the political duty of the people. His talking is always about the rulers. Moreover, Mencius emphasizes repeatedly the importance of benevolence and righteousness instead of benefit when he talks to his present-day kings. It follows that benevolence and righteousness are not the greatest benefits but independent of the consideration of benefits. In my view, hardly Mencius can be considered as consequentialist.[37]

Then, for what reasons do Confucians show such a great concern with the living conditions of the people and the distribution of the wealth? We can observe that Mencius often appeals to the ancient sage kings to inspire the ruler's wisdom and conscience. He says that, 'Yu thought that if any one in the empire were drowned, it was as if he drowned him. Ji thought that if any one in the empire suffered hunger, it was as if he famished him. It was on this account that they were so earnest'.[38] When King Hui of Liang came to Mencius with distress and confusion asking why he did exert his mind to the utmost in the following example that 'If the year be bad on the inside of the river, I remove as many of the people as I can to the East of the river, and convey grain to the country in the Inside' yet his people did not increase, Mencius points out that it is exactly because the King did not try his utmost. Mencius thinks the utmost is not simply avoiding the negative things taking place but positively encourage the people with benevolence and love. In Mencius' words, '[…] when people die, you say, 'It is not owing to me; it is owing to the year.' In what does this differ from stabbing a man and killing him, and then saying—'It was not I, it was the weapon'.[39] His point is to lead the King all the way to understand that every negative thing concerning the people's livelihood happening in his territory is not the fault of Heaven but of the King. What the King should do is to feed his people and protect them from famine in the bad year and to enable them prosperous in good years.

Does Mencius mean to say that the livelihood of the people is so significant that it constitutes the rights of the people and therefore violating the rights will result in the deprivation of the authority of the ruler? To some extent, this interpretation is reasonable, especially in the sense that Confucians appeal to the livelihood of the people almost exclusively when talking about how a ruler can become a true king. However, it is exactly because Mencius talks about a *true king* that offers us a possibly better interpretation. Just as in the case of Aristotelian *telos* where there is no sharp distinction between to be and ought to be, a king in Mencius' mind is not just a ruler in whatever sense but a true ruler who really cares for his people and lives up to the expectation of protecting his people from every danger and damage. This true king is the king who is completely immerged into a moral community in which all members, no matter a ruler or the people, love and care for each other. The community is not an aggregation of interests with the tension between the ruler and the people. It is rather a community in which every part plays its role appropriately. Mencius takes great pains to instruct the kings that in such a community a king must be a true king. So long as the king is the true king, the people will naturally be obedient. If the king

[37]Wang [19].

[38]*Mencius* 8:29.

[39]Ibid., 1:3.

is too far from the true king, then he is no longer a king but a mere fellow. According to Mencius, although Zhou of Yin is the "king" of his age (the last king of Shang Dynasty), as he outraged righteousness, he was actually amounted to a mere fellow. Therefore, when he was put to death, he was cut off just like a mere fellow.[40]

Along this line, we can explain why Mencius repeatedly recommends his present-day kings to follow the ancients who caused the people to have pleasure with themselves and could have the true enjoyment.[41] Only with the presupposition of the moral (and ideal) community can such a proposition be intelligible. This is a community in which all people live together, enjoy together and suffer together. And this kind of community must be grounded on a relational nature of human being. With a relational understanding of human nature in this community, harmony is both a feature and required. There, no one is exempted from the duty but those who are able, intelligent and superior should contribute more than the weak and the inferior do. Mencius often refers to those strong in the family rather than to everyone with the same or equal duty for the family members. In the family, the aged, wife and children must be nurtured. Here, you can identify no individualism.

Then, we can better understand why Mencius is so confident that, 'He who, using virtue, practices benevolence, is the sovereign of the empire'.[42] He who practices benevolence attracts the people who 'followed him looked like crowds hastening to market'.[43] In the Warring States Period when 'A hundred schools of thought contend', scholars are busy with promoting wisdom for governance. Mencius' idea is to get the people' hearts, and the way is 'simply to collect for them what they like, and not to lay on them what they dislike'.[44] In other words, what Mencius demands of his present-day kings is not to consider their own interests as separate from or antagonistic to those of the people. The ideal is that the kings do not prefer their own interests to those of the people, but to take interests of the people as priority, at least not to be inconsistent with their interest. Strictly, there should not be any sharp distinction between the king and the people. The king and the people are in the same community. Mencius is devoted to persuading the kings to take care of the livelihood of the people, rather than to persuading the people to be obedient and satisfied with whatever situation they are in. The reason is that in that community, the king is superior and able while the people remain passive, waiting for the supply from the king. Xunzi urges kings to manage everything well so that the whole country looks like a family in which all the members are nourished while the able nearby do not hide their talents and the people far away do not hate labouring. Each corner of this country is filled with peace and ease.[45]

Although the people are passive, they are the co-builders and at the same time the beneficiaries of the community. In a Confucian ideal or perfect society, everyone does

[40]Ibid., 2:8.

[41]Ibid., 1:2; 2:1.

[42]Ibid., 3:3.

[43]Ibid., 2:15.

[44]Ibid., 7:9.

[45]*Xunzi* 9:16.

his/her duty and every need is taken care of. It means that everyone, no matter the king or the people, will not identify himself/herself without his/her commitment to the community. In this moral community, the king practices benevolent governance and as a result provides the basic condition for the people's learning of virtue.

Therefore, while it is true that Confucians emphasize the importance of wealth and its distribution, the characteristic of the emphasis should be cautiously read. First of all, the importance lies not in meeting individual rights but in fulfilling the precondition of the people's virtue pursuit. Second, Confucians do not talk about the distribution among all people in the society. Instead the distribution in their mind is basically between the king and the people. It is not morally allowed that wealth gathered one-sidedly on the part of the king while the people suffer from starvation. Third, the emphasis is on the people's livelihood (rather than on the distribution), whose justification is a concern for the community's common good through the revelation of benevolent rule.

Seen from this perspective, the so-called Confucian view on social justice is essentially related to Confucian assumptions of human nature, community and more broadly of conception of the good and good life. As Tan expresses, 'Mencian relational ethics requires a more holistic approach to distributive problems'.[46] What the holistic approach appeals to is a society, which, ideally, in Confucius' words, 'has no litigations'.[47] A society with no litigations is surely a harmonious and well-ordered community in which the distribution, if any, will not be based on rights but rather on a communal concern.

At this point, although I am not as ambitious as Yushun Huang who, based on his interpretation of Confucian conceptual framework, does a systematic reconstruction of so-called Chinese theory of justice, I take his argument sound that the real aim of the two principles of justice he figures out is actually a happy (good) life. To understand that kind of happy (good) life, harmony must be taken as its indispensable part.[48] With harmony and a good life as its primary concern, it could be safely inferred that the Confucian understanding of justice is typically grounded on its holistic conception of human nature.

Erin M. Cline discovers that one of the deepest and most important differences between Confucian sense of justice and Rawls' one, is that the former is not limited to the concern of social justice, as in Rawls' case, but actually include concerns with legal justice, and deliberative justice.[49] This demands the Confucian emphasis, as commonly recognized, on the importance of family life and filial piety. As social life in the Confucian sense in its broadest sense shares with the nature of family and community life, a good life can never be separated from the family and the community.

---

[46]Tan [17, p. 503].

[47]*The Analects* 12:13.

[48]Huang [11].

[49]Cline [5, pp. 378–379].

The Modern Relevance of Confucian View of Human Nature and Social Justice

The above discussion has responded partly to various interpretations of Confucian social justice in the first section of this paper. I will try to have more clarifications concerned in this section in order to better understand the characteristic of Confucian position of social justice and its modern relevance.

Social Justice is Part of a Confucian Ideal Society

Let us return to the conceptual background for contemporary theory of social justice. Social justice there basically means the equal distribution of the goods (primary goods in Rawls' words) among the whole society, especially the economic goods. This kind of view is necessarily linked to the presupposition of individual rights. Obviously, without this presupposition, Confucians do not share the contemporary view of social justice. It reminds us of Samueal Fleischacker's argument that although the matter of justice is the competing claims of property, although philosophers for a long time concern themselves with the societal principles of distributing resources, it is not until quite recently that people began to take the basic structure for allocating the resources across the whole society as a matter of justice. In its earliest Aristotelian sense, Fleischacker states, "distributive justice" refers to ensure that those deserving people are rewarded in accordance with their merits, especially regarding their political status.[50] Interestedly and also insightfully, Fleischacker makes a comparison between the ancient and modern principles:

> Above all, the ancient principle has to do with distribution according to merit while the modern principle demands a distribution independent of merit. Everyone is supposed to deserve certain goods regardless of merit on the modern view; merit making is not supposed to begin until some basic goods (housing, health care, education) have been distributed to everyone.[51]

If Fleischacker is correct, then trying to identify the modern sense of social justice in Confucian context will be vain and futile. Detached from the Confucian conceptual framework, such effort cannot be promising. If Confucians do have a perspective on social justice, then that perspective amounts to say what kind of society is good, which must be related to its views on human nature and community. This Confucian view of social justice takes into account the importance of wealth and its allocation, but this concern should be in service of the more comprehensive or broader view of what a good society consists. A mere and exclusive concern with material goods and their allocation does not have any intrinsic value. Certainly, these external and instrumental goods are not dispensable. It is rather the case that neglect of them will

[50]Fleischacker [9, p. 2].

[51]Fleischacker [9, p. 5].

damage the intrinsic value of the whole society. Equally, without taking care of the people's livelihood, the king's benevolence, in this context the intrinsic good of the community, will be out of question.

Therefore, just as Sungmoon Kim argues, 'If there is any room for social justice in Confucianism, it can be found in such public policies that contribute to consolidating decent socioeconomic conditions as the prerequisite of humanity's moral enhancement'.[52] Tan also writes that, Mencius shifts our ethical attention from the popular question for distribution 'who gets what' to 'how should we relate to others'. To this statement, I add that here, the way to relate to others is specified by Confucians almost exclusively as the way a king relates to the people, surely within a distinct conception of the good life and the ideal society or polity.

The Modern Relevance of a Confucian Perspective of Social Justice

Some scholars may be ambitious enough to present Confucian ethics as an alternative to modern ethics in some of its important aspects, including social justice. It is true that with the Confucian lens, one may better find out the characteristics of modern idea of social justice and its defect. Modern theory of social justice typically emphasizes the importance of economic equality. However, as Harry Frankfurt questions during his argument for a "sufficiency" view of social justice, does economic equality itself possess the moral importance? Although economic equality is important, exaggerating its moral importance may be harmful as it is alienating. In his words, 'the doctrine of equality contributes to disorientation and shallowness of our time'.[53] To the contrary, in the doctrine of sufficiency as he advocates:

> the use of the notion of 'enough' pertains to *meeting a standard* rather than to *reaching a limit*. To say that a person has enough money means that he is content, or that it is reasonable for him to be content, with having no more money than he has. And to say this is, in turn, to say something like the following: the person does not (or cannot reasonably) regard whatever (if anything) is unsatisfying or distressing about his life as due to his having too little money.[54]

The sufficientarian view of social justice (or sufficientarianism), presented as an alternative to the principle of equality, does have some advantages. It can help to avoid the problem of distracting from what is truly important, or 'serve as a practical guide for living a happy and principled life'.[55] For an endless pursuit of external goods will reduce people's sense of contentment. However, the problem about sufficientarianism is that sufficiency is a vague concept. What counts as sufficient? We may also worry, among others, that it may become arbitrary and easily manipulated.[56] Sufficiency

[52]Kim [12, p. 28].

[53]Frankfurt [10, p. 23].

[54]Frankfurt [10, p. 37, emphasis original].

[55]Mulligan, [14, p. 1173].

[56]For a detailed discussion of this problem, see Casal [1].

seems not an alternative but supplementary of economic equality. However, these modern principles of social justice, no matter sufficiency or equality, cannot be independent of the presupposition of individual rights and therefore fall into the tension of competing rights. It is reasonable for us to believe that sufficiency is actually derivative in the sense it is something higher than economic equality, which makes the sufficiency possible. And that something goes well beyond distribution and must be gained before distribution. In this context, we may reasonably imagine that without commitment to moral community or a conception of the good life, sufficiency is not able to serve as an independent criterion, neither will the controversies about the criterion cease.

Conclusion

Returning to what Confucians say about social justice, we would be reminded that a harmonious society requires exactly that we voluntarily give up some of our rights and show our commitment to community. The modern sense of social justice may be the basic factor of a harmonious society but not the whole. Confucians convince us that a purely modern principle of social justice should be enlarged to and located in a broader picture of what a substantively good society is.

A society which prioritizes individual freedom may be full of tensions, while a society prioritizing commitment to the community may terrify us with the potential of violations of human rights. To be sure, taking the communal life as valuable, advocating a strong commitment to the community may sometimes need to set restrictions on the enjoyment of individual rights, in order to better value the harmonious relationship and to achieve a happy (good) life. This kind of restrictions may not be everywhere welcomed but could be well justified. In modern societies where prioritization of individual rights is taken for granted, Confucian deliberation on justice and its underlying assumptions of human nature and a good life not only appears intelligible by itself, it will call attention to something essentially needed for our age.

References

1. Casal, P. (2007). Why sufficiency is not enough. *Ethics, 117*(2), 296–326.
2. Chan, J. (2009). Is there a Confucian perspective on social Justice. In T. Shōgimen & C. J. Nederman (Eds.), *Western political thought in dialogue with Asia* (pp. 261–277). Lanham, MD: Lexington Books.
3. Chan, J. (2014). *Confucian perfectionism: A political philosophy for modern times*. New Jersey: Princeton University Press.
4. Chen, R. (2006). *Public consciousness and Chinese culture*. Beijing: Xinxing Press.
5. Cline, E. M. (2007). Two senses of justice: Confucianism, Rawls, and comparative political philosophy. *Dao* (6), 361–381.
6. Fan, R. (1997). Confucian and Rawlsian views of justice: A comparison. *Journal of Chinese Philosophy, 24*, 427–456.

7. Fan, R. (2010). *Reconstructionist confucianism: Rethinking morality after the west.* Springer.
8. Fan, R. (2011). *Contemporary Confucian bioethics*. Beijing: Beijing University Press.
9. Fleischacker, S. (2004). *A short history of distributive justice.* Cambridge, MA: Harvard University Press.
10. Frankfurt, H. (1987). Equality as a moral ideal. *Ethics, 98*(1), 21–43.
11. Huang, Y (2009). An outline of Chinese theory of justice. *Journal of Sichuan University (Philosophy and Social Science Edition), 5,* 32–42.
12. Kim, S. (2010). The secret of Confucian Wuwei statecraft: Mencius's political theory of responsibility. *Asian Philosophy, 20*(1), 27–42.
13. Liu, C., & Luo, Z. (1992). Chinese and English four books. (J. Legge, Trans.). Changsha: Hunan Press.
14. Mulligan, T. (2015). On Harry Frankfurt's 'Equality as a Moral Ideal'. *Ethics, 125*(4), 1171–1173.
15. Rawls, J. (1971). *A theory of justice*. Cambridge, MA: Belknap Press of Harvard University Press.
16. Shen, S. (2013). A reasonable justice: Together with on problems of Confucian justice. In *Confucian thoughts and social justice*, edited by Confucian Institute for Advanced Study in Shangdong Province, China Confucius Foundation and China Research Center in Hawaii University (pp. 154–168). Jinan: Shandong Renmin Press.
17. Tan, S. (2014). The concept of Yi (义) in the Mencius and problems of distributive justice. *Australasian Journal of Philosophy, 92*(3), 489–505.
18. Tian, C. (2013). The two 'Name and Word' stories about Chinese and western 'Social Justice'. In *Confucian thoughts and social justice*, edited by Confucian Institute for Advanced Study in Shangdong Province, China Confucius Foundation and China Research Center in Hawaii University (pp. 57–82). Jinan: Shandong Renmin Press.
19. Wang, Y. (2005). Are early Confucians consequentialists? *Asian Philosophy, 15*(1), 19–34.

Yunping Wang is Professor of Ethics and Political Philosophy at School of Public Affairs in Xiamen University, China. Her academic qualifications are in the subjects of Confucian Ethics and Public Administration Ethics. She is the author of *Ethics in Public Administration* (Beijing, 2018). Her articles on Confucian ethics and public administration ethics have appeared in several journals including the *Journal of Chinese Philosophy*, *Asian Philosophy*, *Philosophical Researches* (in Chinese), *Chinese Public Administration* (in Chinese). Her current research interest is in exploring the relationship between (Confucian) virtues and the effectiveness of public administration.

Chapter 2
Confucianism and the Foundation of Human Rights

Yong Li

Abstract This chapter argues that Confucianism is compatible with the idea of human rights. In the first section, I survey the current debates on whether Confucianism is compatible with the idea of human rights. In the second section I discuss the virtue ethics reading and the role ethics reading of Confucian moral theory. In the third section I argue that regarding one possible foundation of human rights, human dignity, Confucian idea of human nature and virtues can provide a better foundation than the idea of autonomy. In the last section I address some of the objections to this argument.

Introduction

David Wong argues that Confucianism, which has been the guiding ideology of traditional Chinese society, is a virtue-based and community-based approach that orients us towards how to become a good person and build a good society.[1] However, liberalism, which is the guiding ideology of modern western society, is a rights-based and individual-based approach that orients us towards how to become an autonomous individual and build a just society.[2] One may easily discard the above contrast as superficial and stereotypical since both traditions are complex and share elements of each set of values. However, if we look at Confucianism and liberalism as pure philosophical theories, the contrast becomes clear and powerful.

[1]An extended version of this paper was originally published by *International Philosophical Quarterly*, vol. 59: 2 (2019), pp. 175–192. Thanks also to the Institute of Sino-Christian Studies in Hong Kong for hosting my visit for writing this paper from September to December of 2017. Funding for this paper was provided by MOE (Ministry of Education in China) Project of Humanities and Social Sciences (Project No. 18YJC720009) and "the Fundamental Research Funds for the Central Universities" of Wuhan University.

[2]Wong [33, 35].

Y. Li (✉)
School of Philosophy, Wuhan University, 299 Bayi Road, Wuhan, Hubei 430072, P. R. China
e-mail: liyonginwuhan@yahoo.com

Z. Xie et al. (eds.), *Human Dignity, Human Rights, and Social Justice*,
https://doi.org/10.1007/978-981-15-5081-2_2

There are many aspects of this contrast if both are treated as philosophical theories, such as different understandings of virtues, justice, family, or government. Most comparisons would not end up implying that one theory is better than the other. However, it might seem that Confucianism lacks the resources to justify the concept of human rights, at least to the extent that Confucianism prioritizes virtues, family, and the good of the community over other values. This paper will discuss the question of whether Confucianism can embrace the idea of human rights. I will argue that Confucianism can provide a basis for human rights.

In this chapter, a human right is primarily understood as a protection. In the first part of this paper I will survey the current debates on the issue of whether Confucianism can embrace the idea of human rights. In the second part I will explain what interpretation of Confucianism and what kind of Confucianism I want to focus on. I will explore the possible resources from Confucianism and examine whether the core values of Confucianism are compatible with the idea of human rights. In the third part I will argue that Confucianism not only is compatible with human rights but also provides a foundation for human dignity, which is a basis for human rights. I argue that the Confucian virtue-based approach can overcome certain challenges that are faced by autonomy-based approach to human dignity and human rights. In the fourth part I will address some objections to this view.

Current Debates on Confucianism and Human Rights

In the current literature there are three different camps on the issue of whether Confucianism is compatible with the idea of human rights.[3] The first group claims that the idea of human rights assumes certain fundamentalism of human nature. The idea of human rights assumes that we are rational and autonomous individuals. A just society consists of rational and autonomous individuals. This group believes that the fundamentalism of human rights is wrong. A just society is rather based on relational individuals. Let's call this group Confucianism First (CF) group.[4]

A related but different claim made by the CF group is that Confucianism provides a superior alternative to this rights-based conception of the state that prioritizes human rights. People in the first camp believe that, due to various problems of liberalism, such as the difficulty of forming a cohesive community out of isolated individuals, Confucianism, which prioritizes family and relationships, can build a stronger and more flourishing community. In other words, Confucianism as a social ideal is better than the rights-based ideal society. Craig K. Ihara argues that rights are not necessary for a good community or society. For example, in a basketball team, a ballet group

[3]Stephen Angle believes that there could be three different approaches to the relation between Chinese tradition and human rights: an obstacle, an alternative, or a source. See Stephen Angle, 'Human Rights in Chinese Tradition', forthcoming [4]. My following categories are slightly different from his.

[4]I believe that Henry Rosemont [22], Daniel Bell and Roger Ames belong to this group. See also de Bary and Weiming [9]; Also, Liang [19].

or a ceremony, cooperation and the good of the team are more important. Rights are not necessary in those contexts.[5] Why can't we imagine society as a whole being organized in a similar way?

In my opinion, whether human beings by nature are rational and autonomous is an empirical question. Whether the idea of human rights derives from a particular understanding of human nature is a conceptual question. Whether a just society is based on rational and autonomous individuals is a normative question. For the empirical question, we can examine the facts and find out whether we are indeed rational and autonomous. For the conceptual question, we may find out whether there is a conceptual connection between the idea of human rights and this particular understanding of human nature. For the normative question, it would depend on how we understand the "just society".

I agree with the CF group that the fundamentalism of human nature is wrong. I do not think that human beings by nature are rational and autonomous. Recent research on developmental psychology supports more of a relational understanding of human nature.[6] However, I disagree with the CF group that Confucianism as a social ideal is better than the rights-based ideal society. If we do not have an absolutism view of a just society, rather a pluralistic view, we would recognize the plural values among different decent societies.[7]

The second group believes that Confucianism is straightforwardly incompatible with the idea of human rights.[8] However, according to this group, the incompatibility of Confucianism and rights is a reason for abandoning Confucianism, not abandoning rights. Let's call this the Human Rights First group (HRF). This was the view of Chinese intellectuals of the May Fourth Movement of the early twentieth century and continues to be the view of Chinese liberals today. As Joseph Chan points out, advocates of HRF claim that there are four Confucian reasons for rejecting the idea of human rights.[9] First, in Confucianism, there are only contextual individuals and role-based ethics. Confucianism treats each individual as the composition of different social roles. Relations define the personhood of each individual. There are no autonomous or isolated individuals. Second, an ideal society for Confucianism is an extended family. The relations among citizens are not egalitarian. Rights do not play any significant role in virtuous relationships. Rights might be only regarded with "a fallback apparatus" in the event that social norms fail.[10] Third, Confucianism advocates hierarchy and submission. There is a strong paternalism element in the Confucian concept of family, marriage and government. This is inconsistent with

[5]Ihara [15].

[6]Coplan and Godie [7].

[7]A further problem with some formulations of the CF view is that their anti-essentialist interpretation of Confucianism which does not seem well supported by classical Confucian texts. See Yu [36], Sim [24] and Wilson [32].

[8]Most liberalists in China hold this view.

[9]Chan [6].

[10]Ibid., p. 221. Justin Tiwald explores the complications with regard to the view that rights fit into Confucian institutions as a fallback apparatus. Cf: Tiwald [28]. Also, see Tiwald [27].

the egalitarian nature of human rights. Fourth, Confucianism emphasizes harmony rather than disagreement and competition. However, in an egalitarian society, citizens with rights are expected to compete for their own interests, which ends up producing litigation and many conflicts.

Seung-hwan Lee also presents three similar reasons to explain why Confucianism does not develop the idea of human rights.[11] First, the idea of self in Confucianism is closely connected to one's roles in a hierarchical society. Thus, the idea of equal human rights is not acceptable to Confucians. In other words, the kind of equality embedded in the very idea of human rights by principle is in tension with the Confucian social ideal of a hierarchical society. Second, in Confucianism, the good of a community is always more important than the good of each individual. Therefore, the demand of one's individual interests supported by the idea of human rights conflicts with the Confucian idea of an ideal community. Third, the Confucian ideal of harmony praises submission and compromises, which is in tension with the unconditional priority of one's own self-interest.

I agree with the HRF group that some concepts in Confucianism, such as society as an extended family or the social ideal of a hierarchical society, do pose prima facie challenges to an egalitarian conception of rights. However, there are many different conceptions of what rights are and how they are justified. Some of them will be consistent with certain conceptions of social harmony or hierarchy. For example, Confucian idea of universal human nature, such as Mengzi's idea of compassion, can be developed into and channeled with the idea of human rights. Also, Confucians discuss more about elitism in governing, which is different from overall paternalism. In general, I think that the HRF group has not shown that we must discard Confucians merely because Confucians historically have not developed the idea of human rights or because there are prima facie tensions between certain concepts in Confucianism and the idea of completely egalitarian rights. I do not think that Confucianism and human rights are in rivalry or exclusive with each other.

The third group believes that Confucianism is compatible with the idea of human rights. Let's call this group Confucianism and Human Rights Compatibilism group (CHRC). They claim that the fundamentalism of human rights is wrong. And Confucianism has concepts that can channel the idea of human rights.[12] However, there are several different approaches to the above thesis. Some advocates of CHRC argue that there is already a concept of rights in Confucianism. Others argue that while Confucian virtue-based ethics is completely distinct from a rights-based approach, the two systems are complementary, and a society can consistently realize both. Finally, some claim that we can find in Confucianism the resources for constructing a new foundation for rights. One of those who argue that Confucianism already appeals, at least implicitly, to a conception of rights is William Theodore de Bary. He argues that at least in Song and Ming Neo-Confucianism, human dignity and equality were well respected. Human dignity is expressed in the respect for others

[11]Lee [17].

[12]I believe that Joseph Chan, William Theodore de Bary, Sumner Twiss, and Stephen Angle belong to this group.

that is embodied in different social relationships, such as respect for elders in the family. However, Confucianism holds that differences in age, gender, social status, and political positions are relevant to justice in unequal social relationships. De Bary calls this equity rather than equality in social relationships.[13] I think that this idea of equity presents a tension with the value of equality embedded in the idea of human rights. This tension renders the above historical approach less attractive comparing to the following approaches.

Another approach to the thesis that Confucianism is compatible with the idea of human rights is to argue that Confucianism does include the idea of rights even without the terminology. Seung-hwan Lee points out that, even if there is the alleged distinction between virtue-based morality and rights-based morality, Confucianism, recognized as a virtue-based morality, still has the concept of rights. Lee argues that without the concept of rights, institutions of property and the practice of promise and contract would not have been possible in Chinese traditional society. Lee believes that the concept of rights is 'normatively necessary for a moral life (even for a fully communitarian society) and also for an ethics theory (even for a virtue-based theory)'.[14] Lee argues that despite not using the exact term "rights", Confucianism provides a good understanding of the institution of property and contract rights. For example, Mengzi claims that if a promise is made between two friends or a business contract between two contractors, both parties have obligations to fulfill the promise or the contract.[15] Lee argues that there is a working understanding of rights-duty relationship in Confucianism even though there is no straightforward expression of the term "rights". Furthermore, Lee points out that according to Mengzi, 'a government has an absolute duty of nourishing the people and maintaining peace and stability in the country, and people have rights to welfare and social security. If the government fails in its responsibilities, then the people not only need not be loyal to it, but also can make a claim against it'.[16]

However, Lee believes that individual assertion of equal rights is not encouraged in Confucianism because Confucianism values more the common good and social harmony. In response, I think that there is a clear difference between a general concept of rights and a moral specific concept of human rights. The practice of respecting private property or business transactions does not imply respecting human rights. For many countries with numerous human rights violations, they do respect private property and business transactions.

May Sim presents a third approach to the compatibility thesis between Confucianism and human rights. Sim does believe that there is a false dilemma for Asian people to choose between accepting traditional ways, such as Confucianism, and rejecting rights, and accepting rights and rejecting their traditions. Sim proposes to use A. I. Melden's idea that human rights are not based on a fixed human nature. Melden recognizes that human beings are inter-related and that every moral agent

---

[13] de Bary [8].

[14] Lee, 'Was There a Concept of Rights?, p. 242.

[15] Lee, 'Was There a Concept of Rights?', p. 247.

[16] Lee, 'Was There a Concept of Rights?', p. 248.

needs support from each other and needs to recognize each other's moral agency. Melden also looks into family as a way to explore the importance of relationship and community. Thus, Melden does not base rights on autonomous individuals. Humans are not pure Cartesian subjects of experience, immune to changes. Humans are not pure Cartesian subjects merely connected by memory either. Rather, a human being 'is born into a family and gradually extends his relations from the family to friends, acquaintances, colleagues, and strangers'.[17] Sim believes that there is a common ground between Confucianism and Melden's view on human rights.

I am sympathetic to Sim's approach. However, even if there is a common ground between Confucianism and Melden's view, we still need establish whether the relational approach to human rights is a plausible approach or an alternative to the autonomy-based approach. This needs further discussion.

A fourth approach to the compatibility thesis between Confucianism and human rights is to explore a different foundation for human rights in Confucianism. This is the approach that I endorse in this paper and will discuss in more depth later. It provides a more universal basis for human rights than other approaches, which makes Confucianism relevant in the discussion about the foundation and justification of human rights. Heiner Roetz points out that seminal figures in the development of the modern notion of rights, including Francisco Suarez, Thomas Hobbes, and John Locke all had a quite different understanding of human beings from their ancient intellectual ancestors. They derived the idea of rights from moral agency with free will. However, Roetz proposes that Confucianism could derive the idea of rights from moral agency with the potential capacity to act morally. Roetz disagrees with Roger Ames and Randall Peerenboom that moral agency can only come from achievements.[18] Roetz further explores the Confucian understanding of human dignity. In addition, Roetz argues that Mengzi's theory of human nature provides a direct connection between Chinese classical philosophy and the modern idea of human rights. And this is the only link for Roetz.[19] Mengzi argues that our empathetic capacity as the essence of human beings enables us to care for those who are not related to us. Human beings cannot be treated like other animals because of this noble moral capacity. Each individual deserves our respect due to their empathetic human nature. The moral potential in each human being to become a gentleman or a sage is the source of human dignity, which is the basis for human rights.[20] Mengzi believes that our human nature, the inner moral capacity, renders us with dignity, which provides the basis for respect and human rights. Irene Bloom further develops the idea of human moral potentials as the basis for human rights. Bloom points out that a fundamental similarity among human beings, especially a common human moral potential, 'implies a respect for persons that goes beyond, and tends to undermine, class distinctions'.[21] But Bloom believes that 'recognizing a common humanity and

[17]Sim [24, p. 341].

[18]Roetz [21].

[19]Roetz [20].

[20]Zhang [37, 38].

[21]Bloom [5, p. 98].

a similarity in moral potential implies no commitment on the part of Confucius to ultimate equality or treatment because he recognizes that the many variables involved in the process of human development may lead to different behavioral outcomes'.[22]

I am sympathetic to Roetz's and Bloom's efforts to find a Confucian foundation for human rights. However, I think that there is a tension between common humanity and unequal treatment in Confucianism. For the idea of human rights, I believe that common humanity should be treated with priority. However, the idea of unequal treatment is very complicated in Confucianism. It appears that for Confucians people should be treated differently in terms of their moral (and social) achievements. If we take a weak reading of this differential treatment, such as we treat children differently from the way we treat elders, the ideal of differential treatment sounds attractive. However, if we take a strong reading and assign rights, such as political rights, based on one's moral or social achievements, it would be problematic for an egalitarian society.

A fifth approach to the compatibility thesis is that some scholars argue that Confucianism and human rights are complimentary. They claim that virtue-based morality represented by Confucianism and rights-based morality expressed in the discussion on human rights are complimentary for a good life. Seung-hwan Lee points out that 'rights are such a dominant moral currency in our time that not only problems between one human and another human but problems between human and nonhuman subjects are also treated in terms of rights'.[23] In contrast to this liberal, rights-based morality, Confucianism provides a morality based on the virtue of caring and benevolence. Lee believes that the right is over the good for rights-based morality but that becoming a good person is over being a right-claimer for virtue-based morality. Lee concludes that it 'is not a simple choice of either rights or virtues, but a harmonious coordination of rights (as basic requirements of morality) and virtues (as counsels of moral wisdom)'.[24]

Confucianism

Whether Confucianism is compatible with the idea of human rights also partly depends on how we understand Confucianism. Historically, Confucianism went through different developments. For example, in the Song and Ming Dynasties, Confucian scholars emphasized the potential of becoming sages in each individual, promoted autonomy in local administration, and set the boundary of royal powers. All those ideas seem to be compatible with the idea of respecting each individual citizen and granting them dignities.[25]

[22]Ibid.

[23]Lee [18].

[24]Ibid., 376.

[25]Some may argue that this is far from the practice of human rights. However, those ideals make Confucianism more compatible with the idea of human rights.

As previously discussed, W. Theodore de Bary argues that at least in Song and Ming neo-Confucianism, human dignity and equality were respected to a certain degree. Seung-hwan Lee also argues that even without using the term of human rights, the institutions of property and practice of promise and contract would not have been possible in traditional Confucian society without the idea of rights. Stephen Angel also gives a thorough discussion on how the idea of rights is expressed through Confucian history. He points out that prior to the nineteenth century there was no Chinese word to translate as "rights". He also believes that there were ideas and institutions 'served functions similar to those served by rights'.[26] He explores how Confucians around nineteenth century proceed from recognizing the legitimate desires to introducing the idea of rights from Europe, then to having sustained engagement between Western and Chinese rights discourses.[27]

Besides the historical developments of Confucianism as a cultural tradition, it is also true that Confucian scholars have different interpretations of the core values of Confucianism. Take Confucian ethics for example. Bryan Van Norden reads Confucian ethics as similar to Aristotelian virtue ethics.[28] However, Roger Ames reads Confucian ethics as role-oriented moral theory.[29] Since virtue ethics seems to value individuals more while role-oriented moral theory emphasizes community, the virtue ethics reading of Confucianism seems to be more compatible with the idea of human rights.[30] However, this does not imply that the virtue ethics reading is a more accurate reading of Confucianism. Which reading is more accurate is a different question from which reading renders Confucianism more compatible with the idea of human rights.

The question whether Confucianism is compatible with the idea of human rights is a complex one. A simple answer is yes. Since there are many readings of the idea of human rights and there are different developments of the idea, how to answer the question depends on which reading, and interpretation is used. It is also true on the side of Confucianism. How to answer the question partly depends on which reading of Confucianism one endorses. In the following section I will endorse the virtue ethics reading of Confucianism and will argue that Confucianism provides an alternative foundation for human rights.

---

[26] Angle [2, p. 74].

[27] Angle, 2002. Angle discussed important Confucians, such as Huang Zongxi, Gu Yanwu, and Dai Zhen in 17th century, and Chen Duxiu in 20th century. In a different book, Angle also discussed 20th century Confucian Mo Zongsan. Angle [3].

[28] Van Norden [30].

[29] Ames [1].

[30] Some may argue that the role ethics understanding of Confucianism may be more compatible with the idea of human rights. For example, according to Pan-Chiu Lai, "Confucianism can offer an alternative interpretation of human rights that is more communitarian than individualistic, affirming human rights without neglecting responsibility to one's family and wider society". Lai [16, p. 138]. As I explained, if we take the thick idea of human rights with the human nature assumption, the individual oriented virtue ethics understanding of Confucianism seems to share the focus on individuals. Another complication is the subtle difference between role ethics and communitarian reading of Confucianism. Valuing community itself does not lead to defining personal identity as compositions of social roles.

Human Dignity as the Foundation of Human Rights: Virtues or Autonomy?

In recent decades, scholars prefer to ground human rights in human agency and autonomy. Alan Gewirth argues that having a life for a human being requires having freedom and well-being, which demands that others must respect her freedom and well-being.[31] This is the basis of human rights. James Griffin shares this idea and argues that agency and autonomy to pursue freedom and well-being would demand respect from others.[32] This is where human dignity comes from. I believe that the concept of autonomy discussed here is closely related to reason and rationality, which refers to a person's capacity to make a rational choice with regard to the ends and how to achieve the ends.[33]

In my view, the core argument that Gewirth and Griffin share is the following. Autonomy-based human rights indeed respects human agency and dignity. Here is the thread of the argument. We have human rights because we have human dignity.[34] We have human dignity because we have autonomy. We believe that the kind of autonomy that human beings have to a great degree makes human beings different from other animals. This explains why human beings deserve respect.

In general, the autonomy-based concept of human dignity and human rights faces two substantial challenges: the rights-holder problem and the incompleteness problem. If we only ascribe rights to those autonomous agents who are rational and able to make free choices, how about those who are not autonomous, such as children or mentally disabled? Also, the list of rights has expanded, and it is difficult to differentiate them from mere personal interests.[35] For example, people demand rights for public nudity. It is hard to decide which demand should be included if autonomy is the basis to justify rights.

I would challenge the view that the autonomy-based view of human dignity can successfully respond to the rights-holder problem or the incompleteness problem. Instead, I think that virtue-based human dignity theory inspired by Confucianism can meet these two substantial challenges. If we endorse the virtue ethics reading of Confucianism, the dignity of human agency can come from Confucian understanding of human nature, which is not autonomy-based. It is beyond the scope of this paper to argue which Confucian, Mengzi or Xunzi, has the correct understanding of human nature, or to argue for moral potentials or moral achievements as the key to define Confucian perception of human nature. Thus, I am making a conditional statement here: if Mengzi's understanding of human nature is correct, and if moral potentials are

---

[31] Gewirth [11].

[32] Griffin [13].

[33] I do not think that the idea of autonomy here is restricted to a moral sense. It is closely related to a broader notion of rational choice. I believe that this is quite different from the concept of autonomy in Kantian discussion, a free will subject only to self-legislated but universal laws. Cf. Guyer [14].

[34] An extensive survey of this approach can be seen in Gilabert [12].

[35] Here the challenges can be directed to moral rights or human rights. The following discussion can be applied to both moral rights and human rights.

the key to define Confucian perception of human nature, the Confucian virtue-based idea of human rights can meet the above two challenges.

Concerning the first challenge of the rights-holder problem, since moral potentials, such as empathetic capacities, have nothing to do with age, gender, race, education, culture and religion, moral potentials can attribute dignity to almost all human beings, which would then justify human rights.[36]

Regarding the incompleteness challenge, I believe that the normative ideal of being virtuous and cultivating those moral capacities can help to set a boundary of interest claims. Morality can be understood as having intrapersonal and interpersonal dimensions.[37] Moral codes are supposed to help moral agents to build personal integrity and coordinate with others. Being moral is both self-regarding and other-regarding. A virtuous person is not only concerned with one's own interests and freedom, but also is concerned with the other's well-being and freedom. So, the list of rights based on virtues would not expand along with personal interests and preferences.[38] Concern for others would set a boundary of interest claims.

Objections and Replies

My conditional statement was that, if Mengzi's understanding of human nature is correct, and if moral potentials are the key to defining Confucian perception of human nature, Confucian virtue-based conception of human rights can meet the above two challenges against the autonomy-based conception of human rights.

One can easily point out that the virtue-based human rights theory would face a new rights-holder problem. For example, if we identify empathetic capacity as the potential moral capacity for being a virtuous person, then those without empathetic capacity would not be given rights. This is against our intuition. For example, people with autism are believed to be without the empathetic capacity. Should people with autism not be given human rights? Obviously, people with autism should be accorded human rights. Thus, virtue-based human rights theory seems to be as vulnerable as autonomy-based human rights theory.

I believe that the above challenge only shows that empathetic capacity is not the defining feature of moral capacity; it does not show that virtue-based human rights theory fails. The general challenge to any ethical justification of human rights, which is to provide an anthropological property to differentiate human beings from other

[36]Since "moral potentials" brackets all the discussion of moral codes, moral relativism would not be seen as an imminent challenge to this view. The cultural or moral diversity has been regarded as a challenge to universal human rights.

[37]Wong [35].

[38]I am aware of the complications of using the terms "virtues" or "virtuous persons" here. I just focus on Confucian understanding of moral potential and moral virtues. I do believe that there are similarities among different views about virtues.

animals, is how to make the anthropological property as inclusive as possible.[39] If any human being who lacks this property is excluded from being given rights, the particular theory has to justify this exclusion.

If Jeremy believes that any human being deserves human rights, then Jeremy would not need any ethical justification of human rights. If Jeremy believes that even a moral monster, such as Hitler, deserves human rights, then Jeremy does not need to find the defining feature of human beings. Any defining feature of human beings could easily leave some people out. I believe that Jeremy has a default assumption of the special status of human beings. As long as we are human beings, we deserve human rights.

I recognize that the connection between human dignity and human rights could be understood differently. Also, there are various understandings of human dignity. For example, Jeremy Waldron points out, 'Dignity is intimately connected with the idea of rights—as the ground of rights, and the content of certain rights, and perhaps even the form and structural character of rights'.[40] However, Waldron does not think that dignity should be understood as moral worth. He embraces the conception of dignity as universalized social rank, which is a special social status. Apparently, this approach to dignity is different from the ethical approach to human dignity that relies on certain human traits.

I would therefore propose that the Confucian virtue ethics approach to human dignity can respond to the new rights-holder problem. I believe that acting morally does need a motivational component, which could be emotional or rational. For those who lack empathetic capacity, such as people with autism, they may be motivated by following moral rules.[41] The potential moral capacity refers to the emotional or rational capacity that fulfills the motivational function of a moral action.[42] I believe that most people, including people with autism, do have either a (potential) emotional or rational capacity to act morally.[43]

---

[39] There might be a generality problem. If the feature is too inclusive, the theory collapses to the "rank" idea that if one is a human being, one has human rights. If the feature is too exclusive, the theory might exclude those who should have been included.

[40] Waldron [31, p. 15].

[41] As Uta Firth points out, people with autism lack the ability to engage reciprocal social interaction, communication. They engage repetitive activities and act with narrow interests. Due to neurological deficiency, they have challenges to show joint attention. But they can learn to follow rules. Firth [10].

[42] Some may point out that I am taking a very liberal understanding of Confucian understanding of moral agency. I believe that Confucians, such as Mengzi, do have the emotional and rational component of human moral agency. For example Mengzi's discussion of the heart/mind of compassion, respect, shame, right and wrong with regard to the ethical ideals of benevolence, propriety, ritual and wisdom can be read as having emotional and rational component. Cf. Sung [26].

[43] I realize that there are many borderline cases, such as senior people who are not in a lucid state of mind. I believe that even if they cannot come back to a lucid mind, it does not imply that they do not have the (moral) ground to be given rights. In some sense, they still have moral memories or moral knowledge. Another challenge is the case of severely mentally underdeveloped. I do not think that the care for these people is based on the idea of rights, rather on the idea of needs. They

One may also point out that the virtue-based human rights theory does not provide a reasonable answer to the incompleteness problem. People may claim that it is ridiculous to set up a moral boundary for the list of rights. For example, the rights to life or property seem to be irrelevant to our moral cultivation, just like the right to freedom of religion is irrelevant to our moral cultivation either. However, Confucian virtue theorists can claim that any plausible candidate for a right should be conducive to the growth of virtues. Otherwise, it should not be included in or added to the list of rights. For example, it seems that the claim to public nudity is not conducive to one's moral growth, thus, it should not be added to the list. How about the rights to life or property? I believe that the rights to life or property are indispensible for our moral cultivation. Some of those rights are pre-conditions for our moral cultivation. The right to freedom of religion is relevant to our moral cultivation since spiritual pursuit is part of one's building of personal integrity, which is indispensible for moral cultivation. I understand that there is a danger of moralizing all our choices implied by this view. But I do believe that this is a plausible way to set the boundary for the list of rights.

Conclusion

This chapter reviews the current debates on the question of whether Confucianism is compatible with human rights with the aim of examining some of the different understandings of human rights and Confucianism relevant to this topic. My proposal mixes the good and the right, or the private and the public. Some may argue that virtues as goods belonging to the private domain, but human rights belong to the public domain. They should be separated. Whether one wants to cultivate one's moral potentials is a private decision. I believe that this objection misunderstands the proposal here. I am not arguing that one must cultivate one's moral potentials. Rather, I argue that in Confucianism our moral potentials can be the foundation of human dignity, which justifies human rights. I do not believe that moral cultivation is a categorical imperative here. Whether or how to cultivate morality is indeed in the private domain. However, I do propose that morality sets a boundary of the list of rights. This in a sense does regulate the right with the good.[44]

Confucianism can provide an alternative foundation for human rights and dignity grounded in human moral capacities. In addition, the virtue-based rather than autonomy-based idea of human rights would solve the challenges that face the latter. Confucianism is indeed compatible with the idea of human rights.

---

need protection. They need to be cared for. Treat them with dignity does not imply that we should not hospitalize them or that we should leave them alone.

[44]I believe that this is in the spirit of Confucianism. However, to discuss the complication of this implication is beyond the scope of this chapter.

References

1. Ames, R. T. (2011). *Confucian role ethics: A vocabulary*. Honolulu: University of Hawaii Press.
2. Angle, S. C., Rights, H., & Thought, C. (2002). *A cross-cultural inquiry*. Cambridge: Cambridge University Press.
3. Angle, S. C., & Philosophy, C. C. P. (2012). *Toward progressive Confucianism*. Cambridge: Polity Press.
4. Angle, S. C. (Forthcoming). *Human rights in Chinese tradition*.
5. Bloom, I. (1998). Fundamental intuitions and consensus statements: Mencian Confucianism and human rights. In W. T. de Bary & T. Weiming (Eds.), *Confucianism and human rights* (pp. 94–116). New York: Columbia University Press.
6. Chan, J. (1999). A Confucian perspective on human rights for contemporary China. In J. R. Bauer & D. A. Bell (Eds.), *The East Asian challenge for human rights* (pp. 212–237). New York: Cambridge University Press.
7. Coplan, A., & Godie, P. (Eds.). (2011). *Empathy: Philosophical and psychological perspectives*. Oxford: Oxford University Press.
8. de Bary, W. T. (1988). Neo-Confucianism and human rights. In L. S. Rouner (Ed.), *Human rights and the world's religions* (pp. 183–198). Notre Dame: University of Notre Dame Press.
9. de Bary, W. T., & Weiming, T. (Eds). (1998). *Confucianism and human rights*. New York: Columbia University Press.
10. Firth, U. (2008). *Autism: A very short introduction*. New York: Oxford University Press.
11. Gewirth, A. (1982). *Human rights: Essays on justification and application*. Chicago: University of Chicago Press.
12. Gilabert, P. (2019). *Human dignity and human rights*. Oxford: Oxford University Press.
13. Griffin, J. (2008). *On human rights*. Oxford: Oxford University Press.
14. Guyer, P. (2005). Kant on the theory and practice of autonomy. In *Kant's system of nature and freedom* (pp. 115–146). New York: Oxford University Press.
15. Ihara, C. K. (2004). Are individual rights necessary? A Confucian perspective. In K. Shun & D. B. Wong (Eds.), *Confucian ethics: A comparative study of self, autonomy, and community* (pp. 11–30). Cambridge: Cambridge University Press.
16. Lai, P.-C. (2013). Human rights and Christian-Confucian dialogue. *Studies in Interreligious Dialogue, 23*(2), 133–149.
17. Lee, S. (1992). Was there a concept of rights in Confucian virtue-based morality? *Journal of Chinese Philosophy, 19,* 241–261.
18. Lee, S. (1996, July). Liberal rights or/and Confucian virtues? *Philosophy East and West, 46*(3). Seventh East-West philosophers' conference (pp. 367–379).
19. Liang, T. (Ed.). (2016). *美德与权力 (Virtues and Rights)*. Beijing: China Social Science Press.
20. Roetz, H. (1999). The 'Dignity within Oneself': Chinese tradition and human rights. In K.-H. Pohl (Ed.), *Chinese thought in a global context* (pp. 236–261). Leiden: Brill.
21. Roetz, H. (2002). Confucianism and some questions of human rights (in English). In L. Shuxian (Liu Shu-hsien) & L. Yuehui (Lin Yueh-hui) (Eds.), *Xiandai Rujia yu Dongya Wenming: Wenti yu Zhanwang* (Modern Confucianism and East Asian civilization: Problems and prospects) (pp. 155–182). Taipei: Academia Sinica, Institute of Chinese Literature and Philosophy.
22. Rosement, H. J. (1991). Rights-bearing individuals and role-bearing persons. In M. I. Bockover (Ed.), *Rules, rituals, and responsibility: Essays dedicated to Herbert Fingarette* (pp. 71–101). La Salle, Illinois: Open Court.
23. Sensen, O. (2009). Kant's conception of human dignity. *Kant-Studien, 100*(3), 309–331.
24. Sim, M. (2004). A Confucian approach to human rights. *History of Philosophy Quarterly, 21*(4), 337–356.
25. Sim, M. (2007). *Remastering morals with Aristotle and Confucius*. New York: Cambridge University Press.
26. Sung, W. (2016). Mencius and Xunzi on Xing (Human Nature). *Philosophy Compass, 11*(11), 632–641.

27. Tiwald, J. (2012). Confucianism and human rights. In T. Cushman (Ed.), *Handbook of human rights* (pp. 244–254). New York: Routledge.
28. Tiwald, J. (2016). Confucian rights as a fallback apparatus. In T. Liang (Ed.), *美德与权力 (Virtues and Rights)* (pp. 86–103). Beijing: China Social Science Press.
29. Twiss, S. B. (1998). A constructive framework for discussing Confucianism and human rights. In W. T. de Bary & T. Weiming (Eds.), *Confucianism and human rights* (pp. 27–53). New York: Columbia University Press.
30. Van Norden, B. W. (2007). *Virtue ethics and consequentialism in early chinese philosophy*. New York: Cambridge University Press.
31. Waldron, J. (2012). *Dignity, rank, and rights*. New York: Oxford University Press.
32. Wilson, S. A. (2002). Conformity, individuality, and the nature of virtue. In B. W. Van Norden (Ed.), *Confucius and the "Analects": New essays* (pp. 94–118). New York: Oxford University Press.
33. Wong, D. (1984). *Moral relativity*. Berkeley: University of California Press.
34. Wong, D. (2004). Rights and community in Confucianism. In K. Shun & D. B. Wong (Eds.), *Confucian ethics: A comparative study of self, autonomy, and community* (pp. 31–48). Cambridge: Cambridge University Press.
35. Wong, D. (2006). *Natural moralities: A defense of pluralistic relativism* (pp. 37–59). New York: Oxford University Press.
36. Yu, J. (2007). *The ethics of Confucius and Aristotle: Mirrors of virtue*. New York: Routledge Press.
37. Zhang, Q. (2012). *为了人的尊严 (For Human Dignity)*. Beijing: Zhongguo Mingzhu Fazhi Press.
38. Zhang, Q. (2016). *Human dignity in classical Chinese philosophy*. New York: Palgrave Macmillan.

Yong Li is Associate Professor of Philosophy at Wuhan University, China. His primary interests are on issues in moral philosophy. He also does comparative study on Chinese Philosophy. He serves as the book review editor for *Dao: A Journal of Comparative Philosophy* and co-editor of the Routledge *Studies in Contemporary Chinese Philosophy* series. He has publications in *Acta Analytica*, *International Philosophical Quarterly*, *Asian Philosophy*, *Dao*, and *Journal of Moral Philosophy*.

Chapter 3
Unspeakable Things: Drawing upon the Nanjing Massacre to Read Crucifixion as an Assault on Human Dignity

David Tombs

Abstract What might be gained from a reading of crucifixion in light of an atrocity like the Nanjing massacre? This chapter suggests that an acknowledgment of the 'unspeakable things' of the 1937 Nanjing massacre offers important insights into Roman crucifixions. Drawing on Iris Chang's influential book, *The Rape of Nanking* (1997), it suggests a number of features in the violence at Nanjing that might help towards a more informed reading of the biblical accounts of crucifixion as assaults on human dignity.

The Nanjing Massacre

Japanese expansion into mainland Asia in the early twentieth century led to the occupation of Korea in 1910 and Manchuria in 1931. A truce over Manchuria signed with the Nationalist Government in China in 1933 led to an uneasy piece over China's north-eastern border which lasted for a few years. The Marco Polo Bridge (Lugou Bridge) incident near Beijing on 7 July 1937 started a new stage in the conflict. Efforts to de-escalate hostilities after the incident failed, and fighting quickly widened into the Second Sino-Japanese War (1937–1945). Following the fall of Beijing (8 August 1937) a further incident in Shanghai was used to justify an attack against Shanghai by the Japanese Shanghai Expeditionary Force (August–November 1937).

[1]The name Nanjing is used throughout this chapter, expect in citations of other works (including Chang's book) that use the term Nanking.

[2]IMTFE [19, p. 1011], On the Tokyo trials, see Brackman [2].

A version of this chapter was presented under the title "The Massacre at Nanking, Crucifixion, and Public Theology" at *Religion and Social Justice Symposium*, Tongji University, Shanghai, 30 October 2015. I am grateful to Prof. Monhong Lin (Nanjing Union Theological Seminary) and other participants at the symposium for their discussion of the paper. The term 'unspeakable things' in the chapter title is taken from the writing of the missionary and Nanjing eye-witness John Magee.

D. Tombs (✉)
Center for Theology and Public Issues, University of Otago,
PO Box 56, Dunedin 9054, New Zealand
e-mail: david.tombs@otago.ac.nz

Z. Xie et al. (eds.), *Human Dignity, Human Rights, and Social Justice*,
https://doi.org/10.1007/978-981-15-5081-2_3

Nanjing (or Nanking as it was widely known in English) was at this time the capital city of the Republic of China and was an obvious target for the Japanese.[1] At the end of November 1937, Japanese forces marched inland towards Nanjing from three directions, and the Chinese government moved its seat of government from Nanjing to Chongqing. The population of Nanjing was largely left to fend for themselves. The International Military Tribunal for the Far-East (IMFTE), which organized the Tokyo War Crimes Trials (May 1946–November 1948), subsequently reported:

> As the Central China Expeditionary Force under command of [General] Matsui approached the city of Nanking in early December 1937, over one-half of its one million inhabitants and all but a few neutrals who remained behind to organize an International Safety Zone, fled from the city. The Chinese Army retreated, leaving approximately 50,000 troops behind to defend the city. As the Japanese forces stormed the South Gate on the night of 12 December 1937, most of the remaining 50,000 troops escaped through the North and West Gates of the city. Nearly all the Chinese soldiers had evacuated the city or had abandoned their arms and uniforms and sought refuge in the International Safety Zone, and all resistance had ceased as the Japanese Army entered the city on the morning of 13 December 1937.[2]

Most westerners had evacuated the city before the Japanese arrived, but a small group of about twenty or so Christian missionaries, business leaders, and medical professionals, had intentionally stayed on. This group worked with Chinese colleagues to create the Nanjing Safety Zone, which was established on 22 November 1937. The Safety Zone was intended to be a demilitarized area to locate refugee camps that would give some protection to Chinese civilians in the city centre.[3] The International Committee to oversee the Safety Zone was led by a German businessman, John Rabe, a member of the German Nazi party.[4] Despite the obligation on the Japanese to respect civilians, the official status of the Safety Zone was precarious. The Committee hoped that Rabe might use the pact between Germany and Japan to provide some restraint on the Japanese military. The Committee could do little to prevent incursions into the Safety Zone, but they could protest and publicize some of the frequent breeches that occurred. Through the Committee's persistent efforts, it is estimated that the Safety Zone saved many thousands of lives, and significantly reduced the frequency of rapes that were common in many other parts of the city.[5]

Despite the relative success of the Safety Zone, the Japanese invasion had a devastating impact on the city. The IMTFE estimated that 100,000–200,000 Chinese died at Nanjing.[6] In March 1947, the Military Tribunal in Nanjing (held by the Chinese)

---

[3]This was the same day that the Japanese airplanes first attacked the city, shortly before the ground assault began on 1 December; for a chronology, see Zhang [52, p. 411]. On the Westerners who stayed and their work for the International Committee and documenting the massacre, see Lu [26], Brook [3], Hu [16], Vautrin and Tsen [44].

[4]Rabe [32]. See also the film, based on the diaries: *City of War: The Story of John Rabe* (2009), directed by Florian Gallenberger. Chang discovered references to Rabe's diaries during her research and persuaded Rabe's granddaughter to publish it; see Chen [9].

[5]Gin Ling college was intended to serve 2700 women, but filled to 10,000 women; see Vautrin and Tsen [44].

[6]On p. 1014 the Tribunal report appears to endorse an estimate of 200,000: 'Estimates made at a later date indicate that the total number of civilians and prisoners of war murdered in Nanking

gave an estimate in excess of 300,000 or even more.[7] Since the 1960s the estimated number of deaths has become highly contentious and often highly politicized.[8] Some Japanese historian have accepted relatively high figures, but others put the number much lower.[9] Some ultranationalist Japanese critics have gone as far as to dispute whether there ever was a civilian massacre, and accuse the Chinese of fabricating the evidence. In China these accusations are viewed as part of Japan's wider failure to take responsibility for their actions in the war. In reaction to the controversy, the Chinese government now stand firmly behind the 300,000 number indicated at the Nanjing Military Tribunal. Some Chinese historians put the number even higher.[10] The disagreement over the numbers killed and a highly publicized dispute over the presentation of the war in Japanese text-books in 1982 prompted the Chinese authorities to begin work a few years later on the Nanjing Memorial Hall, to preserve the memory and publicize the extent of the massacre.[11]

---

and its vicinity during the first six weeks of the Japanese occupation was over 200,000. That these estimates are not exaggerated is borne out by the fact that burial societies and other organizations counted more than 155,000 bodies which they buried. They also reported that most of those were bound with their hands tied behind their backs. These figures do not take into account those persons whose bodies were destroyed by burning, or by throwing them into the Yangtze River, or otherwise disposed of by Japanese.' However, in the IMTFE verdict against General Iwane Matsui, this appears to be revised, or at least rephrased, to 'more than 100,000'; IMTFE, Judgment, p. 1180.

[7]See Kitamura and Gold [23], Yang [47, 48].

[8]Some of the difference depends on how the massacre is delineated in terms of the timespan and geographical area, and whether the figure includes only civilian deaths or both civilian and military deaths. Harold Timperley, an Australian journalist who worked for the British *Manchester Guardian* and reported on the Nanjing massacre from Shanghai, sent a despatch on 16 January 1938 indicating that 300,000 Chinese civilians had been killed in the Nanjing-Shanghai area; see Lu [24, pp. 58–63). In April 1938 Timperley left for London, and in July 1938 he published edited testimonies and documents as the first book to address the massacre. This offered the relatively modest figure of 40,000 as those killed in Nanjing itself; Timperley [38].

[9]On the hisotoriography and the surrounding controversy, see especially Fogel [12], Liet al. [24], Yoshida [49], Seraphim [35].

[10]Bob Wakabayashi warns that the history is more complicated than any simple numbers or single perspectives allow. Wakabayshi himself offers the range from over 40,000 to under 200,000; see Wakabayashi [45].

[11]The site is also known as the 'Memorial for Compatriots killed in the Nanjing Massacre by Japanese Forces of Aggression'. In 2015, despite objections from Japan, China persuaded UNESCO to add documents from the massacre and the post-war investigation to the Memory of the World Register, a program established in 1992 to preserve and ensure access to documentary heritage of world significance.

The Cross at the Nanjing Memorial Site

The memorial site is located in the Nanjing suburb of Jiangdongmen. It is near an excavated execution and burial site known as the Mass Grave of 10,000 Corpses.[12] The memorial complex occupies quite an extensive footprint, which includes a large exhibition hall (which contains historical documents, photos, and educational displays),[13] a separate building for the preservation and display of skeletal remains (taken from a smaller mass grave subsequently excavated from beneath where the site is located),[14] and an extensive outdoor area which includes a peace park, artwork and sculptures, and open spaces.

One of the most striking structures in the outdoor area, near to the entrance to the exhibition hall, is the enormous concrete Christian cross, over 12 m in height.[15] The horizontal cross-beam of the cross bears the dates of the massacre in large characters, (13 December 1937–January 1938), as a reminder to visitors. At the foot of the cross is a square filled with cobblestones to symbolise the bones of victims.

The reasons for including a cross in such an important site are not specified. It might be an acknowledgment of the contribution that western Christian missionaries made to the Safety Zone and to the protection of civilians. Or the cross may have been included because it is associated in Christianity with extreme suffering. It might be seen as directing visitors, especially Christian visitors, to frame the atrocities it commemorates in terms of the suffering of the innocent. It seems to invite visitors to read the massacre in the light (or in the shadow) of the cross.

There is much that might be said about the massacre by looking it at in the light and shadow of the cross, but this chapter takes the opposite approach. Instead of reading 'from cross to massacre' it explores what might be gained in a reading 'from massacre to cross' and with particular attention to the atrocities that accompanied the massacre as presented by Iris Chang.[16] Both the events of the Nanjing Massacre, and the way they were largely written out of history, can serve as valuable resources for reading the crucifixion. However, before turning to Chang's work, the next section offers a brief summary of previous work on relationship of Roman crucifixion and sexual abuse or sexual violence.[17]

---

[12]A foundation stone was laid on 13 December 1983, and construction began in 1984. The site was opened in 1985. A second phase of major development took place in 1995, and since then a number of further renovations and enlargements have been added; Logan and Reeves [25].

[13]The exhibition hall itself is a very distinctive building, which some commenators compare to a tomb, since it built partly beneath the ground, and has a very sombre atmosphere, which visitors descend into.

[14]In 1998, further skeletal remains were discovered in a burial pit underneath the site. This pit was protected and incorporated into a display hall; Logan and Reeves [25].

[15]The cross was added in 1995 as part of the second phase of development; Logan and Reeves [25]. Despite its considerable height and prescence, it is eclipsed by the very tall flag pole in the middle of the sqaure, which flies the national flag.

[16]Chang [7].

[17]Some of the most creative contextual readings of scripture draw on the personal experience and the immediate cultural background of the interpreter or scholar. By contrast, this chapters stands

Crucifixion, State Terror, and Sexual Abuse

The experience of state terror, torture, and political violence under dictatorships and military regimes in Latin America from the 1960s to 1990s offers a thought-provoking context for reflection on the use of crucifixion in the Roman Empire. In particular, it points to the widespread use of sexual humiliation and sexual violence in torture and prisoner abuse in Latin America, which invites biblical scholars to a deeper investigation of sexual violence and crucifixion.[18]

My earlier publications on crucifixion may be broadly summarised in four points. First, crucifixions had a wider political purpose as state terror, and served as more than the punishment of an individual. Second, Roman tortures often involved sexual humiliations, and these commonly included stripping and naked public exposure as part of crucifixion. Third, other forms of sexual violence were also associated with crucifixion. Fourth, this sexual violence has been rendered largely invisible and unspeakable in Christian tradition, but it should be acknowledged and named as sexual violence or sexual abuse.

The Roman historian Seneca writes on what he saw in Bithynia:

> I see crosses there, not just of one kind but fashioned in many ways: some have their victims with head down toward the ground; some impale their private parts; others stretch out their arms on their crossbeam.

Martin Hengel's influential work on crucifixion mentions this passage in passing (as well as other passages referencing impalement) but Hengel does not name or address the overtly sexualised element.[19] There is no suggestion in Hengel's work that sexual violence might be relevant to an understanding of Roman crucifixion. Likewise, a number of recent scholarly works on crucifixion offer detailed and insightful investigations of many aspects of crucifixion, yet somehow manage to avoid its sexual dimension.[20] This is particularly strange since so much of the debate between Cook and Samuelsson has focussed on the relationship between impalement and crucifixion, which might be expected to foreground concerns for sexual violence.[21]

The lack of sustained attention to past and present torture practices in biblical studies may explain why although the stripping of Jesus is widely acknowledged, it is rarely given significant attention. The cultural and political context of enforced stripping are often ignored, even though these would shed light on the meaning and significance of what is involved. References to crucifixion as a form of torture have

---

one step removed from the context it seeks to draw upon, and relies on perspective provided in Chang's disturbing work.

[18] See, Tombs [41, 40, 42].

[19] Hengel's German title *Mors turpissima crucis* ('most vile death of the cross') echoes the words of North African theologian Origen (c. 185–254) in his *Commentary on Matthew* (on verse 27.22 and following). Hengel is especially interested in understanding Origen's description of the cross 'as most vile death' but he does not explore the possibility that the sense of horror might be due to an association of crucifixion with extreme forms of sexual violence; see Hengel [14].

[20] Chapman [8], Samuelsson [34], Cook [11].

[21] Samuelsson [34], Cook [11].

become relatively common in recent years, but there is still very little work on what insights more systematic studies of torture and abuse of political detainees might offer into crucifixion.[22]

A careful reading of Matthew 27:26–31 indicates that Jesus was stripped multiple times. Matthew explicitly records two strippings in the *praetorium* (Matthew 27:28 and 27:31). In addition, Jesus was probably also stripped for flogging (Matthew 27:26) before being taken into the *praetorium*. Furthermore, since crucifixion usually took place with the victim naked, so Matthew 27:31 points to a further stripping. There is little reason to think that Jesus would have been an exception to this, and no suggestion in the text that he was anything but fuller naked on the cross. This is clearest in Jn 19:23–24, which records that after putting Jesus on the cross the soldiers took his clothes to divide amongst themselves, and that these included his undergarment for which they cast lots so as not to tear it.[23] Therefore, the implied stripping for flogging, the two strippings stated in the *praetorium*, and the stripping at the cross means that Matthew records four strippings.

Mark 15:15–20 also records multiple strippings, but Mark is less clear than Matthew on whether Jesus is stripped prior to being dressed in purple (15:17), or if he was brought into the *praetorium* already naked from the flogging (15:15). Nonetheless, this still amounts to at least three strippings: the first for the flogging (15:15), or for dressing in purple (15:17), then after the mockery (15:20a), and subsequently at the cross (15:20b).

Jesus's crucifixion is seen as the pivotal moment in the Gospels, and the central event for Christian theology. Even though the nakedness of Jesus on the cross was widely known, the *Crucifixion, State Terror, and Sexual Abuse* article appears to have been the first time that the stripping and exposure of Jesus were presented as sexual humiliation. It was also the first time that this element of crucifixion was used to name what should be a self-evident fact, that if Jesus was subjected to stripping and forced exposure he should therefore be acknowledged as a victim of sexual abuse. Furthermore, stripping and exposure is a form of sexual abuse that very often leads to and enables other forms of sexual abuse. It is therefore appropriate to consider whether or not there is evidence of other forms of sexual abuse or sexual violence connected with Roman crucifixions, and if so, whether these might shed further light on the Passion narratives.

---

[22]Two partial exceptions to this are: Cavanaugh [5], Neafsey [31]. However, neither Cavanaugh nor Neafsey link the sexual violence that commonly accompanies contemporary torture practices to the sexual violence that accompanied crucifixion. Neafsey mentions the use of rapes and other sexual violence in torture, for example, *Crucified People*, p. 22, 66. He also cites (p. 11) the work of Elizabeth Johnson, which argues that victims of sexual violence can find a positive value in the cross; see Johnson [20, pp. 263–264]. However, Neafsey does not identify or discuss sexual violence as an element of Roman crucifixion or as a part of the historical experience of Jesus. Other valuable collections that address the use of torture from an ethical and theological perspective is Hunsinger [18], and *Theology Today* 63(3) (October 2006). However, none of the contributions connects the sexual element of torture to crucifixion.

[23]The synoptic gospels (Mk. 15.24, Mt. 27.35 and Lk 23.34) are less explicit, and simply refer to the division of his clothes by lots, but they do not provide evidence to suggest that Jesus was allowed to remain partially clothed.

In light of what ancient authors say about Roman torture and treatment of prisoners, it would not have been unusual if Jesus' crucifixion had been preceded by other forms of sexual violence, such as rape with a weapon or object, or other forms of sexual assault. The Gospel accounts indicate that Jesus was taken into the *praetorium* and was mocked and mistreated in front of the whole assembled cohort (500 or more soldiers). The account of this mistreatment that is presented in the Gospels gives the impression that it was relatively mild and restrained, at least compared to the accounts of the mistreatment of other condemned Roman prisoners. It is unlikely that there will ever be sufficient evidence to draw firm historical conclusions one way or the other on what really happened in the Roman *praetorium*. However, it would not be out of keeping with Roman practice if further abuses occurred. On the contrary, in view of the Roman wish to humiliate and shame the prisoner so that no vestige of dignity remained, it would be strange if further abuses did not happen. It will never be known for sure, but it is quite possible that the gospels have passed over this further unspeakable violence in silence.[24] Acknowledging the possibility may allow insights that deepen awareness of what the scandal of the cross may have been. To this end there is value in considering how accounts of more recent abuses might inform a reading of the biblical text.

Iris Chang and 'The Rape of Nanking'

Iris Shun-Ru Chang (1968–2004) was a Chinese-American writer whose grandparents had fled Nanjing shortly before the Japanese invasion. Growing up in the United States, Chang had heard stories about the Nanjing massacre, but it was not until she attended a conference in California on Japanese war atrocities in 1994 that she made it a focus of her attention.[25] At the conference she was shocked by an enlarged photo display of Japanese war crimes in China. She felt that there was little public awareness or memory of the atrocity in the United States, and that it was neglected in historical accounts of the war. She decided to research and publicize the story of Nanjing by writing a book that would describe the events and explain why they should be remembered.[26] After working intensively for three years of research and writing her book was published in December 1997.[27] The timing of the publication, which intentionally coincided with the 60th anniversary of the massacre, and the strong interest in the Chinese–American community helped the book to become a best-seller. It featured on the *New York Times* best-sellers list for a number of weeks,

[24] See Tombs [41, pp. 104–107].

[25] For biographical background on Chang's life, written by her mother, see Chang [6].

[26] Chang [7].

[27] In 1989 Chang had graduated from the University of Illinois where she had majored in journalism. She worked briefly as a journalist before becoming an author. She was only 29 when *The Rape of Nanking* was published. Her research included a visit to China in 1995 to interview victims, and a period at the library of Yale Divinity School, where many of the documents from western missionaries who had been in Nanking were deposited.

and parts of it were serialized in *Newsweek*. To publicize the book further Chang undertook extensive and exhausting public speaking and promotional work.

The book's title, *The Rape of Nanking,* echoed what had been a common expression for the massacre in 1938, and also reflects Chang's decision to highlight the sexual violence associated with the mass killings.[28] The book draws on the letters and documents of the westerners who remained in the city. Chang's sources include the missionary James McCallum, who reported in his diary for 19 December 1937:

> It is a horrible story to try to relate; I know not where to begin nor to end. Never have I heard or read of such brutality. Rape! Rape! We estimate that at least 1000 cases at night and many by day. In case of resistance or anything that seems like disapproval there is a bayonet stab or bullet. We could write up hundreds a day ... Women are being carried off every morning, afternoon and evening. (James McCallum, December 19, 1937)[29]

Chang also cites the Episcopalian missionary John G. Magee who records many instances of rape in his letters to his wife, the English missionary Faith Backhouse.[30] For example, on 2 February 1938 Magee wrote: 'For some reason we have again had a great many cases of complaints about rape—it is not the complaints that are strange, but the increased number of cases'.[31]

More than twenty years before Chang's book, Susan Brownmiller had already drawn attention to the widespread use of rape at Nanjing in her pioneering feminist work *Against Our Will* [4].[32] Even so, Chang's sustained and graphic documentation

---

[28]See especially Chang [7, pp. 89–99].

[29]Chang [7]. McCallum worked for the United Christian Mission Society and was an administrator at the hospital. This passage was submitted to the IMTFE. A copy of McCallum's diary was discovered in Shanghai in 1995. If anything, Chang's quotation from McCallum slightly downplays the original diary entry. The version in McCallum's diary, published in a collection [28], has an even more emphatic threefold repetition 'Rape! Rape! Rape!'; James H. McCallum, 'Account of the Japanese Atrocities at Nanking During the Winter of 1937–1938' (19 December 1937) in Zhang [52].

[30]Magee [27, pp. 166–195]. Magee returned to the United States in 1940 and was the Episcopalian chaplain at Yale University from 1946 until his death in 1953. Magee described what he saw in letters to his wife and managed to take photos of some of the atrocities and made a sequence of short films. When these were smuggled out of the city they became the first available visual documenation of what had happened. On the films, Magee writes: The pictures herewith give but a fragmentary glimpse of the unspeakable things that happened following the Japanese occupation of Nanking on December 1937; Zhang [52]. Two of the surviving reels (Nos. 1 and 9) lasting about 22 min were later donated by his grandson to the archive at Yale Divinity School. These have now been digitized and are available at the Divinity Library Nanking Massacre Project website http://web.library.yale.edu/divinity/nanking.

[31]Magee [27]. Chang does not cite this particular letter, but might nonetheless have been influenced by it. She reports that she consulted Magee's papers during her research at Yale Divinity School library, along with the papers of Robert Wilson (a doctor at a Nanjing hospital), Lewis Smythe (a professor of sociology teaching at the University of Nanjing), and Minnie Vautrin (who taught at Ginling Women's College).

[32]Brownmiller [4, pp. 57–61]; see also Chang [7]. Brownmiller notes (p. 57, 58) that rape and sexual violence were excluded from the 60-page report that the International Committee submitted in June 1938 in her discussion of rape in World War II (*Against Our Will*, pp. 48–78), but were included in submissions to the IMTFE and were acknowledged by the Tribunal.

of sexual violence was ground-breaking. Wartime rape and other sexual violence were becoming more widely known and discussed in the 1990s due to reports of rape in Bosnia, Rwanda and other conflicts in the first-half of the decade. Despite this, for most people, sexualized violence is a highly stigmatised subject and this impedes public debate. Likewise, sexualized violence during war is rarely discussed in depth as an important subject for theological or biblical investigation.

Chang notes that estimates of the number of women raped at Nanjing range from 20,000 to 80,000 women.[33] Whilst these numbers, along with the numbers killed, are disputed as part of the wider controversy around the massacre, there is no question that widespread rape and sexual violence accompanied the killing.[34] Her book provides extensive examples of how the public display of humiliation and shame was used against the Chinese civilians, and how sexual violence was central to this.

For the purposes of this chapter, it will be suggested that four features of Chang's presentation of the rape and sexualized violence that accompanied the massacre are worthy of note by theologians and biblical scholars. First, the apparent enjoyment and recreational pleasure that Japanese soldiers took in humiliating Chinese civilians; second, the use of sexualized impalements to degrade and dehumanize the Chinese; third, the use of sexualized violence against male victims as well as female victims; fourth, the targeting of religious figures for special treatment. Each one of these features identifies an aspect of the Nanjing experience that might be pursued in relation to Roman crucifixions. Although Nanjing cannot offer definitive answers it can help raise important questions. As Chang notes, the massacre at Nanjing can serve as a 'metaphor for unspeakable evil'.[35] However, to address the unspeakable in her work raises difficult ethical questions on the appropriateness of repeating descriptions of extreme violence and horror. There are risks that many of the passages which follow might be confronting.[36] The dangers of complicity with an unhealthy voyeurism and sensationalism also have to be recognised.[37] The decision to include such passages below, despite the risks and dangers involved, reflects a belief that if theologians and biblical scholars are to understand Roman crucifixions they need to recognise the deeply disturbing and offensive character of sexual violence as a weapon of war and how it operates as a common practice in the abuse of detainees. Theologians cannot reflect with honesty and integrity on crucifixion until the disturbing elements

---

[33] Chang [7]. The IMFTE estimated: 'Approximately 20,000 cases of rape occurred within the city during the first month of the occupation.' IMFTE, *Judgment*, p. 1011.

[34] Even prominent Japanese sceptics appear to accept that sexual violence was widespread, and focus their criticisms on the numbers killed, for example, Tanaka Masaaki author of 'Nankin Gyakusatsu' no Kyoko [*'Rape of Nanking' as a Ficition*] in 1984; see Yamamoto [46]. Furthermore, as a perspective for reflection on crucifixion, Chang's descriptions of different forms sexual violence are more important than quantifying the overall numbers.

[35] Chang writes: 'Throughout my childhood *Nanjing Datusha* remained buried in the back of my mind as a metaphor for unspeakable evil'; Chang [7, p. 8].

[36] In light of Chang's subsequent mental health difficulties and suicide, some have suggested that her efforts to uncover and address this unspeakable violence took a heavy toll on her health. See McLaughlin [29].

[37] On the dangers of such voyeurism, see Sontag [36].

it involved have been named and recognized. The testimonies of abuse and violence from Nanjing can help in this process.

Exploring these questions is not to suggest that such direct and frank discussion of the sexualised violence of Roman crucifixions is always appropriate. The sexualised violence of crucifixion will often be an inappropriate subject for a specific audience or for a wider discussion of the cross. There will therefore be many occasions when the sexualised violence of crucifixion does not need to be referenced or explicitly mentioned. For example, in church settings and services, it will often be better to acknowledge it in a less direct way.[38]

Recreational Spectacles of Humiliation

According to Chang, Japanese soldiers found inventive ways to entertain themselves by mistreating Chinese civilians. For example, in some cases they doused people in gasoline, and then set them alight and watched them run away in flames.[39] In other cases, the abuse involved rape and other forms of sexualized violence.[40] In some instances, girls were tied naked to chairs, beds, or poles to be readily available for repeated rape.[41] Chang writes of 'recreational rape':

> There seemed to be no limit to the Japanese capacity for human degradation and sexual perversion in Nanking. Just as some soldiers invented killing contests to break the monotony

[38]Cavanaugh's discussion of torture and the broken body in *Torture and Eucharist* might provide a basis for exploring how the liturgy of the eucharist could be drawn upon to offer one appropriate way to include a subdued acknowledgment of sexualised violence in memory of the breaking of the body.

[39]Chang [7, p. 94]. Chang [7, p. 88, 89] comments: 'The incidents mentioned above are only a fraction of the methods that the Japanese used to torment their victims. The Japanese saturated victims in acid, impaled babies with bayonets, hung people by their tongues. One Japanese reporter who later investigated the Rape of Nanking learned that at least one Japanese soldier tore the heart and liver out of a Chinese victim to eat them. Even genitals, apparently, were consumed; a Chinese soldier who escaped from Japanese custody saw several dead people in the streets with their penises cut off. He was later told that the penises were sold to Japanese customers who believed that eating them would increase virility'.

[40]Brownmiller also drew attention to the dis-robing of Jewish women as a form of shaming. She cites Sala Pawlowicz, a Polish Jew who survived Bergen-Belsen, who described the disrobings as a humiliation that Germans staged for their 'diversion'. Pawlowicz writes: 'They forced us to undress and lie on the ground as they walked by, laughing and making lewd comments. Then we were beaten with whips on our bare backs and chased through the ghetto. Their actions shamed me.'; cited Brownmiller [4]. Brownmiller also points to a widespread pattern of rape, sexual tortures, and humiliations against Jewish women during World War II and the Shoah; Brownmiller [4, pp. 49–56]. These abuses received very little attention in most histories of the war, perhaps because of a naive and mistaken assumption that the anti-Semitic 1935 Nuremberg race laws would have prevented them. In fact, sexual violence against women and children was widespread and varied; see, Hedgepeth and Saidel [13].

[41]Chang [7, p. 93].

> of murder, so did some invent games of recreational rape and torture when wearied by the glut of sex.[42]

Describing these acts as 'recreational rape' is not to suggest that this was merely incidental to what was happening in the military campaign, or in any way less important than other acts of killing or abuse. 'Recreational rape' is embedded within a complex set of gender dynamics and power relationships. In recent decades, feminist scholars, starting with Susan Brownmiller, have drawn attention to ways that some forms of violence, in particular sexual violence against women, have been marginalized from accounts of war.[43] This was often on the mistaken assumption that rapes and other violence against women during conflicts were incidental acts, without public or political significance in military campaigns.

Since Brownmiller, the prevalence of sexual violence in armed conflicts has received much more attention. The extent to which rape is an intentional strategy might vary in different conflicts. In some cases, it is clear that the use of sexual violence was ordered by those in power as a deliberate strategy, using rape as a weapon of war or ethnic cleansing. In other cases, the sexual violence might not have been intentionally planned or organized at a command level, but have been more opportunistic or 'recreational'. However, opportunistic or recreational rape can still have significant political consequences, especially when it is widespread or well known. Even in conflicts where those in command did not order or encourage the use of sexual violence, a failure to do more to prevent it or prosecute it suggests that it was seen of minimal concern, and in some cases might have been tacitly condoned.[44]

The Japanese soldiers' apparent enthusiasm for macabre acts of violence against defenceless civilians at Nanjing raises a question as to whether the Roman soldiers in Jerusalem might have derived some perverse enjoyment or satisfaction from the mistreatment of prisoners. The abuse of those who were without protection or recourse to justice could offer a welcome diversion to soldiers who were in Jerusalem to prevent disturbances during the Passover Festival. In all likelihood, the Roman soldiers faced boredom and frustration in their duties, and any diversion might have been welcome. Any opportunity to express their anger and contempt against a prisoner who disturbed the peace, and therefore made their presence in Jerusalem all the more necessary, is understandable.

Josephus describes something close to this in his account of the crucifixions of those who attempted to flee Jerusalem during the siege by Titus in 70 CE:

> Scourged and subjected before death to every torture, they were finally crucified in view of the wall. Titus indeed realised the horror of what was happening, for every day 500—sometimes even more—fell into his hands… But his chief reason for not stopping the slaughter was the hope that the sight of it would perhaps induce the Jews to surrender in order to avoid the same fate. The soldiers themselves through rage and bitterness nailed up their victims

[42]Chang [7, p. 94].

[43]Brownmiller [4, pp. 31–113].

[44]Even if the sexual violence at Nanjing was the result of a break-down in Japanese military discipline, and not an intentional instrument of terror, there is little evidence of Japanese commanders seeking to prevent or punish what happened, despite their obligation to protect civilians.

> in various attitudes as a grim joke, till owing to the vast numbers there was no room for the crosses, and no crosses for the bodies.[45]

The enthusiasm of Roman soldiers for a 'grim joke' might in turn shed light on the mistreatment of Jesus before his public execution. For example, both Mark and Matthew state that the 'whole cohort' was assembled to witness the degrading mistreatment of Jesus in the *praetorium*. If the whole cohort was assembled, it suggests that whatever happened was not just the action of a few disgruntled soldiers, but a more formal and organized spectacle. In addition, it suggests that the humiliation itself would be a serious and dramatic action. The purpose would have been to humiliate and shame the prisoner, but quite possibly this doubled as an opportunity to provide recreational amusement for the soldiers. In the same way that gladiatorial fights and the execution of *noxii* (condemned prisoners or criminals) provided entertainment at arenas for blood-thirsty crowds throughout the Roman world, so the abuse in the *praetorium* might have been entertainment for the Roman soldiers. There are reference in ancient writers to different tortures that preceded or accompanied Roman crucifixions. These included: covering victims wholly or partially in pitch and setting them alight, castrating or otherwise mutilating the prisoner, and forcing the prisoner to wear macabre and dehumanizing costumes, including animal skins. The mistreatment and mockery of Jesus may therefore have included other humiliating acts of abuse that have not be preserved in the narrative.

Dehumanization and Impalement

Many of the most disturbing testimonies of sexual violence at Nanjing describe humiliations that seem to have been intentionally designed to degrade and dehumanize.[46] This dehumanization is reflected in the language used by Japanese soldiers, in which Chinese women were referred to by inhuman or sub-human terms, such as 'toilets' or 'pigs', as well as a wide variety of acts described by Chang. In many cases, the degradation and dehumanization were associated with sexual violence.

Chang's description indicates that the rapes and other sexual abuses were closely linked to other forms of violence that humiliated the victims and treated them as less than human. She also shows that these were often enacted and displayed in public.

> Many soldiers went beyond rape to disembowel women, slice off their breasts, nail them alive to walls. Fathers were forced to rape their daughters, and sons their mothers, as other family members watched. Not only did live burials, castration, the carving of organs, and the roasting of people become routine, but more diabolical tortures were practiced, such as hanging people by their tongues on iron hooks or burying people to their waists and watching them get torn apart by German shepherds. So sickening was the spectacle that even the Nazis in the city were horrified, one proclaiming the massacre to be the work of "bestial machinery."[47]

---

[45] Josephus [22, p. 314].

[46] Chang [7].

[47] Chang [7, p. 6].

Sexual violence is a particularly potent way to dehumanize and shame a victim, since sexuality and sexual identity are so closely connected to personal identity. Chang describes how the Japanese used sexual impalement to reinforce the humiliation and dehumanization of women and girls.

> Perhaps one of the most brutal forms of Japanese entertainment was the impalement of vaginas. In the streets of Nanking, corpses of women lay with their legs splayed open, their orifices pierced by wooden rods, twigs, and weeds. It is painful, almost mind-numbing, to contemplate some of the other objects that were used to torment the Nanking women, who suffered almost unendurable ordeals. For instance, one Japanese soldier who raped a young woman thrust a beer bottle into her and shot her. Another rape victim was found with a golf stick rammed into her. And on December 22, in a neighbourhood near the gate of Tongjimen, the Japanese raped a barber's wife and then stuck a firecracker in her vagina. It blew up and killed her.[48]

The extensive wider literature on sexual violence in conflict, which has emerged since the 1990s, suggests sexual violations of this type are connected with gendered notions of power and identity. Rape and sexual violence are used as an assertion of military potency and as a tool for political subjugation. Genital impalement represents one of the most extreme ways of displaying military conquest through sexual vulnerability and sexualised violence.[49] The examples described by Chang demonstrate misogynistic conceptions of masculinity, power, and conquest, which were intended to emphasize the vulnerability and shame of the victims, in contrast to the 'power, control, and virility' of the conquerors.

The passages cited from Chang mention only the impalement of women, but it is also possible that men and boys were also impaled, either as a form of execution or as a humiliating display after some other cause of death. Chang's awareness of sexual violence against male victims is shown in her reference to castrations, and will be discussed further in the next section. The same underlying symbolism of power and shame is involved in the sexual impalement of men, as it is in the impalement of women. However, in many societies the taboo associated with sexual violence against men is even greater.

There is a scholarly consensus that Roman crucifixion developed out of earlier impalement punishments in Assyria and Persia, and that the impalement of male victims could be through either the abdomen or through the rectum.[50] The sexualized element of impalement through the rectum added an additional sense of humiliation and psychological suffering to the physical pain of impalement. As noted in the earlier discussion above, there are a number of references in ancient texts that suggest Roman crucifixions could include genital impalement in some form. Rather than replacing impalement with crucifixion it is possible that crosses were designed to include genital impalement but to do so in ways that would prolong the death of the victim rather than speed it. There is nothing in the New Testament texts that directly

---

[48] Chang [7, p. 6].

[49] On the relationship of power and conquest in the 1960–1996 conflict in Guatemala, and its expression through sexual violence, see Tombs [39].

[50] See for example, the History Channel television programme *Crucifixion* (2008) directed by Jon Taylor on the historical origins of Roman crucifixion.

suggests that this was an element in the crucifixion of Jesus of Nazareth, but nor is it explicitly excluded. The association of some Roman crucifixions with genital impalement might shed light on why crucifixion was seen as not just supremely painful but also as a deeply shameful death. In addition, it would align with the custom of victims being exposed and displayed naked, which is explicitly attested in the Gospel accounts of Jesus' death.

In addition to impalement, Chang's account of atrocities at Nanjing also mentions instances of crucifixion.

> The Japanese not only disembowelled, decapitated, and dismembered victims but performed more excruciating varieties of torture. Throughout the city they nailed prisoners to wooden boards and ran over them with tanks, crucified them to trees and electrical posts, carved long strips of flesh from them, and used them for bayonet practice.[51]

Such crucifixions may differ in some ways from the Roman style of crucifixion typically represented in Christian art, but it is still significant that at Nanjing impalement and crucifixion were both used. There is a scholarly consensus that Roman crucifixions grew out of earlier impalement executions. However, Samuelsson's recent work argues that it impossible to draw clear distinctions between references to crucifixion and impalement in Greek and Latin accounts of executions.[52] Chang's reports on both impalements and crucifixions at Nanjing might therefore prompt further investigation into the relationship between impalement and crucifixion, and whether crucifixions might have found ways to incorporate genital impalement.

Sexual Violence Against Male Victims

Whilst the most frequent victims of rape at Nanjing were women and girls, it is also clear that men and boys were also targeted for rape and humiliation. Chang writes:

> But not all of the victims were women. Chinese men were often sodomized or forced to perform a variety of repulsive sexual acts in front of laughing Japanese soldiers. At least one Chinese man was murdered because he refused to commit necrophilia with the corpse of a woman in the snow.[53]

Although conflict-related sexual violence against women is now much more widely recognized and discussed than it was previously, the acknowledgment and discussion of sexual violence against men, is still quite unusual. The barriers to men disclosing sexual abuse are at least as high as for women, and self-censorship and under-reporting is generally seen as an even greater issue for male victims.[54] Furthermore, many human rights reports include sections on sexual violence or gender-based violence against women, but rarely include a corresponding section

[51] Chang [7, p. 87].

[52] Samuelsson [34].

[53] Chang [7, p. 95].

[54] Jones and Zotto [21].

on sexual or gender-based violence against men.[55] Men's experience is sometimes referenced in passing in sections dealing with women's experiences. Likewise, there are far fewer references to male victims in the media, and even when male victims are featured their experiences are often treated superficially without further adequate context, explanation, or analysis. There is good evidence and reason to believe that the majority of conflict-related sexual violence is directed against women and girls. Nonetheless, recent reports on sexual violence against male victims in conflicts in Bosnia, Sri Lanka, Sudan, and elsewhere, demonstrate that conflict-related sexual violence against male victims is a widespread issue.[56] Abuses can be especially prevalent in torture practices and can serve as a powerful weapon to break down a prisoner's sense of identity.[57] This is not limited to male rape, but includes a much wider range of abuses. Common practices include: enforced nudity; beatings or shocks to genitals; castrations and mutilations; penetration with weapons or instruments; forced oral sex or masturbation; and humiliating sexual relations. One study of 434 male political prisoners in El Salvador found that 76% reported being subjected to at least one form of sexual torture.[58]

The examples that Chang offers from Nanjing, along with much other evidence from both the Ancient world and more contemporary settings, indicates that it is not at all unreasonable to ask if there is evidence that Jesus might have experienced some form of sexual abuse as a prisoner, either before or during crucifixion.

Sexual Violence Against Religious Figures

In one revealing passage, Chang describes how a Buddhist Monk was subjected to sexual violence.

> The Japanese also delighted in trying to coerce men who had taken lifetime vows of celibacy to engage in sexual intercourse. A Chinese woman had tried to disguise herself as a man to pass through one of the gates of Nanking, but Japanese guards, who systematically searched all passing pedestrians by groping at their crotches, discovered her true sex. Gang rape followed, at which time a Buddhist monk had the misfortune to venture near the scene. The Japanese tried to force him to have sex with the woman they had just raped. When the monk protested, they castrated him, causing the poor man to bleed to death.

The monk's status as a religious figure was no protection. Indeed, although it cannot be known for sure, it is possible that his religious identity (which would have included a vow of celibacy) was the reason that he was picked out to be coerced into

---

55 See for example, the, Archdiocesan Human Rights Office (ODHAG) report on the Recovery of Historical Memory Project (REMHI) presented on 24 April 1998 and translated as REMHI [33]. The presentation of sexual violence against males in this reports is discussed in Tombs, 'Honour, Shame and Conques'.

56 See Stemple [37, especially p. 613, 614], Zalewski et al. [50]. On Bosnia, see also Zarkov [51]; On Sri Lanka, see especially Human Rights Watch [17].

57 Agger [1, pp. 311–12].

58 Comision de derechos humanos de El Salvador [10], cited Agger [1].

raping the woman. If so, rape by a monk would both demean the woman and also serve to humiliate and defile the monk. Since the monk protested against the rape, the soldiers probably saw castration as an especially apposite punishment.

This too raises a question as to Roman practices. The gospels seem to go out of their way to give a benign interpretation of Roman actions and exonerate the Romans for responsibility for the crucifixion. Mark reports that the Roman centurion at the cross even declared ‘Truly this man was the Son of God’ (Mk 15.39).[59] However, this positive picture of the Romans has to be treated with suspicion, and the political motives behind shifting responsibility for crucifixion have been widely recognised.[60] It is also naïve to think that Romans soldiers would treat a religious figure with piety, fairness or respect. It is usual to understand the centurion’s words as intended by Mark as a genuine confession of faith, they might also have been (at least if they capture an original utterance) a highly sarcastic remark.[61] In much the same way that the Japanese soldiers may have taken pleasure in humiliating the Buddhist monk, likewise the Roman centurion could have seen crucifixion as the ultimate degradation and desecration of a Jewish Rabbi, who claimed to be King of the Jews, and Son of God. The abuse and execution of Jesus would have been an excellent opportunity for Roman soldiers to express their contempt and hostility not just against an individual, but against Jewish religious faith and the Jewish people as a whole.

Conclusion

The huge cross at the Nanjing Memorial site invites important theological questions. How is the Nanjing massacre to be seen in the shadow of the cross, and how is the cross to be seen in the context of the Nanjing massacre? More generally, how is Christian theology to remember and speak of the unspeakable things of the past, and also address unspeakable things that continue today?

This chapter has explored how the atrocities at Nanjing and the atrocity of the cross might be read together in ways that open up new avenues on the meaning and implications of crucifixion. Building on previous work, it has used Chang’s account of the Nanjing massacre to identify questions to consider in seeking a fuller understanding of the crucifixion as an historical event.

Given the graphic and disturbing nature of the subject, care needs to be taken in how the issues are best addressed. First, any investigation of Roman crucifixion from the perspective of other atrocities will involve scholarly care to ensure that the investigation is well-grounded and not a mistaken and anachronistic distortion of

---

[59]This translation is KJV. The NRSV read ‘Truly this man was God’s Son!’. In Mt. 27.54 the same statement is made by the centurion guarding the tomb, but it is placed later in the narrative. In Matthew it is prompted by the earthquake and breaking open of tombs, whereas in Mark it is when Jesus gave a loud cry and breathed his last.

[60]The shifting of blame to the Jews as ‘Christ killers’ has contributed to a horrifying legacy of anti-Semitism in Christian tradition.

[61]See Horsley [15], as discussed in Moore [30, pp. 95–110, 107].

one historical period through the lenses of a different history. Second, it will involve ethical and cultural sensitivity, to avoid a simplistic appropriation of a painful event in Chinese history to serve a Christian theological interest, which might seem as alien and insulting to the victims of the massacre. Third, it will involve a pastoral care for those who might find the direction of research disturbing, and also care for those who carry out the research.[62]

How can further work on the subject make a constructive contribution, and have a positive benefit for wider discussions of sexual violence? If the historical amnesia on crucifixion is to be overcome, theologians will need to take up the sexual humiliation and sexual abuses of the cross in a way that serves a positive purpose. If the churches actively embrace this challenge, they might offer significant leadership for a global response to sexual violence in conflict, as a contribution to social justice in the twenty-first century.[63] A better understanding of crucifixion might offer powerful Christological resources to address this, and to affirm human dignity in face of even seemingly 'unspeakable things'.

References

1. Agger, I. (1989). Sexual torture of political prisoners: An overview. *Journal of Traumatic Stress, 2*, 305–318.
2. Brackman, A. C. (1987). *The other nuremberg: The untold story of the Tokyo war crimes trials*. New York: William Morrow.
3. Brook, T. (Ed.). (1999). *Documents on the rape of nanking*. Ann Arbor, MI: University of Michigan Press.
4. Brownmiller, S. (1975). *Against our will: Men, women and rape*. New York: Simon and Schuster.
5. Cavanaugh, W. T. (1998). *Torture and eucharist: Theology, politics and the body of Christ*. Challenges in Contemporary Theology. Oxford: Blackwell.
6. Chang, Y.-Y. (2011). *The woman who could not forget: Iris Chang before and beyond. A memoir by Ying-Ying Chang*. New York: Pegasus.
7. Chang, I. (1997). *The rape of Nanking: The forgotten Holocaust of World War II*. New York: Basic Books.
8. Chapman, D. (2008). *Ancient Jewish and Christian perceptions of crucifixion*. Grand Rapids, MI: Baker Academic; Tübingen: Mohr Siebeck.
9. Chen, D. W. (1996, December 12). At the rape of Nanking: A Nazi who saved lives. *New York Times*, p. 3.
10. Comision de derechos humanos de El Salvador (CDHS). (1986). *La tortura en El Salvador. Penal "La Esperunzu" Ayutuxtepeque, San Salvador*. San Salvador: CDHS.
11. Cook, J. G. (2014). *Crucifixion in the mediterranean world*. Tübingen: Mohr Siebeck.
12. Fogel, J. A. (Ed.). (2000). *The Nanjing Massacre in history and historiography*. Berkeley, CA: University of California Press.

[62]It is possible that Chang herself was so deeply disturbed by her research, and the intensity with which she pursued it, that it may have affected her mental health and possibly contributed to her depression and suicide in 2004.

[63]See Tombs [40, 43].

13. Hedgepeth S. M. & Saidel, R. G. (Eds.). (2010). *Sexual violence against Jewish women during the holocaust*. Waltham, MA: Brandeis University Press.
14. Hengel, M. (1977). *Crucifixion: In the ancient world and the folly of the message of the cross* (trans. J. Bowden). Philadelphia: Fortress Press; London: SCM. Enlarged and revised from German orig. (1976). *Mors turpissima crucis*: Die Kreuzigung in der antiken Welt und die "Torheit" des "Wortes vom Kreuz. In J. Friedrich, W. Pöhlmann, & P. Stuhlmacher (Eds.), *Rechtfertigung. Festschrift für Ernst Käsemann zum 70. Geburtstag*; Tübingen: J.C.B. Mohr; Göttingen: Vandenhoeck and Ruprecht.
15. Horsley, R. A. (2001). *Hearing the story: The politics of plot in Mark's Gospel*. Minneapolis: Fortress Press.
16. Hu, H.-l. (2000). *American goddess at the rape of Nanking: The courage of Minnie Vautrin*. Carbondale, IL: Southern Illinois University Press.
17. Human Rights Watch. (2013). *We will teach you a lesson: Sexual violence against Tamils by Sri Lankan security forces*. New York: Human Rights Watch.
18. Hunsinger, G. (Ed.). (2008). *Torture is a moral issue: Christians, Jews, Muslims and People of conscience speak out*. Erdmans: Grand Rapids, MI.
19. International Military Tribunal for the Far East (IMTFE) (1948, November 1). *International military tribunal for the far east: Judgment*. Retrieved May 25, 1948, from http://www.ibiblio.org/hyperwar/PTO/IMTFE/index.html.
20. Johnson, E. A. (1992). *She who is: The Mystery Of God in feminist theological discourse*. New York: Crossroad.
21. Jones, A., & Zotto, A. D. (2002) Male-on-male sexual violence in Wartime: Human rights' last Taboo? Paper presented to the Annual Convention of the International Studies Association (ISA), New Orleans, 23–27 March 2002. Retrieved May 22, 2015, from http://adamjones.freeservers.com/malerape.htm.
22. Josephus. (1970 [1959]). *Jewish war* (trans. G.A. Williamson, Revised ed.). Harmondsworth: Penguin Books.
23. Kitamura, M., & Gold, H. (2007). *The politics of Nanjing: An impartial investigation*. Lanham, MD: University Press of America.
24. Li, F. F., Sabella, R., & Liu, D. (Eds.). (2002). *Nanking 1937: Memory and healing*. Armonk, NY and London: M.e. Sharpe.
25. Logan, W. S., & Reeves, K. (2011). *Places of pain and shame: Dealing with 'Difficult Heritage'*. London: Routledge.
26. Lu, S. (2004). *They were in Nanjing: The Nanjing Massacre witnessed by American and British nationals*. Hong Kong: Hong Kong University Press.
27. Magee, J. G. (2001). Letters to wife (12 December 1937—5 February 1938). In K. Zhang (Ed.), *Eyewitnesses to Massacre* (pp. 166–227). London: Routledge.
28. McCallum, J. H. (2001). Account of the Japanese atrocities at Nanking during the Winter of 1937–38. In K. Zhang (Ed.), *Eyewitnesses to Massacre* (pp. 228–242). London: Routledge.
29. McLaughlin, K. (2004, November). Iris Chang's suicide stunned those she tried so hard to help—The survivors of Japan's "Rape of Nanking". *SFGate*. Retrieved May 12, 2015, from http://www.sfgate.com/entertainment/article/Iris-Chang-s-suicide-stunned-those-she-tried-so-2634180.php.
30. Moore, S. D. (2008). Deconstructive criticism: Turning mark inside out. In J. C. Anderson & S. D. Moore (Eds.), *Mark & method* (pp. 95–110). Minneapolis: Fortress Press.
31. Neafsey, J. (2014). *Crucified people: The suffering of the tortured in Today's World*. Maryknoll, NY: Orbis.
32. Rabe, J. (1998). *The good man of Nanking, the diaries of John Rabe* (trans. J. E. Woods & Ed. E. Wickert). New York: A. A. Knopf.
33. Recovery of Historical Memory Project. (1999). *Guatemala: Never again!* Maryknoll, NY: Orbis Books; London: Latin America Bureau and Catholic Institute for International Relations.
34. Samuelsson, G. (2011). *Crucifixion in antiquity: An inquiry into the background of new testament terminology*. Tübingen: Mohr Siebeck.

35. Seraphim, F. (2006). *War memory and social politics in Japan, 1945–2005*. Harvard University Asia Center. Cambridge, MA and London: Harvard University Press.
36. Sontag, S. (2003). *Regarding the pain of others*. New York: Farrar, Giroux and Strauss.
37. Stemple, L. (2009). Male rape and human rights. *Hastings Law Journal, 60,* 605–647.
38. Timperley, H. J. (1938). *What war means: The Japanese terror in China: A documentary record*. London: Victor Gollancz.
39. Tombs, D. (2002). Honour, shame and conquest: Male identity, sexual violence and the body politic. *Journal of Hispanic/Latino Theology, 9*(4), 21–40.
40. Tombs, D. (2014). Silent no more: Sexual violence in conflict as a challenge to the worldwide church. *Acta Theologica, 34*(2), 142–160.
41. Tombs, D. (1999, Autumn). Crucifixion, state terror and sexual abuse. *Union Seminary Quarterly Review, 53,* 89–109.
42. Tombs, D. (2017). Lived religion and the intolerance of the cross. In R. Ganzevoort & S. Sremac (Eds.), *Lived religion and politics of (In)tolerance*. Palgrave Studies in Lived Religion and Societal Changes (pp. 63–83). London: Palgrave Macmillan.
43. Tombs, D. (2019). Confronting the stigma of naming Jesus as a victim of sexual violence. In C. Pearson (Ed.). *Enacting a public theology* (pp. 71–86). Stellenbosch: Stellenbosch University Press.
44. Vautrin, M., & Tsen, S. (2010). *The undaunted women of Nanking: The wartime diaries of Minnie Vautrin and Tsen Shui-fang* (trans. and Eds. H. Hu & L. Zhang). Carbondale, IL: Southern Illinois University Press.
45. Wakabayashi, B. T. (2007). Leftover problems. In B. T. Wakabayashi (Ed.), *The Nanking atrocity, 1937–38: Complicating the picture* (pp. 357–393). New York: Berghahn Books.
46. Yamamoto, M. (2000). *Nanking: Anatomy of an atrocity*. Prageger: Westport, CT.
47. Yang, D. (1990). A Sino-Japanese controversy: The Nanjing atrocity as history. *Sino-Japanese Studies, 3*(1), 14–35.
48. Yang, D. (1999). Convergence or divergence? Recent historical writings on the rape of Nanjing. *American Historical Review, 104*(3), 842–865.
49. Yoshida, T. (2006). *The making of the 'Rape of Nanking': History and memory in Japan, China and the United States*. New York and Oxford: Oxford University Press.
50. Zalewski, M., Drumond, P., Prügl, E., & Stern, M. (Eds.). (2018). *Sexual violence against men in global politics*. New York: Routledge.
51. Zarkov, D. (2007). *The body of war: Media, ethnicity and gender in the break-up of Yugoslavia*. Durham: Duke University Press.
52. Zhang, K. (Ed.). (2001). *Eyewitnesses to Massacre: American missionaries bear witness to Japanese atrocities in Nanjing*. Armonk, NY and London: East Gate Books.

David Tombs is the Howard Paterson Chair of Theology and Public Issues, at the University of Otago, Aotearoa New Zealand. He has a longstanding interest in contextual and liberation theologies and is author of *Latin American Liberation Theology* (Brill, 2002). His research is on religion and violence, and his current writing focusses on crucifixion. He is originally from London and has previously worked in Britain (University of Roehampton, London) and in Ireland (Irish School of Ecumenics, Trinity College Dublin).

Chapter 4
When Religious Freedom Was Under Attack: A Study of Four Christians' Responses in Modern China

Zhifeng Zhong

Abstract In this chapter, I have selected two Chinese Christians, Mingdao Wang and Y. T. Wu, and two missionaries Hudson Taylor and Timothy Richard to illustrate Christian leaders' various approaches to ensuring religious freedom protection. Theology, political capital and personal experiences of church-state encounters are used to examine their various positions on protection of rights as regards religious freedom. The study shows turning to political authorities was a common approach for addressing these rights. Both Richard and Taylor believed without external pressure, the Chinese officials would not stop their hostility, nor will they take any action to protect religious rights. Both Wu and Wang considered the state as a potential helper who can turn to because they believed there was common ground between Christianity and Communism. Theology played a very limited role in shaping their approaches. In contrast, political capital and previous experiences in church-state encounters had a much larger impact.

Introduction

Since 2014, a cross removal campaign was launched in Zhejiang province which caught much attention across the world.[1] The Chinese state tightened its control on religion fearing the subversive potential of the powerful independent house churches. A revised version of the *Regulations on Religious Affairs* became effective in February 2018. Many observers and church leaders were concerned that a new round of political campaigns targeting the churches would be launched in the near future. How to respond to the state when religious freedom is under attack become an urging issue. Examining some influential Christian leaders' responses to religious attack will shed light on the contemporary situation.

[1]Ying [28], Cao [3].

Z. Zhong (✉)
School of Philosophy, Renmin University of China, Rm. 3051, Qingnian Gongyu, 100872 Beijing, China
e-mail: gracez2001@163.com

Z. Xie et al. (eds.), *Human Dignity, Human Rights, and Social Justice*,
https://doi.org/10.1007/978-981-15-5081-2_4

In the history of Chinese Christianity, Hudson Taylor (1832–1905) and Timothy Richard (1845–1919) were two of the most influential missionaries who greatly shaped the missionary movement in China while Mingdao Wang (1900–1991) and Y. T. Wu (1893–1979) were two of the most important church leaders who had enormous impact on the development of Christianity after 1949.[2] In the past, these four figures were put into stark dichotomy. For example, Taylor was labeled as a conservative Christian who represented a bottom-up approach of evangelism while Richard was regarded as a liberal missionary who adopted an elitist approach.[3] Wang was considered as a hero of the confessing house church while Wu was treated as the head of the co-opted Three-self church. People usually attribute their different choices to their theologies. Under religious repression, only two extreme approaches were identified: martyrdom or surrender. However, this dichotomic perception distorts the complex reality and prevents us from grasping the similarities they shared in their thinking and action.

Nowadays more and more literatures which revaluate the legacy of missionaries and some controversial figures such as Mingdao Wang and Y. T. Wu have emerged.[4] Missionaries are not totally condemned as cultural imperialists but recognized as important promoters of modernization and cultural exchanges. As a result of this positive turn, many biographies and primary sources of missionaries have been published.[5] The stark black and white picture of Wang as a martyr of faith and Wu as a co-opted destroyer of the church, or vice versa Wang as the trouble-maker of unity and Wu as a prophetic figure to unite the churches, has been revised. However, these literatures seldom touch their attitudes and actions towards right protection. This chapter will concentrate on this important issue, hoping to contribute to these revaluation literatures.

In this chapter, religious freedom refers to an individual's or community's right to practice one's religion or exercise one's beliefs without the state's intervention. It usually includes the right of worship, observance, conversion, preaching and proselytizing. In dynastic China no religious freedom was sanctioned by law, and the fate of religion was always under the hand of the emperors and local governors. Since the Republican era, religious freedom has been written into the Constitution. However, it was constantly challenged by political campaigns in reality. Response to the state's attack on religious freedom is a very important issue in the history of Christianity in China. The main questions are: When religious freedom was under attack, what kinds of approaches did Christians use? What are the main similarities and differences? How theology, political capital and previous experiences of church-state encounters shaped these various responses?

---

[2]For more information, please see Bohr [1], Evans [7], Soothill [16], Stanley [17, pp. 567–568].

[3]Cohen [5].

[4]Gu [8], Pfister [12], Ying [26, 27].

[5]There are three most important series of missionaries' biographies: (1) The Protestant Missionaries Series edited by Zhenhe Zhou, (2) the Salt and Light Series edited by Carol Lee Hamrin; (3) and the Cosmic Care Biographical Series edited by Lin Zhiping.

Methodological Note

I look at Mingdao Wang, Y. T. Wu, Hudson Taylor and Timothy Richard and compare their various approaches to religious freedom protection. The rationale of these individuals is threefold.

First, they are very influential Christians in the history of Christianity in China. Wang has been considered as one of the three giants of faith and the spiritual leader of the house church movement.[6] Wu who greatly shaped the fate of Chinese Christianity since 1949 has been recognized as the founding father of the Three-self Patriotic Movement. Hudson Taylor and Timothy Richard were two influential missionaries who represented two different missionary approaches: a top-down approach which pays more attention to the elites, and a bottom-up approach which emphasizes more on the mass.

Secondly, all of them were attacked by the state. In 1900, mobilized by Empress Dowager Cixi and some local governors, the boxers killed thousands of missionaries and Chinese Christians, which severely damaged the Taylor's CIM and the Taiyuan churches built by Richard. After the founding of the People's Republic of China in 1949, another round of church-state conflict began. Many churches were confiscated, and Christians were put in jail.

Thirdly, they were quite different in term of theology, political capital (connection with governmental officials) and personal experiences of church-state encounters. Comparing their responses to the state's attack can help us understand how theology, political capital and previous personal experiences shaped their approaches of right protection.

This chapter therefore covers two different political settings of church-state encounters: the late Qing and the early People's Republic of China. The former represented a period of turmoil. The crisis of the dynasty, the progressive advance of the missionary enterprise and feverous reaction of the local elites all contributed to the church-state conflict. The latter represented a period of insecurity. The nascent authoritarian state felt threatened by any autonomous groups. In order to consolidate the regime, a series of political movements were launched, targeting any suspected groups which included Christianity. In order to make comparison more focus, for Hudson Taylor and Timothy Richard, I will compare their responses to the same incident: the Gengzi Massacre (also called Gengzi Incident or Boxer Rebellion). As for Mingdao Wang and Y. T. Wu, I will compare their attitudes towards religious attacks from the state. I use their biographical materials and published works to reconstruct their approaches to right protection.

---

[6]Lyall [11].

Hudson Taylor's Response to the Gengzi Massacre in 1900

Hudson Taylor was the founder of the China Inland Mission (CIM, now Oversea Mission Fellowship International), an interdenominational Protestant mission society which dedicated to the evangelization in China's inland provinces. He established a faith mission paradigm which emphasized faith and prayer. He was famous also due to his adoption of the Chinese clothes (quite rare at that time) and his offspring continue his missionary enterprise till now. His theological position was very conservative. He emphasized personal salvation and regarded evangelization as the main task of missionaries. Under his impact, CIM also redrew from the ecumenical yet liberal Christian Council of China in 1926.

If we want to understand Hudson Taylor's response to the Gengzi Massacre, we need to first go back to the Yangzhou Riot. The Yangzhou Riot was a serious challenge to the nascent China Inland Mission, which established by Taylor in 1858. The missionary station of CIM in Yangzhou were encircled by a riot on August 22, 1868. They attempted to kill the missionaries, loot their poverty and burnt their houses to the ground. Hudson Taylor escaped from the encircled houses and went to the local magistrate's house to look for help. The magistrate unwillingly sent his officials and polices to stop the riot. Later, some CIM missionaries also reported this riot to Sir Walter Henry Medhurst, the British Envoy to China. Sir Medhurst wanted to use this event to pressure the Chinese officials. With the strong intervention of the British envoy backed by the British Navy, the CIM got some compensation from the local government.[7] At that time, relying on foreign authority and urging them to pressure the Chinese officials was a typical method for religious rights protection among the missionaries. However, the intervention of foreign power also aroused hatred and resentment, which in the end escalated hostility. In this case, although the Yangzhou magistrate did give in under pressure, this intensified the conflict between the local church and the local government which made evangelization became more difficult. Furthermore, this also triggered enormous criticism from the members of parliament in the Great Britain. They complained that the missionaries not only damaged the fragile British-Sino relations and did severe harm to the bilateral trade, but also put the lives of British citizens in danger. The controversy resulted from the settlement of the Yangzhou Riot in 1868 changed Hudson Taylor's approach to church-state conflict. Later, the CIM developed the following principle to handle church-state conflict:

> Too great caution cannot be exercised by all Missionaries residing or journeying inland to avoid difficulties and complications with the people, and especially with the authorities. Every member of the Mission must fully understand that he goes out depending for help and protection on the LIVING GOD, and not relying on an arm of flesh. While availing himself of any privileges offered by his own or the Chinese government, *he must make no demand for help or protection* though in emergencies he may need to ask for it as a favour. *Appeals to Consuls or to Chinese officials to procure the punishment of offenders, or to demand the vindication of real or supposed rights, or indemnification for losses, are to be avoided* (italicized by the author). Should trouble or persecution arise inland, a friendly

[7] For more detail information about this event, please see Steer [18, pp. 156–164].

representation may be made to the local Chinese officials, failing redress from whom, those suffering must be satisfied to leave their case in GOD'S hands. *Under no circumstances may any Missionary on his own responsibility make any written appeal to the British or other Foreign authorities*. Should such an appeal be thought necessary, it must first be submitted to the China Director or his Deputy, through the Superintendent, and receive his authorization.[8]

The Gengzi Massacre took place in 1900. It was an anti-imperialist movement launched by an indigenous heretical sect called boxer. It originated in Shandong province, then spread to many provinces in northern China. A slogan of supporting the Qing court and wiping out the foreigners appeared in various places. Boxers was exploited by a local governor and the Empress to undermine imperialism. They selected Christianity as the scapegoat and killed thousands of missionaries and Chinese converts.[9] It claimed seventy nine lives of missionaries and their children from the CIM.[10] Though the CIM suffered more than any other Protestant mission societies in China, Taylor refused to accept the compensation for the loss of property or life, as a way of showing the "meekness and gentleness of Christ".[11]

Timothy Richard's Response to the Taiyuan Massacre in 1900

Timothy Richard was a famous British missionary to China. He was remembered not only as a missionary, but also a statesman and reformer who had great impact on China's modernization in the late nineteen century and early twentieth century.[12] When he arrived in China in 1870, he adopted a common approach to evangelize: to preach in the street and distribute Christian pamphlets. However, this approach had very limited success. He abandoned this method and shifted to a more elitist approach which not only built up his social capital but also opened a door for him to influence China's reform. His theological position was quite different from his British colleague Hudson Taylor. Richard adopted a liberal position which emphasized religious dialogue and social reform. He was a pioneer in Christian-Buddhist dialogue. He also actively engaged in educational and political reform in late Qing China.

Due to Richard's engagement in disaster relief and Chinese reform, he established personal connections with some influential governors such as Li Hongzhang and Zhang Zhidong.[13] Even though many officials in the Qing court and in the locals were xenophobes, Richard still found some helpful officials who he can turn to. For example, when he was in Qingzhou, Shandong, a retired official tried to trigger

[8]China Inland Mission [4].

[9]For more information of the Boxer rebellion see Esherick [6].

[10]Taylor [19, p. 135].

[11]Steer [18, pp. 258–262], Broomhall [2].

[12]Reeve and Glover [13], Johnson [9].

[13]Richard [14, pp. 206–207, 234–241, 256–260].

social hostility towards him by accusing him of kidnapping children. When he sent a letter to the local magistrate to complain about this false accusation, the magistrate put on a public notice to stop this kind of false accusation.[14] This eased social harassment of Richard and enable him to continue his missionary work peacefully. In another instance, a local magistrate tried to stop him renting a house in his prefecture. Richard reported this to the British consul and the consul brought this case to the local governor. The governor also issued a public notice, which not only criticized the plaintiff but also confirmed Richard's right to rent a house. Richard learnt two lessons from these successes in protection his religious freedom: (1) regardless of general suspicion and hostility among Chinese officials, there were always some pragmatic officials he could turn to; (2) Foreign intervention and pressure from above could be conducive protection of religious freedom.

If these previous incidents only made missionaries' life and work more difficult, the Gengzi massacre put many missionaries' lives in danger. Due to Richard's previous success, this approach was also used during the Gengzi massacre. At that time, he was attending missionary conferences in the United States of America (USA). Before the massacre took place, he tried to persuade the USA to take action to prevent the killing. He brought a report of Chinese situation to John Hay, the State Secretary of the United States. When he learnt that without the support from two third of the senators, the White House can do nothing towards China; he approached Mr. Hoar, the Chair of the Senate, for help. Mr. Hoar informed him that the Senate still could not make any initiative without the majority support of the senators. He went to New York to seek support but unfortunately, his attempt failed.[15] He then turned to British officials for help. He sent a telegraph to the consul general for the Great Britain at Shanghai, and asked him to suggest to Sir Salisbury, the then Prime Minister of Great Britain, to send a telegraph to the Chinese governors to urge them to guarantee the safety of British citizens in China. A telegraph was sent but it reached Shanxi late, and the killing had already began claiming more than 5700 missionaries' and Chinese Christians' lives in Shanxi. However, the message from the British government did stop many potential killings in other provinces. For example, the governor in Shaanxi sent a troop to protect the foreigners leaving for Wuhan while governor in Sichuan hided the killing order from the Qing court and used his influence to protect foreigners.[16]

After the Gengzi Massacre, Richard was invited by Prince Qing and governor Li Hongzhuang to Beijing to deal with the compensation issue. As one of the representatives of the missionary societies, he proposed to use 500,000 liang of the indemnity to build a modern university for he believed the missionary society should not exchange the lives of missionaries for money, but using the indemnity to support modern education so as to get rid of the ignorance and superstition of the people

[14] *Ibid.*, pp. 84–85.

[15] *Ibid.*, pp. 295–296.

[16] Richard [14, pp. 279–280]; Soothill [16, pp. 244–252].

which caused this horrible massacre. This was the origin of Shanxi University. Later, building a university in each province also became the official policy of the Qing court.

Y. T. Wu's Approach to Ensure Religious Freedom

The founding of the People's Republic of China marked a new era of church-state relations. Although religious freedom had been incorporated into *The Common Program* of the Chinese People´s Political Consultative Conference (CPPCC), many local churches still forbore enormous attacks from local governments. As Wu mentioned in a report, the most common violations of religious freedom were as follow: church buildings were occupied, property was confiscated, religious activities were intervened, and religious personnel was arrested.[17]

Wu's theology was also very liberal. He was greatly influenced by the social gospel. He converted to Christianity after he attended some public lectures by Sherwood Eddy (1871–1963), an influential missionary from Young Men's Christian Association (YMCA) of the USA. He later became a sectary of the national YMCA in China who mainly responsible for student movement and publication. He undertook theological training from the liberal Union Theological Seminary in New York. Although there was tension between theism and atheism, he believed this was a conflict among the people (人民内部矛盾) rather a conflict between people and their enemies (敌我矛盾, and Christians and communists shared a common ground on 'building the country, defending peace and advancing the happiness of humanity'.[18] His previous exchange with Prime Minister Zhou and the incorporation of five Christians into the CPPCC seemed to support this idea. Wu used to be a Christian leader who criticized the communist movement. From the 1920s to the late 1930s, Y. T. Wu moved from pacifism to a limited synthesis of communism and the Christian social gospel. He believed Communism was a very useful tool to diagnose the contemporary situation while Christianity could provide a better practical solution to the problem. During the anti-Japanese War, he closely worked with some left-wing activists and participated in some patriotic organizations promoted by communist intellectuals. As a result of the ideological appeal of Communism and social networking with communists, he became an ally of the Chinese Communist Party (CPC). Before the founding of People's Republic of China in 1949, he had three personal meetings with high ranking communist officials Zhou Enlai, one in Hankou and two in Chongqing.[19] After these meetings, he learnt the CPC's attitudes towards Christianity and built trust with CPC leaders.

As a church leader, he was very concerned at the time about the recent violation of religious freedom by local governments. He wanted to use the political power

[17]Wu [24, p. 211].

[18]Wu [23, p. 380].

[19]Zhao [29, pp. 494–495].

of the delegates to urge the local officials to guarantee the implementation of the *Common Program*. He also tried to collect the local appeals to Beijing to bring out a national settlement. Therefore, together with some influential church leaders, he formed several delegations.

Their visits had three main goals: to help the local church leaders to build up relationship with local officials, to propagate the main message of the CPPCC to the local churches, and to pressure the local governments to stop attacking the churches. The delegations to Central China made some significant achievements. For example, the Hubei Provincial Government issued a general order to implement religious freedom protection policy in December 1949. In January 1950, the Ministry of Internal Affairs of the Central Government gave a guideline maintaining that governmental organs and armies shall consult the churches before borrowing their buildings. According to this guideline, the Hubei Provincial Government sent out a notice to its government departments on respecting religious freedom and protecting the churches.[20] However, it was only a tactic to establish Wu as a national leader of the churches so that the state could use him to promote the later government-lead church reform.[21] Once Wu's status was established, local governments stopped granting Wu's delegates respect. For example, the Delegation to visit East China did not receive any attention from the local governments.

The success of further delegations was still very limited. Wu's office continued to receive many petitions from local churches. More than one hundred and sixty cases of violation were received by Wu which were sent to various government authorities. Due to the substantive amount of violation, he believed that a national settlement was needed. Therefore, after the successful visit to Central China, together with other church leaders, Wu formed another delegation—The Delegation to Visit North China. This delegation reached Beijing, and brought their cases to Premier Zhou, hoping that a grand settlement will be made with the central government. However, the meeting with Premiere Zhou Enlai changed the direction from ensuring religious freedom to self-reform.

His previous success and personal meeting with Zhou made him believe that he could persuade the central government to issue a general order to protect religious freedom. He had prepared a document entitle *Guanyu Chuli Jidujiao Wenti de Chubu Yijian* (A Preliminary Suggestion to Settle the Christian Problems) for the meeting with Zhou. Although this document also included a section on how to eliminate imperialist force and boost national morale, the main parts of this document were related to the registration of Christian associations, the methods to deal with the occupied church buildings, provisions on religious freedom and issue on establishing a national religious association.[22] After three meetings with Premier Zhou, he understood the most important issue was not to urge the governments to correct the violation of religious freedom, but to reform the churches to make it acceptable to the state. He pointed out:

---

[20] Shen [15, p. 86].

[21] Jun [10, pp. 114–115].

[22] Wu [25, p. 231].

> After three conversations with Premier Zhou, our thoughts had changed. Problems need to be solved, but this is not the most urgent issue. As for the method to solve the problem, at the beginning we want to ask the central government to issue a general order to urge local officials strictly implement religious freedom decree in the *Common Program*. However, later we realized this method might not get the result we expected. If Christianity cannot get rid of people's prejudice against it, even though the government issue an order, the basic situation will not change.[23]

He dropped the religious freedom protection sections in a later revision of this document, and naively believed that once Christianity reformed itself, all the problems would be settled automatically. However, even after the *Three-self Movement*, a state-led reform movement had been consolidated, enormous violation of religious freedom continued to exist. He addressed this in *Guanyu Guance Zongjiao Zhengce de Yixie Wenti* (About Some Issues on the Implementation of Religious Policy), a speech delivered at the Third Plenary of the Second CPPCC in 1957. After pointing out the violation of religious freedom in small cities and the countryside, Wu maintained that the main problem was not from the church but the state. He attributed this to the lack of concrete legal framework to implement the Constitution and the existence of some hostile propaganda. He recommended two suggestions to better implement the religious freedom policy: central and local governments pay more attention to religious affairs, and produce systematic and efficient propaganda promoting religious freedom protection; and do more supplementary legislation to the religious freedom clause (article 88 in the 1954 constitution).[24] He continued to believe that the state was the main player of religious freedom protection. But he relied more on legislation rather than his connection with high ranking officials.

Mingdao Wang's Response to the Counter-Revolution Imprisonment

Mingdao Wang was an indigenous preacher who had great influence on the house church movement in contemporary China. As a conservative preacher, he denounced modernist Christians such as Wu and some other *Three-self church* leaders as non-believers and false prophets. Due to this theological difference, he rejected jointing the *Three-self Patriotic Movement*. As a result, Wang was condemned as the head of a counter-revolution movement (the *Wang Mingdao Counter-revolution Clique*) and was imprisoned for more than twenty years. Some of his followers had also been criminalized as counter-revolutionaries and imprisoned. After the Cultural Revolution, he was released from prison. Even though many cases where people had been unjustly charged had been overturned, but Wang's case was not one of these. He wrote many petition papers to Jianghua, the then Chief Justice of the People's Supreme Court of the People's Republic of China, hoping to correct his unjust case

[23]*Ibid.*

[24]Wu [23, p. 380].

and restore the reputation of his followers. However, due to opposition from his wife, these letters were not sent out.

The petition papers are letters written by Wang to Jianghua from 1982 to 1983. Wang expressed his views on the unjust case of *Wang Mingdao Counter-revolution Clique*, his conflict with the *Three-self Movement* as well as some information about his imprisonment and dramatic release.[25]

He was exclaimed as the hero of the church for his defiance of the Japanese Occupation Authority and the communist state by not jointing their sanctioned church organizations. In 1942, he refused to join the *Huabei Zhonghua Jidujiao Tuan* (Chinese Christian mission in North China) promoted by the Japanese Occupation Authority. Ten years later, he also rejected to join the *Three-self Movement* steered by the communist state. The reasons why he did not join these two movements were because he believed authentic Christians should not yoke with unbelievers, and he considered the leaders in these two movements to be false prophets. He also believed that due to the independent nature of his Christian Tabernacle, there was no need to join these movements to distance himself from the missionaries:

> I strongly argue that churches cannot collude with the secular people, God's servants cannot be controlled by the unbelievers. I strongly maintain that churches which strongly believe God's salvation cannot united with the churches ran by unbelievers. God's servants cannot collaborate with false prophets and false teachers.[26]

His previous success in not joining the Chinese Christian mission in the North made him believed that he also kept his independent spirit.[27] The logic is very simple: even the ruthless Japanese occupation authority tolerated his non-collaboration, and he would be more likely to be spared in a more democratic government in the New China. Although the Soviet Union's religious repression and atheism troubled him, he was convinced him that this kind of attack on religion would not happen in China because of the good discipline of the liberation army, and the slogan of religious freedom in the Concession of Tianjin, a sign of departing from Soviet Union and willingness to protect religious freedom.[28]

His views on the Communist Party also had great impact on his action. His optimism not only supported his not lining with the *Three-self Movement*, but also his petition to the Supreme Court for justices.

> My views on the Communist Party had shifted several times. From 1949 to 1950, I was very optimistic and had great hope on the Party. After that, disappointment and pessimism increased year by year. In 1966, I changed from disappointment to despair. I thought China would fell beyond redemption. But since the Gang of Four had been defeated, my optimism and hope towards China's future has come back again. And for almost one year, my optimism and hope has increased enormously.[29]

---

[25]For more detail, see Ying [27, pp. 6–37].

[26]Wang [22, p. 148].

[27]For more information about this episode please see Wang [21].

[28]Ying [27, pp. 54–55].

[29]*Ibid.*, p. 157.

After the Cultural Revolution, the state changed its ultra-left policy, and corrected many unjust cases. This aroused his optimism again.[30] Jianghua was the Chief Justice of the Supreme Court who in charge of overturning the unjust cases. For Wang, Justice Jianghua was like Justice Bao (包青天) in ancient China who could right the wrongs and restore justice. Sending an appeal to the righteous judge is a very traditional way to restore injustices in China. He believed this petition was not only for himself but for many Christians who were put in jail only because of their relationship with him. However, his wife stopped him sending these petition papers because she believed all injustice was allowed by God and beneficial to the victims.[31] She spiritualized the case and trusted God in heaven rather than Justice Bao in the world as the ultimate source of justices and redemption. Under her prevention, Wang gave in and let these petition papers unsent.

Four Approaches to the Protection of Rights

The approaches of these four men to the protection of religious rights share some similarity though with some noticeable differences. The main similarities and differences of these four Christian approaches I've summarized in Table 4.1.

Although there were significant differences between liberal Christians such as Richard and Wu and conservative Christians such as Taylor and Wang, they shared a common approach of rights protection by turning to political authorities for help. All four figures in this study sought help from the state when religious freedom was under attack. Even though the regime was not friendly to Christianity, they still tried to involve the state in rights protection, either by pressure or persuasion. In other words, turning to 'Caesar' was a common approach. Environment rather than theology can better explain this similarity. Their similarity in rights protection cannot be explained by their divergent theology but by some common contextual factors. China is a country where the state dominates society. The state is the problem as well as the solution. Freedom violation usually comes from the state. However, in order to correct this violation, people must turn to the state. Although Taylor and Richard were quite different in theology (modernism vs. conservatism) and approach in evangelization (elitist vs. bottom-up), both turned to Chinese authorities and foreign power for help.

Wu and Wang also have significant differences in attitudes towards modernism and *the Three-self movement*. However, their approaches towards freedom protection were very similar. Both Wang and Wu considered the state as the main protector of religious freedom. When religious freedom was under attacked, both turned to central government for help. Although this common approach was used by these four figures at the beginning, some changed their methods later. Then the question is not why some Christians seek help from the state while other did not, but what kinds of factors

---

[30]*Ibid.*, p. 160.

[31]Wang [20, p. 122].

Table 4.1 Four Christian approaches for right protection

	Wu	Wang	Richard	Taylor
Approach	Turn to central government for right protection, forming delegation to pressure local government to implement the central policy	Appeal to the chief justice to overturn his unjust case	Ask foreign governments to pressure local governors, find a win-win solution for both	Not turning to Caesar, refuse indemnity
Theology	Liberal	Conservative	Liberal	Conservative
Political capital	Many	Few	Some, both internal and external	Few
Personal experiences	Cooperation with left-wing intellectuals, meeting with high rank communist leaders and participating in the CPPCC	Success in not joining the Chinese Christian mission in North China	Some meeting and cooperation with the Chinese officials	Conflict and controversy resulted from the settlement of the Yangzhou Riot

stimulated or discouraged people to continue this approach. Previous encounter and political capital are two important factors.

At the beginning, Hudson Taylor engaged political authorities to settle down the Yangzhou Riot. However, this not only intensified the church-state conflict in the local, but only triggered controversy, which severely undermined the evangelization of the CIM. As a result, CIM developed a principle of not involving with foreign power and not pressuring the Chinese authorities. Under this guideline, CIM refused to receive any compensation from the Chinese government for the loss of lives and property in the Gengzi Massacre.

Richard also sought help from political authorities when the churches were under attack by the boxers. Engaging with state authority was supported by his liberal theological position. His previous encounters with the state also made him believed that political authorities could be potential collaborators. They can not only be a negative force to prevent conflict, but also be a positive force to advance some common goods such as disaster relief and modernization. Because he had connections with both the British Government and some Chinese officials, he used this political capital to help stop the massacre of the Boxers. Using foreign power to pressure the Chinese officials was also a key aspect of this approach. One thing to be noted is that his handling with the compensation of the Gengzi Massacre in Shanxi was not based on a retributive philosophy but an ancient wisdom of returning good for evil.

Why do people still turn to a hostile regime for help? There are two possible answers: first, this is the only way can make things work; secondly, people do not treat the regime as a whole and believe some part of the government is good. For example, even today many Chinese still believe the central government is just and benevolent though the local governments are harsh and corrupted. In a state-dominant society, it is very natural to resort to the state for solution. China also has an idiom for this: only the person who tie the bell can untie it. Here I will provide more explanation to the second answer. Although both Y. T. Wu and Mingdao Wang realized there were many violations of religious freedom in the People's Republic of China, they believed the main intent of the central government was to protect religious freedom. They shared a similar optimism toward communism. Both believed Christianity was compatible with communism and religious freedom would be protected by the state. For Wu, this came from his conversations with the high-ranking officials in the Communist Party. For Wang, this came from the good impression of the Liberation Army. He also believed that the Communist Party would correct the mistakes made by the Soviet Union as well as the mistakes made in the Cultural Revolution.

Believing there was a common ground between Christianity and Communism, Y. T. Wu tried to persuade the central government to issue a general order to stop the violation of religious freedom in the locals. He also used his positional power of representative of CPPCC and National People Congress to pressure the local officials to conform to the religious freedom clause in the *Common Program* and the Constitution by forming national delegation to the locals. However, this top-down approach had very limited success. The central government did not issue the general order he expected. Instead it pushed Wu to reform the church. Even after Wu had launched a Three-Self Movement to transform the church into a loyal organization, the state's attacks did not end.

As for Wang, his previous success in not joining the Chinese Christian mission in North China under Japanese occupation made him believed that his Christian Tabernacle could be spared by the communist state. At that time, his impression of communist rule was very optimistic. He believed the communists' religious freedom policy was sincere and not lining with the *Three-Self Movement* was possible in New China. But the sudden attack of the state and his long-term imprisonment drove out this optimism. After the Cultural Revolution, under the guideline of restoring things to order (拨乱反正), many unjust cases were overturned, and religious freedom was enshrined in the 1982 Constitution. A new wave of optimism rose up which stimulated him to write petition papers to Jianghua, the chief justice of the Supreme Court to correct his own unjust case. This kind of optimism not only supported his not lining with the *Three-self Movement*, but also his petition to the Supreme Court for Justice. This repeated an ancient repertoire that an unjustly treated person turned to the Justice Bao for justices. However, due to his lack of political capital and the objection from his wife, he gave up sending his petition papers.

Conclusion

In this chapter, I have examined how theology, political capital and personal experiences influenced four Christians' responses to two main attacks by the state: the Gengzi Massacre in the late Qing period and the communists' attack in the 1950s. In each attack, religious freedom was severely violated. In the Gengzi Massacre, churches were destroyed, property was looted, and thousands of Christians were killed. In the latter, religious venues and items were confiscated, worship services were suspended, and hundreds of Christians were denounced and put into prison. As church leaders, Timothy Richard, Hudson Taylor, Y. T. Wu and Mingdao Wang tried to response to the state to protect the religious freedom of the Christian community. Their theology was quite different, but it mainly impacted their methods in evangelization and their attitudes towards pubic engagement, not in the domain of freedom protection. Both Richard and Wu believed social reform was important component of salvation while Taylor and Wang believed the most important thing was personal salvation. As a result, while Richard and Wu actively engaged in social reform movement, Taylor and Wang put aside public engagement and concentrated on their evangelization work.

However, these theological differences did not prevent them from taking a very similar approach to right protection. All believed that the state could play a positive role on protecting religious freedom, and all turned to the Chinese government when freedom was violated. Compare to theology, political capital and previous experiences in church-state encounters had much larger impact. Lack of political capital and negative experience in church-state encounter discouraged Wang and Taylor from keeping appealing to the state while political capital and positive encounters stimulated Wu and Richard to continue this approach.

References

1. Bohr, P. R. (1972). *Famine in China and the missionary: Timothy Richard as relief administrator and advocate of national reform, 1876–1884*. Cambridge: East Asian Research Center, Harvard University.
2. Broomhall, M. (1901). *Martyred missionaries of the China Inland Mission with a record of the perils and sufferings of some who escaped*. London: Morgan and Scott.
3. Cao, N. (2017). Spatial modernity, party building, and local governance: Putting the Christian cross-removal campaign in context. *The China Review, 17*(1), 29–52.
4. China Inland Mission. (1903). Principle and practice of the China Inland mission. Retrieved October 11, 2019, from http://digitallibrary.usc.edu/cdm/ref/collection/p15799coll14/id/33181.
5. Cohen, P. (1957). Missionary approaches: Hudson Taylor and Timothy Richard. *Papers on China, 11*, 29–62.
6. Esherick, J. W. (1988). *The origins of the boxer uprising*. California: University of California Press.
7. Evans, E. W. P. (1945). *Timothy Richard, a Narrative of Christian Enterprise and Statesmanship in China*. London: The Carey Press.

8. Gu, C. (2005). *Cong Ma Lixun dao Shitu Leideng* (From Robert Morrision to John Leighton Start). Shanghai: Shanghai Bookstore Press.
9. Johnson, E. V. (2014). *Timothy Richard's vision: Education and reform in China, 1880–1910*. Eugene: Pickwick.
10. Jun, S. (2017). *Making choices in the midst of change*. Hong Kong: Christian Study Center on Chinese Religion and Culture.
11. Lyall, L. (1973). *Three of China's mighty men: Leaders of Chinese church under persecution*. London: OMF International.
12. Pfister, L. (2003). Re-thinking mission in China: James Hudson Taylor and Timothy Richard. In A. Porter (Ed.), *The imperial horizons of British protestant missions, 1880–1914* (pp. 183–212). Cambridge: William B. Eerdmans.
13. Reeve, B., & Glover, R. (1911). *Timothy Richard, D. D. China missionary statesman and reformer.* London: S. W. Partridge & Co.
14. Richard, T. (1916). *Forty-five years in China*. New York: Frederick A. Stokes Co.
15. Shen, D. (1989). *Wu Yaozong Xiaojuan* (A Short Biography of Y. T. Wu). Shanghai: TSPM Press.
16. Soothill, W. E. (1924). *Timothy Richard of China, seer, statesman, missionary & the most disinterested adviser the Chinese ever had.* London: Seeley, Service & Co.
17. Stanley, B. (1998). Timothy Richard. In G. H. Anderson (Ed.), *Biographical dictionary of Christian missions*. New York: Macmillan Reference USA.
18. Steer, R., &Taylor, J. H. (2006). *A man in Christ*. Beijing: China Friendship Publishing House.
19. Taylor, J. H. (2015). *A retrospect*. Abbotsford: Aneko Press.
20. Wang, C. (2005). *You Sishi Nian* (The Last Forty Years). Hong Kong: Chenxin Chubanshe.
21. Wang, M. (2019). *Zai Huoyao yu Shizi Xue Zhong* (In the Fire Kiln and the Lion Dense). Retrieved October 11, 2019, from http://wellsofgrace.com/messages/wmd/lion.htm.
22. Wang, M. (2005). *Wushi Nian Lai* (Fifty Years On). Hong Kong: Chenxin Chubanshe.
23. Wu, Y. T. (2010). Guanyu Guance Zongjiao Zhengce de Yixie Wenti (A Preliminary Suggestion to Settle the Christian Problems), in *Wu Yaozong Wenxuan,* edited by China Three-self Patriotic Movement Committee (pp. 378–384). Shanghai: TSPM Press.
24. Wu, Y. T. (2010). Jidujiao Fangwentuan Huazhong Fangwen Ji (A Report of the Christian Delegation's Visit to Central China), in *Wu Yaozong Wenxuan,* edited by China Three-self Patriotic Movement Committee (pp. 210–218). Shanghai: TSPM Press.
25. Wu, Y. T. (2010). Zhankai Jidujiao Gexin de Qizhi (Raising the Flag of Christian Reform), in *Wu Yaozong Wenxuan,* edited by China Three-self Patriotic Movement Committee (pp. 219–234). Shanghai: TSPM Press.
26. Ying, F.-T. (Ed.). (2011). *Da Shidai de Zongjiao Xinyang: Wu yaozong yu Ershi Shiji Zhongguo Jidujiao* (Abiding Faith for A Nation in Crisis: Y. T. Wu and Twentieth Century Chinese Christianity). Hong Kong: Christian Study Center on Chinese Religion and Culture.
27. Ying, F.-T. (Ed.). (2013). *Wang Mingdao de Zuihou Zibai* (Wang Mingdao's Last Confession). Hong Kong: Logos Publishers.
28. Ying, F.-T. (2016). Chai shizijia de zhengzhi—Zhejiangsheng sangaiyichai yundong de zongjiao-zhengzhi fenxi (The Politics of Cross Removal—A Religious-Political Analysis on the "Three Rectifications and One Demolition" Movement), *Logos & Pneuma*, *44*, 25–59.
29. Zhao, X. (2014). A short chronicle of Y. T. Wu. In X. Zhao (Ed.), *China modern thinkers' papers: Wu Yaozong Juan* (pp. 489–501). Beijing: Renmin University of China Press.

Zhifeng Zhong is a Research Fellow of the Institute for the Studies of Buddhism and Religious Theory and assistant Professor in the School of Philosophy, Renmin University of China. His main research interests are religion and politics in the modern world, as well as the development of Christianity in contemporary China. He has co-edited books on sociology of religion, and religion in contemporary China, and published peer-reviewed articles on church-state relations, and Christianity in contemporary China.

Chapter 5
A Story of Defending Human Dignity as a Right and Virtue, with Reference to the Cross Removal Incidents in China

Lap Yan Kung

Abstract This chapter starts with three questions with reference to the cross removal incidents in China in Zhejiang Province between 2014 and 2016: How did the Chinese authorities violate human rights in terms of freedom of religion and expression? How did Christians respond to what the Chinese authorities did to them? How did Christians view themselves, taking into account the treatment of the Chinese authorities? Apart from human dignity as a right, Christians in their resistance have displayed a dignified manner characterized by non-violence and forgiveness, and this is human dignity as a virtue. Christians in their resistance may have a little impact on the improvement of human rights conditions in China, but they witness to a dignity of life, which can never be deprived by violence and injustice.

Introduction

There is an ongoing debate whether human rights are universal or culture-bound. The Bangkok Declaration (1993) in which the Chinese government is one of the signatories is an example of this controversy.[1] However, Qianfan Zhang, a law professor at Peking University, notes that the notion of human dignity is not completely foreign to Chinese culture, for it has had a very long history in classical Chinese philosophy. Zhang examines the three classical Chinese philosophies, namely, Confucianism, Daoism, and Mohism, and concludes that 'the three schools of thought do converge on a common moral precept that to treat every human being as the end in itself and

[1] See Davis [8].

[2] Zhang [23, p. 200].

This is a revised version of the original article entitled to 'Human Dignity as a Right and Virtue in Practice: A Socio-Theological Reflection from and on the Cross Removal Incidents in China', *Religions*, 2018, 9:138.

L. Y. Kung (✉)
Department of Cultural & Religious Studies, The Chinese University of Hong Kong, Shatin, Hong Kong, China
e-mail: kungly@cuhk.edu.hk

Z. Xie et al. (eds.), *Human Dignity, Human Rights, and Social Justice*,
https://doi.org/10.1007/978-981-15-5081-2_5

not merely as means to other things'.[2] Zhang points out that these three schools of thought affirm that human dignity is an intrinsic value of being human. It is the status of being human that demands our full respect and protection. Moreover, Zhang indicates that these three classical Chinese philosophies, especially Confucianism, consider that the notion of human dignity is reflected in one's dignified manner or bearing.[3] Human dignity, thus, is the expression of a sublime disposition: dignity as virtue. These two dimensions of human dignity as a right and virtue are distinct but related. First, human dignity is an intrinsic value, which we ascribe to all human beings simply in virtue of being human. Second, human dignity is an inflorescent dignity, which people possess to a greater or less extent inasmuch as they lack or possess, gain, or lose special qualities, excellences or virtues. Third, a human being with an inflorescent dignity acts in ways that expresses the intrinsic value of the human.[4] In this chapter, we intend to investigate human dignity as a right and virtue with reference to a traumatic series of events, namely the forced removal of rooftop crosses from church buildings in China's Zhejiang Province since early 2014. The three dimensions of human dignity in practice will be addressed by examining three questions: First, how do the Chinese authorities violate human dignity in terms of freedom of religion? Second, what have Christians done in order to defend their dignity violated by the Chinese authorities? Third, what kind of life do they witness to human dignity? These three questions are inspired by M. Rosen's work on *Dignity*.[5] Finally, we will correlate the findings from these three questions which is also based on fieldwork, including interviews, to a general enquiry of human dignity practice in China.

The Cross Removal Campaign

In early 2014, the Chinese authorities began a campaign to demolish crosses on the rooftops of churches as well as churches in Zhejiang Province.[6] It is estimated that the number of affected churches is about 1500 and around twenty of them are completely demolished.[7] Most affected churches are found not in the cities but in towns and villages. They are mostly members of the Three-Self Patriotic Movement (TSPM, an approved Protestant organization), Catholic churches, and a few non-registered churches (house churches). Though the demolition campaign has been relatively quiet since April 2016, it has not come to a complete stop. The government explains that the demolitions being conducted are all part of the government's intent to implement the policy of 'Three Rectifications and One Demolition' (hereafter

---

[3]Zhang [23, pp. 56–58].

[4]Sulmasy [16, pp. 937–944].

[5]Rosen [15].

[6]Cook [7, pp. 43–65].

[7]*List of Affected Churches in Zhejiang and Wenzhou (2014–16)*, https://docs.google.com/document/d/1bx5XNC-WEt7EJ0zwpmvkrcPjeUbqCTEMFyqbeJINvmE/edit. Accessed 18 November 2019.

referred to as TROD) that was endorsed in December 2012 by the Zhejiang provincial government, which aims to address the increasing number of illegal constructions.[8] The government further clarifies that a construction can be considered as an illegal construction when the 'construction is without approval and construction is beyond the size of approval'. Some churches are involved in illegal construction, but this cannot explain in what sense the crosses on the rooftops of churches are illegal construction. I would consider that the TROD has a political agenda.

The introduction of the program of 'Five Entries and Five Transformations' in late 2015, cross removals in other provinces since 2016, and the introduction of the 'Revised Regulations of Religious Affairs' in September 2017 convinced people that what happened in Zhejiang Province was a test case for future tightening of religious activities and policy by the government. Apart from the increasing number of illegal constructions being cited as a reason for the implementation of the TROD, another reason being considered is the active religious activities in Wenzhou County. Wenzhou County is known as 'China's Jerusalem' among Chinese Christians, because it has a high concentration of churches and Christians. It was observed that the severe cross removal campaign was carried out as a reaction to a complaint expressed by Baolong Xia, the secretary of Zhejiang Province, as to how a communist country could have so many crosses, which is for him nothing but humiliating to the Chinese Communist Party. In addition, the church, Xia contends, represents foreign beliefs, and is a sign of foreign imperialism.[9] Nevertheless, it is important to note that the TROD has been more devastating to folk religious sites that are labelled as an expression of superstition than to Christian churches.[10] Thus, it may be argued that Christianity is not solely targeted, but rather religion as a whole.

There are two more important reasons causing the cross removals. First, there is a 'holy' tie between the Christian business people and local cadres in Wenzhou County. Without the 'one eye open, one eye blind' unwritten policy of local cadres, Christians would have been unable to build the unapproved churches and organize religious activities publicly. The holy cooperation between the Christian business people and local cadres in Wenzhou County is not a secret. In fact, a number of local cadres are Christians, and some Christian business people are members of the Chinese Communist Party. There is therefore a reciprocity of benefits between the churches and the local government, which has received both material and non-material benefits from churches. Furthermore, the Christian entrepreneurs in Wenzhou County liaise skilfully with the local government in order to promote their faith. Nanlai Cao comments that the Christian business people are 'economically powerful, politically connected, and moralizing Christian entrepreneurs'.[11] This explains the reason why the demolition order came from the provincial government with the support of the central government and not from the local government. Cao succinctly opines that the current campaign, in his view, is a measure adopted by the central government

[8] Exclusive [5].

[9] Wang [18, at p. 795].

[10] Ying [22, at p. 29] (in Chinese).

[11] Cao [3, pp. 33–35].

to strengthen local control and reshape local political-economic order in the context of the party-building work and high-profile commitment to combat corruption.[12]

A second reason for the removal of crosses is the following: since most affected churches are found in towns and villages, it is suggested that the government intends to have tighter control of towns and villages. Traditionally, people in towns and villages have strong blood ties, and the government hardly controls them. The uncontrollable towns and villages can therefore be seen as a threat to the government. A recent example is Wukan village's protests in 2011 and 2016. What concerned the government most, however, was that the village chief showed more loyalty to blood tie relationships than to the government. This was a signal that the village was reaching outside the government's control. Furthermore, one of the characteristics of some towns and villages in Wenzhou County is that the location and the size of church buildings reflects their centrality in the life of the people. The demolition of the crosses served to destabilize the centrality of Christianity in the lives of the people. After the cross removals, the government established People's Centres or Culture Halls in the towns and villages to replace the role of churches in the villages' life. Thus, the TROD is not simply intended to target illegal construction, but has a very strong political agenda. This explains the reason why the government makes no concession to local churches' grievances and appeals.

Freedom of Religion

At its fourth plenary session of the 18th congress in October 2014, the Chinese Communist Party leadership passed a reform plan on the legal system. It presented an ambition to build a system of rule of law in the country. In reality, the legal reform does not change the fundamental nature of the Chinese legal practice, that is, rule by law. The TROD is a test case.

The cross removals themselves are a violation of Christians' freedom of religion. Apart from the concern of building safety, the government argues that it has received complaints against rooftop crosses from *fengshui* (cosmic harmony) believers who claim that the crosses have damaged the local *fengshui* and that the damage of *fengshui* would affect the fate of the people.[13] The government thus explains that the removal of crosses is necessary to bring society into harmony. However, the decision to remove crosses as an appropriate solution to social disharmony is entirely questionable; instead of creating an ambiance of trust and harmony, it creates distrust and hatred. Promoting dialogue is the best course of action in dealing with differences. It requires an invitation to all stakeholders to come together to negotiate—however, the government never consults the churches. Since the number of affected churches is about 1500, it is difficult to be convinced that *fengshui* is the major and real reason for

[12]Cao [4, at p. 36].

[13]Wang [18, p. 795].

the cross removals. In fact, the Chinese government does not take *fengshui* seriously, for it is condemned as superstition.

Fundamentally, the Chinese government has not changed its basic suspicions of religion. Article 4 of the Revised Regulations of Religious Affairs in 2017 states that among the many perils posed by religion there are dangers to 'national security and public health, threats to ethnic and national unity, and the possibility of terrorist activities'. Religion may also 'violate people's civil and democratic rights, obstruct public administration, and invade public or private property'. The government considers that religion always tends to have its own development without accommodating itself to Chinese socialism as well as the 'Sinicization of Christianity'. In addition, some members of the Chinese Communist Party are more tolerant to religion and this consequently weakens and softens the party and government's alertness to the penetration of religion. In order to prevent religious penetration, the government has taken a tight control and non-negotiable policy for handling religion. In an authoritarian government, national security is an excuse to restrict the activities of the imagined enemies more than something truly dangerous to the country. It is not to be denied that there are illegal constructions of churches, but any law should give high priority to ensure the respect and protection of freedom of religion. Obviously, the TROD gives no justified reason to override freedom of religion.

Christian Responses

Some Christians are inclined to see the TROD incident as an opportunity for them to grow spiritually. Some even consider the incident to be God's punishment for the arrogance of churches that focus too much on buildings rather than their spiritual life. Repentance is the first word, not resistance. They argue that the core of the Christian faith is not outer freedom, but Christian living expressed in fellowship, worship, and prayer. This spiritual freedom would not deteriorate even without the outer freedom. They finally conclude that, to a certain extent, the cross removal incidents revealed the spiritual weakness of the churches. An emphasis on inner freedom is an invaluable lesson that the Christian community had learned and developed during the hard times of the Cultural Revolution (1966–1976). During this period, no religious activities were allowed, and Christians were sent to re-education camps. All these adversities did not destroy the faith of Christians. Ironically, their endurance in suffering has become a prevailing source for the rapid growth of churches in China after the Open-Door Policy in 1978. There is truth in this emphasis. Tertullian said, 'The blood of the martyrs is the seed of the Church'. Yet, Christian inner freedom should not be understood as an indifference to violations of freedom of religion and expression. Protecting religious freedom through resistance is not less spiritual than endurance in suffering. Churches are more open to taking a position to defend their right of practicing their faith.

Although the affected churches are in different locations, we confined our research to Wenzhou city. Not all churches in Wenzhou city have been affected by the TROD.

It is estimated that the affected number is about 15–20%. Protestant churches in Wenzhou city are divided into six dioceses, and there are about 150–170 churches in total. All dioceses issued statements in response to the forced removal of crosses.[14] For instance, the statement released by the Diocese of Pingyang Wanquan stated that:

1. We hold prayer and fasting meetings;
2. We organize all churches to have regular church services;
3. We employ lawyers for *weiquan* (rights defense);
4. We make a trip to Beijing for *shangfang* (petition to the central government);
5. We cooperate with other churches;
6. We rebuild the crosses if they are demolished;
7. We rely on God in solidarity, mutual service, and bearing the yoke of Christ.

Holding regular church services and prayer meetings was not only intended for meeting religious needs, but also a strategy to ensure that members were stationed at the church most of the time in order to stop cross removals from taking place. The practice of *shangfang* reflected that their negotiation with the provincial government was futile, and the practice of *weiquan* reflected that they considered the cross removal itself to be unlawful and unconstitutional. More importantly, they called for solidarity among churches.

Apart from issuing statements, the churches organized day and night patrols to protect church buildings from being attacked. Some Christians tied themselves up with the crosses and went on hunger strike. Some rebuilt the crosses when the crosses were removed. For instance, Wuxi Church in Yongxi Diocese rebuilt the cross on 22 August 2015 and invited other churches to come and celebrate. Some, such as Shuangcun Church, exposed the removed crosses up in gardens or in front of churches as a form of protest. Some, such as Shatantou Church, painted crosses on the walls in order to show that the cross was never demolished. Some set up a monument to record how the demolition of the cross took place. This form of protest was employed by Xianqiao Church in Pingyang Diocese, but the monument was forcefully demolished. Some arranged Sunday school classes to be held around the demolished crosses in order to teach younger generations about the event. One favourite biblical story was the story of Daniel in the lions' den. This is about the virtue of courage, non-compliance, endurance, and keeping faith in God. Some unaffected churches joined the affected churches in solidarity to protect their churches. They used different forms of media to spread the news locally as well as internationally in order to put pressure on the government. They held rallies to protest against the cross removals. All of these responses were non-violent. In order to counter the resistance, many pastors and members of the laity were summoned by police for interrogation. Some were beaten, detained for several months and even longer, or imprisoned for different reasons. Apart from these illegal reactions, the police threatened the protestors that their families would be affected if they continued to protest.

A spirit of martyrdom was gradually stirred up and developed among Christians. On 24 July 2015, a prayer letter was circulated among Christians with the heading

[14]China Change [6].

'We are for the Faith.' This phrase was first used by Mingdao Wang, the dean of the house churches, to stand against the intervention of the government into his church in the 1950's. He was imprisoned for his faith from 1955 to 1980. This phrase not only expresses standing firm in one's faith but also signifies a firm non-compliant attitude toward the government.

From Silence to *Weiquan* (a Defence of Rights)

One significant issue in Christian resistance is their association with the *Weiquan* Movement. *Weiquan* literally translates as a defence of rights. It is a broadly based social phenomenon involving all social strata throughout China to assert human rights through individual and collective litigations, petitions, campaigns, and protests.[15] *Weiquan* is fundamentally about human rights, but it does not address human rights directly since it is aware of the political sensitivity of the issue of human rights in China. The features of *weiquan* are that, first, it uses the law to challenge the authorities and their officials in order to push the regime to live up to the promises of its policies and laws. Second, ordinary citizens have become more aware of their constitutional rights, so when those rights get violated by the corruption of local officials they are more willing to speak up. Third, *weiquan* accepts the legitimacy of the existing political system, while the democracy movement does not.[16] Even though *weiquan* is non-violent and is carried out within the boundary of law and order, the authorities still feel uncomfortable and consider it as a possible threat since it has the potential to develop into a nationwide social movement. A recent and significant event occurred on 9 July 2015, when the police arrested more than 300 people related to the *Weiquan* Movement from 25 provinces. This was called the 709 crackdown, and it was a huge blow to the *Weiquan* Movement. The *Weiquan* Movement is not new to churches, because a number of lawyers in the *Weiquan* Movement are Christians and they are motivated by their Christian beliefs to fight for equality, fairness and justice.[17] Due to their illegal status, non-registered churches (house churches) are more engaged in *weiquan* to defend their rights. A small booklet entitled the *Weiquan Handbook for Churches* was published in 2006.

Some TSPM affected churches contacted Kai Zhang, a Christian lawyer committed to *weiquan*. He and other lawyers took the initiative to form the Lawyers for the Protection of the Cross on 14 July 2015, and provided legal advice to the affected churches. Furthermore, Zhang and his team published a small book for the affected churches entitled *A Handbook of Weiquang and the Cross*. He advised the affected churches to take a progressive response instead of a defensive response. He said, 'If more than 10 churches in your town are not able to resist the cross removal campaign,

---

[15]Benney [1].

[16]Hung [11].

[17]Wielander [19, pp. 849–864].

how can you expect a town with one church only to resist it?'[18] Slightly more than a hundred churches out of 150–170 affected churches in Wenzhou city employed him to be their representative. He made four petitions on behalf of these churches:

1. To request compensation for the damage caused to the churches by the government;
2. To accuse the government of blocking electricity and water supplies to the churches;
3. To file a lawsuit against the announcement of the demolition of illegal churches;
4. To request an open hearing of the involved government officials.

However, there are still quite a number of churches, which preferred to be spectators. First, *weiquan*, in whatever sense, was too radical and political for them. This was not only due to the theological position of church-state relations but also a result of socio-political arrangements, for churches were trained not to be engaged in public life. Second, they considered that *weiquan* would not bring them justice, but paradoxically would bring them further damage. In other words, they had unreservedly accepted the realpolitik as an unchallenged reality. Third, they accused some *weiquan* lawyers of taking advantage of the case of religious freedom for their own agenda, namely, an opportunity to express their opposition to the government.

On 23 August 2015, Kai Zhang, and his two assistants, Peng Lui and Xianrui Fang, were held in custody by the government. On 23 March 2016, Zhang was released after he made a televised confession of his wrongdoings on the issue of the cross removals. Zhang released a prayer request on 24 March 2018, in which he mentioned that he had been under different forms of arrest for nearly three years and had no contact with his wife and child. His retreat from this issue has left churches without legal support, but this has not stopped them from continuing different forms of *weiquan* and *shangfang* to protect Christian dignity and their rights. Fenggang Yang comments that the resistance of Wenzhou churches is a sign of churches moving from accommodation to and cooperation with the government to resistance to and even confrontation with the government.[19] It must be noted, however, that only a minority (10%) of the total affected churches took a relatively active role in the resistance. Most churches chose to be passive. Apart from the reasons mentioned above, some church leaders are business people, which is very common in Wenzhou, and they are afraid that their businesses would be negatively affected if they encouraged their churches to take an active role in the resistance against the government. As a result, they are inclined to persuade their church leaders to compromise with the government. Second, many Christians consider that the removal of the crosses is a lesser evil in comparison with the demolition of the church. The case of Sanjiang Church is an example of a non-compromising congregation and, as a result, the whole church was demolished. Moreover, the TROD talks only about illegal construction and says nothing about accountability. In other words, this is a relatively mild suppression. In order to prevent complications of the situation, the best strategy for the churches,

---

[18] Initium [12].

[19] Yang [21, at p. 87].

as felt by some church leaders, is to be silent about the cross removals and just comply with the regulations. The passivity of the majority of churches challenges the optimism of a number of observers about the emergence of civil society among churches, but there is no doubt that the option of resistance as a Christian response is growing.

Another unintended consequence of the cross removal incidents is the establishment of solidarity among churches within and outside of Zhejiang Province. Both the Zhejiang TSPM and Zhejiang China Christian Council, as well as the National TSPM and National China Christian Council, expressed their displeasure with the cross removals. They complained that the cross removals themselves were an unconstitutional act and a violation of the policy of religious freedom; it harmed the feelings of Christians. They strongly requested the Ethnic and Religious Affairs Commission of Zhejiang Province to halt this 'ridiculous' activity. This solidarity act threatened the government. As a result, outspoken pastors were removed from office. An example was Pastor Joseph Gu. He was the former chairperson of the Zhejiang China Christian Council and the former pastor of Chongyi Church in Hangzhou, a church with 10,000 members. His outspokenness, however, caused him to be removed from the office and put in custody from February 2016 to January 2018 on the charge of embezzling funds. The fate of Pastor Gu has left the affected churches isolated from the ecumenicity of the churches in China since many churches and pastors are afraid that they might get into trouble if they show solidarity with the churches in Wenzhou. However, at the same time, Pastor Gu set an example for other churches in the country, demonstrating what it means to be Christ's disciple.

Some Christians have paid a high price for their non-cooperation and *weiquan*. For instance, some churches have been totally demolished, and some Christians have been beaten and detained for months and even years. Still, they do not regret their actions, because they have come to realize that dignity can never be bought or traded. Their stubborn resistance matches the views of Mencius (372–289 BCE) concerning what it is to be a person with integrity. He said:

> To dwell in the wide house of the world, to stand in the correct seat of the world, and to walk in the great path of the world; when he obtains his desire for office, to practice his principles for the good of the people; and when that desire is disappointed, to practice them alone; to be above the power of riches and honors to make dissipated, of poverty and mean condition to make swerve from principle, and of power and force to make bend—these characteristics constitute the great man.[20]

[20]Nothingistic [14].

Human Dignity and the Theology of the Cross

'Near the Cross' was one of the favourite hymns sung by Christians during the cross removal incidents.[21] This hymn echoes the sentimental experience of Christians who have suffered from the incidents of the cross removals. This hymn carries a message that the cross is not a humiliation, but the glory of God (Gal. 6:14). Christian dignity comes through bearing one's own cross, that is, suffering for the sake of Jesus Christ and God's Kingdom. We thus examine how the theology of the cross empowers Christians to interpret their experience and live through it.

First, dignity is not only about the personal ability to control oneself and to determine one's own destiny, that is, autonomy, but it is also experienced in the nature of one's relationships with others, that is, how one is treated and how one treats others. Christians experience dignity in terms of being forgiven, loved, and healed by the cross of Jesus Christ. No matter how one's dignity is humiliated and denied, one's dignity in Jesus Christ will not be eliminated. A passage from the Bible was frequently quoted by Christians during the cross removal incidents: 'A bruised reed he will not break, and a dimly burning wick he will not quench; he will faithfully bring forth justice' (Isa. 4:3). This is not to justify any form of suffering, but a willingness and determination to suffer for a cause, that is, for the Kingdom of God. This is a cause in which certain things mean more to the Christians than to others. By taking care of the things that are important to them, they develop a sense of 'who I am' and 'what I live for'. This realization by Christians in a sense parallels the Chinese motto, 'Morality is doing what is right regardless of what you are told'. In the cross removal incidents, Christians take the cross seriously, for the Christian faith (and Jesus Christ) means more to them than other things in life. They do not regret being beaten, detained, unemployed, or even jailed due to their resistance to the injustice committed against them. The following biblical text is frequently quoted in their struggle: Then Jesus told his disciples, 'If any want to become my followers, let them deny themselves and take up their cross and follow me. For those who want to save their life will lose it, and those who lose their life for my sake will find it' (Mt. 16:24-25). An interviewee reflectively said:

> I wish that I can have a better understanding of the meaning of the fact that Christ calls me to die for him. If the suffering and death of some Christians can calm down the campaign of the cross removals and help our country to move to the rule of law in all areas of life, I am prepared for it. May God strengthen me.

The cross of Jesus Christ empowers Christians not to seek revenge against people who disgrace them, but rather to proclaim the gospel of forgiveness: Jesus said, 'Father, forgive them; for they do not know what they are doing' (Lk. 23:34). Following Jesus, Christians learn to forgive the cadres coming to demolish their crosses, for the cadres are ordered to remove the crosses, and they do not know what they are doing. Christian dignity is expressed in treating others in a dignified manner.

---

[21] *Near the Cross*, https://hymnary.org/text/jesus_keep_me_near_the_cross. Accessed 18 November 2019.

This reminds Christians in China of Xiaobo Liu's Nobel Prize Lecture, *I Have No Enemies—The Final Statement*. He wrote:

> Hatred can rot away at a person's intelligence and conscience. Enemy mentality will poison the spirit of a nation, incite cruel mortal struggles, destroy a society's tolerance and humanity, and hinder a nation's progress toward freedom and democracy. That is why I hope to be able to transcend my personal experiences as I look upon our nation's development and social change, to counter the regime's hostility with utmost goodwill, and to dispel hatred with love.[22]

Liu's message corresponds to the message of the cross of Jesus Christ. It is in the cross that Christians see, judge, and treat themselves and others differently. On the one hand, Christians are the victims of the cross removal incidents. However, they can seek to avoid the tendency toward attitudes of victimization. On the other hand, they have the capacity to forgive their enemies and create an ambiance of mutual respect. They choose non-violence, not because it is a strategy, but because Jesus said, 'Love your enemies', and Liu Xiaobo said, 'I have no enemies'.

Dignity is not an acceptance of finitude, but instead is living in hope. The cross is not just about suffering and crucifixion, but it is the cross leading to resurrection. It is the resurrection of Jesus that gives people hope to live in the midst of injustice and frustration, for they know that the exercise of power, even to the point of putting one to death, is not the final word. Resurrection says no to all kinds of determinism, fatalism, and stoicism. The cross stands for suffering, but it kindles hope in life. However, this is not to suggest that resurrection can only come through suffering. Rather, it is the belief that there is hope in hopelessness. The focus is not on how we can achieve hope, but it is in the resurrection of Jesus Christ that hope emerges and springs forth. Hope is defined by when we do not give in even though we are defeated. Hope is when we do not lose our heart for goodness even though we are powerless to transform injustice. Christians in their resistance to the government are not naïve to believe that they can finally prevent the cross removals. With hope, they resist; with hope, they accept the hostile reality. They accept their failures and defeats, but they do not lose hope in God's justice. In terms of spirituality, this is the dark night of the soul. A favourite biblical message that circulated among churches during the cross removals is as follows: 'I consider that the sufferings of this present time are not worth comparing with the glory about to be revealed to us' (Rom 8:18). William Lynch rightly said that 'hope comes close to being the very heart and centre of a human being'.[23]

Nevertheless, there is always a tendency to stress the essentially otherworldly among Christians. In fact, the theology of pre-millennialism is commonly found in Chinese churches. Social responsibility is less emphasized, as pre-millennialism considers that nothing can be done to improve social conditions. What Christians can do is to pray for divine intervention to rupture the historical process and bring about a radically novel state of affairs. Theologically speaking, Christians who are

[22]Xiaobo [20].

[23]Lynch [13, p. 31].

inclined to be passive in the cross removal incidents cling to the theology of premillennialism. Regarding the matter of hope, Ernst Bloch made a pertinent clarification in distinguishing between the proper imaginative activity of hope and mere fantasizing:

> In the former, hope is often a stretching of the imagination way beyond the limits of what is currently possible. Imagination fuels the engines of our movement into the future. Mere fantasizing is a matter only of projecting our desires on to the blank screen of what may lie beyond.[24]

Real hope liberates and moves us forward while false hope entraps and leaves us where we began. In terms of Bloch's distinction, Christian hope should not be mere fantasy. However, there is a danger of the moralization of eschatology, in which it is believed that the Kingdom of God can be brought about by human action. Christoph Schwöbel reminded that 'the Christian hope distinguishes the eschatological orientation of faith from the open future of humanity's own project, and this is the reason why we can hope that it will not be frustrated when human projects flounder'.[25]

Christians in their resistance have manifested some kind of sublime disposition, but we have to admit that many churches and Christians choose to comply with the TROD. This is not because they agree with the TROD but because they are under different forms of pressure from the government. This is a time of testing of their faith.

Human Dignity and *Mien-Tzu* (Face)

During the time of the implementation of the TROD, there were ongoing formal and informal negotiations among the government, local cadres, and churches. Some local cadres spoke to the churches, 'Don't resist the cross removal. Give us face (*mien-tzu*) and be cooperative so that we can have a good report to the senior. In return, we will not make you suffer too harshly and will give you face on other occasions'. On other occasions, some local cadres said, 'We normally would not interfere with the practice of the churches. But if they do not give us face (*mien-tzu*) by ignoring who the boss is, we will have to punish them severely'.

What does giving face and losing face mean? How is this related to dignity? There are two Chinese words for face, namely, *lien* and *mien-tzu*. '*Lien* is something to which everyone is entitled by virtue of his membership in society and can be lost only though unacceptable conduct'.[26] It focuses on the conduct of oneself. Though this has something to do with the inner qualities of the individual, the public image is the concern. *Mien-tzu* focuses on how one is treated by others in public. Those of lower social status are supposed to defer to those of higher social status, and those

[24]Bloch [2, p. 144].

[25]Schwöbel [17].

[26]Ho [9, at p. 870].

of higher social status maintain face by protecting low-status others.[27] If those of lower social status do not give face to those of higher social status, those of higher social status have no responsibility to protect them. *Mien-tzu* is a reciprocal concept; however, in an asymmetrical relationship, those of higher social status do not need to give *mien-tzu* to those of lower social status. Both *lien* and *mien-tzu* are a kind of a social control, as they are more related to one's position in a social system than to a personal attribute. Face puts a person under pressure to live up to others' expectations, but has little to do with dignity. *Mien-tzu* in particular would not help to build a culture of dignity characterized by self-worth, self-esteem, and respect of others. Nevertheless, there is always confusion between face (*lien* and *mien-tzu*) and dignity in Chinese culture, and this confusion is a hindrance to the development of human rights consciousness. Here, we employ the cross removal incidents to explain this idea.

Like the national flag and national anthem of a country, the cross is the symbol of the Christian faith. Therefore, Christians consider the demolition of the cross as a grave violation against their faith. It is an act of disrespect to and humiliation of the Christian faith. In an interview, a pastor from one of the affected churches said, 'The cross is the symbol of our faith. The forced removal of the cross is a humiliation of our faith and disrespect to the glory of our God. I am not concerned about the stone cross, but it is my conscience calling me to stand up against injustice'. His words were echoed by other Christians. In another interview, a church leader said, 'The cross is not our faith, but an icon of our faith. Why does the government play with our cross? Starting from the end of last year [2013], there are no more lights on the crosses. And starting from this year, most crosses have been demolished. Undoubtedly, this is a challenge to our faith, and also a humiliation'. Are they talking about dignity in the terms of respect of rights or a matter of *mien-tzu*?

Mien-tzu is related to one's position in a social system, and it does not make any sense for those of lower social status to care too much about their *mien-tzu*. Since the Christian churches do not have a high position in the Chinese social system, it is unreasonable to view Christian resistance as being for the sake of retaining *mien-tzu*. On the contrary, we suggest that their resistance is a response to the violation of their dignity as the freedom of religion. There is nothing wrong in the churches giving mien-tzu to the government, but the churches are aware that dignity cannot be traded off, and therefore Christian resistance is an appropriate response to the violation of Christian dignity by the government.

On the other hand, the Chinese government would not consider the cross removals as a violation of human dignity. Its concern is whether the churches give *mien-tzu* to the government, that is, obedience, for the churches belong to a lower social status and have no power to bargain with the government. Christian resistance to the government would not be positively seen as an exercise of their right to protect themselves, but rather as an offensive act against the government. According to the logic of *mien-tzu* culture, compliance and persuasion, instead of resistance, is the appropriate response of those of lower social status to those of higher social status.

[27] Hu [10, at p. 61].

This explains the reason why the government officer said, 'If you [the churches] do not give us *mien-tzu* by ignoring who the boss is, we will have to punish you severely'. Once those of lower social status accept the logic of *mien-tzu* as the foundation of relationships, and resistance to injustice would not be considered as an option, for this would be seen as an inappropriate and disgraceful act to those of higher social status. It cannot be denied that a number of churches choose to comply with the TROD because they consider that giving *mien-tzu* to the government is the best way to protect their interests. But more churches are able to distinguish between dignity and *mien-tzu*, and take that there is no compromise on dignity.

Conclusion

The Chinese government has launched two 'Five Years Human Rights Action Plan' (2012–2016 and 2016–2020) and signed various United Nations Human Rights treaties. (Note: The ICCPR is not legally binding for the Chinese government unless the government ratifies it.) Nevertheless, the case of the cross removal does not reflect how these human rights action plans have obviously improved the human rights conditions in China. We argue that the cross removals have a clear political agenda, that is, to tighten the control of society. Even though the Christian resistance is confined to their sphere in terms of location and interest, their resistance not only provides the churches with a practical experience to reflect on what the church–state relationship should be, what Christian freedom and resistance are, and what Christian responsibility for society is, but it also unmasks the narrative of the empire, which is characterized by the rule by law and the culture of *mien-tzu*. Christians have suffered a great deal in these incidents, but they have expressed an inflorescent dignity embodied by non-violence and forgiveness, persistence in truth, and living in hope.

References

1. Benney, J. (2013). *Defending rights in contemporary China*. New York: Routledge.
2. Bloch, E. (1986). *The principle of hope* (Vol. 3). Oxford: Blackwell.
3. Cao, N. (2011). *Constructing China's Jerusalem: Christians, power, and place in contemporary Wenzhou*. Stanford: Stanford University Press.
4. Cao, N. (2017). Spatial modernity, party building, and local governance: Putting the christian cross-removal campaign in context. *China Review, 17*, 29–52.
5. China Aid. Exclusive: China Aid receives internal government documents confirming Zhejiang campaign to demolish, Rectify 'Illegal' Structures. Retrieved November 18, 2019, from https://www.chinaaid.org/2014/04/exclusive-china-aid-receives-internal.html.
6. China Change. Christian sentiment in Zhejiang against cross removal: Three statements. Retrieved November 18, 2019, from https://chinachange.org/2015/08/07/christian-sentiment-in-zhejiang-against-cross-removal-three-statements/.
7. Cook, S. G. (2017) *The battle for China's spirit*. New York: Freedom House. Retrieved November 18, 2019. (Google. "List of Affected Churches in Zhejiang and Wenzhou, 2014-16").

8. Davis, M. C. (1995). *Human rights and Chinese values*. Hong Kong: Oxford University Press.
9. Ho, D. Y.-F. (1976). On the concept of face. *American Journal of Sociology, 81,* 867–884.
10. Hu, H. C. (1944). The Chinese concepts of face. *American Anthropologist, 46,* 45–64.
11. Hung, C. F. (2010). The politics of China's Wei-Quan movement in the internet age international. *Journal of China Studies, 1,* 331–349.
12. Initium. The War of the Cross. Retrieved November 18, 2019, from https://theinitium.com/article/20150901-mainland-wenzhou-church-protest/.
13. Lynch, W. F. (1965). *Images of hope*. Dublin: Helicon.
14. Nothingistic. *The works of Mencius* (J. Legge, Trans.). Retrieved November 18, 2019, from http://nothingistic.org/library/mencius/mencius21.html.
15. Rosen, M. (2012). *Dignity*. Cambridge: Harvard University Press.
16. Sulmasy, D. P. (2013). The varieties of human dignity: a logical and conceptual analysis. *Medicine, Health Care and Philosophy, 16*(4), 937–944.
17. Schwöbel, C. (2000). Last things first? The century of eschatology in retrospect. In D. Fergusson & M. Sarot (Eds.), *The future as god's gift* (pp. 217–241). Edinburgh: T&T Clark.
18. Wang, S. (2017). Tripartite freedom of religion in China: An illiberal perspective. *Human Rights Quarterly, 39,* 783–810.
19. Wielander, G. (2009). Bridging the gap? Intellectual house church activities in beijing and their potential role in China's democratization. *The Journal of Contemporary China, 18,* 849–864.
20. Xiaobo, L. I have no enemies: My final statement. Retrieved November 18, 2019, from https://www.nobelprize.org/nobel_prizes/peace/laureates/2010/xiaobo-lecture.html.
21. Yang, F. (2017). From cooperation to resistance: Christian responses to intensified suppression in China today. *The Review of Faith & International Affairs, 15,* 79–90.
22. Ying, F. T. (2016). The politics of cross demolition. *Logos & Pneuma, 44*(2016), 17–61. (In Chinese).
23. Zhang, Q. (2016). *Human dignity in classical Chinese philosophy*. New York: Palgrave.

Lap Yan Kung a graduate from the universities of St Andrews and Glasgow (Scotland), teaches Christian ethics, political theology and life education at The Chinese University of Hong Kong since 1996. He has received 4 Book awards, namely, *A Tearless Grief* (2001), *An Abnormal Faith* (2008), *The Cross of Homosexuality* (2013), and *God-Talk in Darkness* (2018). His current research is on memory and religion, embodied spirituality and yoga fever in China, justice and peace in world Christianity. Apart from his academic post, Lap Yan is the honorary general secretary of the Hong Kong Christian Institute (an advocacy NGO).

Chapter 6
Flexible Governance: Petition, Disputes and Citizen's Rights Protection in Contemporary China

Jieren Hu, Tong Wu, and Jingyang Fei

Abstract Blamed as a major threat to an effective judiciary, *Xinfang* not only often fails to resolve social disputes between the petitioners and the Party-state in the authoritarian regime but also exacerbates the conflict. Using two cases of Shanghai, this chapter shows that the innovative mechanism of involving petition social workers (PSWs) in settling disputes is a kind of "flexible governance" (FG) stressing affective care and the use of multi-pronged means of dispute resolution to relieve petition pressure and maintain social stability by the authoritarian state. Facing the surge and intensification of social conflict in recent years, "flexible governance" reflects the corporatist relations between social organizations and the local state with the state's intensive political control over the society.

Introduction

Discontent and frustration caused by political and economic hardship, which forced the weak and poor to fiercely protest, substantially explains the increasing number of petition cases and mass movements in China.[1] *Xinfang* (信訪), broadly known

[1] This paper uses the terms "petition" and "*Xinfang*" interchangeably, hereafter.

[2] Minzner [18].

[3] Hu and Zheng [12].

This chapter is a revised version of the original article "Flexible Governance in China: Affective Care, Petition Social Workers, and Multi-Pronged Means of Dispute Resolution" appeared in *Asian Survey* (58: 4) 2018: 679–703.

J. Hu (✉)
Law School, Tongji University, Siping Road, Shanghai 200092, P. R. China
e-mail: besthujieren@bnu.edu.cn

T. Wu
School of Social Development, East China University, Shanghai, P. R. China

J. Fei
School of International Relations and Public Affairs, Fudan University, Shanghai, P. R. China

Z. Xie et al. (eds.), *Human Dignity, Human Rights, and Social Justice*,
https://doi.org/10.1007/978-981-15-5081-2_6

as petition or *Letters and Visits* in English, includes a variety of practices that parallel, overlap, and in some cases replace formal legal channels. Petitioning effort aimed at triggering the discretionary involvement of key Party leaders in the relief of popular contention is an alternative to formal judicial way that Chinese citizens can seek to redress their disputes.[2] Given the internal flaws of the *Xinfang* system and the political pressure of disputes resolution and stability maintenance, the Chinese Communist Party (CCP) has deployed a diversified mechanism of dispute resolution to contain social conflicts and defuse popular grievances more flexibly and effectively.[3] For example, "grand mediation", "active judiciary", "judges mediating community disputes" and, the "grid management" in urban China and the "carrot and stick policy" in the rural area are actually a kind of "flexible governance" (柔性治理 *rouxing zhili*) under the authoritarian rule that tries to contain social grievances and maintain social stabilities.[4] Why does the Party-state continuously encourage and promote the social innovative programs in dispute resolution in local China? What are the characteristics of this kind of "flexible governance" and to what extent is it effective in addressing *Xinfang* disputes? What's the implication of the "flexible governance" to the state-society relations?

We try to answer these questions by studying a new practice of involving social workers in *Xinfang* disputes resolution in Shanghai. It finds that the PWSs represent a typical example of the "flexible governance" through which the local governments adopt comprehensive/multi-pronged means to relieve long-frustrated petition disputes as well as maintain social stability. Flexible governance provides buffers and all kinds of innovative dispute resolution methods to relieve petition pressure and increase the dispute resolution rate. "Flexible governance" adds credibility to the current *Xinfang* system and local government since it can successfully redress intractable disputes between petitioners and the local government by bypassing the limitations in the current law and policies and taking the psychological and humanistic care into concern. Facing the surge and intensification of social conflict in recent years, the flexible governance reflects the corporatist relations between social organizations and the local state with the state's intensive political control over the society.

Methodology

Started in 2008, social workers with professional knowledge and skills in Shanghai began to manage and settle disputes between the petitioners and the local government. PSWs apply their professional knowledge and skills to address petition disputes through casework, psychological counseling, group work, and community activities after getting connection with the petitioners and their families. Shanghai is chosen for studying the processes and features of social workers' intervention in petition disputes resolution since it took the first step in China to invite social forces to manage social disputes, appease popular grievances and reduce the number of collective disputes.

[4]Hu [10], Su [25], Chen and Kang [2].

After the practice in Shanghai and the witness of PSWs' positive outcomes on the petition disputes resolution, it has been extensively practiced in many other cities and provinces in China in the recent years, including Beijing, Shenzhen, Guangdong and Shanxi, etc.[5] The introduction of PSWs reflects a new state-society cooperation by a coordinated mechanism of *Xinfang* bureaus, administrative agencies and social forces to address social disputes and maintain social stability in China.[6]

Qualitative case analysis is applied, and the cases are selected based on both analytical purposes and practical concern of the successful and failed ones. As one of the most international and prosperous yet conflict-ridden city, Shanghai is a typical city that adopts the "flexible governance" to contain petition disputes and achieve social governance innovation and social stability maintenance at local place. The practice of involving social workers in petition dispute resolution provides a window to probe the state-society relations, i.e. the interaction between the local government and social forces.

We got contact with the officials in Civil Affairs Bureau and the Women's Federation government in Shanghai by our personal ties. Staffs in the municipal government also assisted us to contact the social workers and the local petitioners. We collected our data from 78 *Xinfang* cases with social workers' intervention in petition disputes resolution in Shanghai during 2012–2016. Forty-two in-depth interviews were conducted, this included twenty social workers who participated in citizens' dispute resolution, three judges and four officials in the Civil Affairs Bureau and Women's Federations who have managed the *Xinfang* cases, fourteen petitioners having contacted by social workers and one lawyer. Extensive background information was also derived from government documents, case files and media reports.

Regime Type and "Flexible Governance"

Social governance is a perennial issue in the study of state-society relations. And the type of political regime, to a large extent, shapes the state's response to popular resistance.[7] Democratic countries pursue good governance and provide more opportunities for political skills to be developed among a much broader range of people than centrally organized institutions.[8] Given that repression undermines the regime's legitimacy, although authoritarian regimes are less reliant on legitimacy for survival than their democratic counterparts, they certainly have incentives to build and strengthen their legitimacy by promoting social governance and improving citizen's recognition and support to the government.[9]

[5] Lee and Zhifen [15], You and Qianmin [29].

[6] Manning [16].

[7] Goldstone and Tilly [6].

[8] Pratchett [20].

[9] Cai [1].

Orthodox justifications on social governance include the state-centered theories, which stress the omnipotent state with top-down control and the binding of organizations into various forms of state patronage[10]; society-centered theories, which seek to explain the pluralizing social forces devise strategies to negotiate with the state and pursue their members' interests[11]; and the social corporatism or state-in-society approach, which argues that continued state control through indirect mechanisms of coordination and co-optation coexists with the opening-up of social space.[12] These approaches, however, have been criticized for the risk of obscuring the dynamics of change in China and the capacity of the "co-opted groups" to influence the policy-making processor to pursue the interests of their members.[13]

In the Chinese setting, the period of "decentralized authoritarianism"[14] from Deng Xiaoping, Jiang Zemin to Hu Jintao is actually characterized by a "state-led civil society", or even more properly, a "state-led social pluralism" where local governments and society enjoy increasing responsibility over policy development and implementation with the dominant control by the central government.[15] Pluralism is only possible with the central's permission and directions. In spite of recent promising changes in polities at both national and provincial levels, the party-state always attempts to enhance stability in China's increasingly volatile cities in recent years. Known as consultative authoritarianism, social organizations in China have been encouraged by local officials to provide social services and improve public policies, yet they may also be treated as threats that may challenge social stability and regime legitimacy.[16] Therefore, although the Chinese government has adopted pragmatic and problem-solving approaches in response to the complicated and challenging social situation in the name of innovation in social governance, the reforms in China have not produced straightforward decentralization since the state's surveillance and control over the society remains pervasive and effective to a large extent.[17] Rather, alternative governing paths, driven by the pressure of social development at local place and the quest for stability maintenance and legitimacy enhancement, have been devised to realize public participation and good governance.

Facing the surging number of social conflicts in recent years, the CCP has adopted diversified mechanisms of dispute resolution and innovative social governance through non-binding rules in addition to rigid way of litigation and suppression. The various kinds of local mechanisms are, in essence, a kind of "flexible governance" which relied upon the use of multi-pronged means and task-specific arrangements to achieve dispute resolution. It is a strategy of stability maintenance that (1) operates beyond law but within policy boundary; (2) employs various cooperation between

[10]Reuschemeyer and Evans [22].

[11]Dahl [3], Diamond [5].

[12]Migdal [17], Unger and Chan [27], Schmitter [24].

[13]Saich [23].

[14]Landry [14].

[15]Hu [11].

[16]Teets [26].

[17]Hu and Zheng [12].

the state and society in the form of purchasing services by the government;(3) hinges upon a circuitous way of dispute resolution focusing on the petitioners' emotion, psychological feeling, empathy and humane sympathy. Flexible governance is the development of "emotional governance" in state building and social construction during the revolutionary era in China[18] and entails the innovative way of unification of government and social organizations at present to manage social disputes at local place under the authoritarian political system which puts social stability and regime legitimacy as the primary task.

It is a rational choice for both the local government to use social forces to relieve social grievances under a flawed judicial system and meet the political tasks of stability maintenance from above and the social organizations to justify their legal status, continue their institutional development and get financial support from the government. The cases of ISWX illustrate how "flexible governance" works in addressing social conflicts in urban China and identify the features of the flexibility in the practice and its internal limitations. However, despite a reduction of petition disputes and the petitioners' positive attitude towards the local government at the moment, how long can the flexible governance be effective is still in question.

Petition Social Workers and Dispute Resolution

Social workers try to ensure social welfare and security for those affected by social disadvantages such as poverty, provide psychosocial care to the mentally and physically disabled people, and raise voices against social injustice during the social reforms through casework, research, psychological counseling, policy planning, community development, direct practice and crisis intervention.[19] The central documents of the *Opinions on Strengthening the Construction of Professional Social Workers in 2011* and the *Medium and Long-term Plan on Constructing Professional Social Workers' Team (2011–2020)* in 2012 were promulgated to promote innovation in social governance in China.[20] Since then, local governments in China have launched more collaborative projects with social organizations in various areas and tried to improve social workers' ability in problem-solving and helping the weak groups in society. With the hope of relieving tensions at moments of high strain, the Shanghai Civil Affairs Bureau and Women's Federation has cooperated with PSWs in 11 districts to settle difficult petition cases since 2008. Table 6.1 illustrates the Xinfang projects with PSWs' intervention in Shanghai, with each project containing a number of petition cases managed by social work agencies.[21]

[18]Perry [19].

[19]Reamer [21].

[20]Government of the Republic of China [7].

[21]Source: From the authors' field work in 2014, Shanghai. For privacy all the names of the petitioners and the PSWs are pseudonyms.

Table 6.1 *Xinfang* projects with PSWs' intervention in Shanghai

Xinfang projects	Period	Client	Agent
Petition case of Mrs. Chen	May 2008–2011	Shanghai Civil Bureau	Shanghai Social Work Firm A
Family service for petitioners of land expropriation in K District retired cadres from enterprises	2009–2011	Women's Federation in P District	Shanghai Social Work Firm B
Retired cadres from enterprises	2011–2012		
Petition case of Vietnam War Veteran-Mr. Li	2012	Shanghai Civil Bureau	Shanghai Social Work Firm C
Petition case for Mrs. Du's family in Anhui	2012		
Magnolia Happy Home—Intimate Mama	2008–2013	Women's Federation in Shanghai	Various Social Work Institutions in Shanghai

Using K district in Shanghai as an example, the District Civil Affairs Bureau and Women's Federations entrusts social workers firms to mediate *Xinfang* cases usually paid by installment, lump-sum payment. Moreover, social workers who are able to settle intractable disputes will get an additional bonus based on the nature of the case. According to our data in K district, the number of social workers has increased from 7,044 in 2008 to 8,973 in 2013. To mobilize social workers' intervention in dispute resolution, the local state has continued to increase their annual income after 2010, with a surge in 2010 and a stable increase of over 3,000 yuan per year afterwards (see Fig. 6.1).[22]

Detailed cases will be expatiated on how social workers manage and settle petitioners' disputes while interacting with the local government.

Magnolia Happy Home—Intimate Mama Project

In December 2011, Shanghai Civil Affairs Bureau, Shanghai Women's Federation and Shanghai *Xinfang* Bureau started a petition dispute resolution project called "Magnolia Happy Home—Intimate Mama" (MHHIM) (白玉蘭開心家園—知心媽媽 *baiyulan kaixin jiayuan, zhixin mama*) in the form of purchasing services from social workers' firms in Shanghai. Professional social worker institutions signed a three-year contract with the Street/Town Women's Federations in 11 local districts. The social workers need to manage and resolve protracted (usually over 5 years)

[22]Source: K District Statistical Yearbook [13].

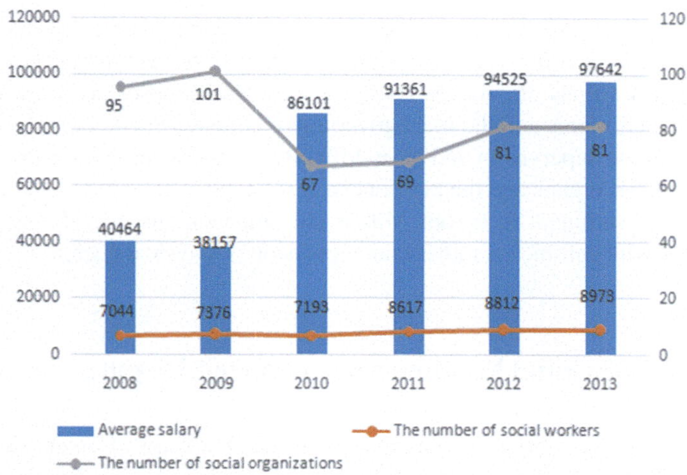

Fig. 6.1 Statistics of the number of social organizations, social workers and their salaries, 2008–2013

and intractable *Xinfang* cases in their districts with salaries around 95,000 yuan per year paid by the Women's Federation. Third-party evaluation from independent and professional organizations is conducted to appraise PSWs' performance in the project. The independent evaluation team is comprised of professors/experts of Social Work, Sociology and Psychology from outstanding universities in Shanghai. The evaluation standards are based upon the scope of the service covered, the number of petition times and the dispute resolution rate. Meanwhile, petitioners' change of attitude toward the PSWs even if the problems have not yet been resolved would also be taken into consideration during the appraisal. Social work organizations also have the rights to select cases they would like to handle. Particularly, two elements are of key concerns for them: unreasonable/unlawful demands and no solution according to law and policy. In other words, if the cases transferred to PSWs from the local Women's Federation and District Civil Affairs Bureaus cannot be resolved by laws and policies, the social work institutions can turn them down and choose those they are capable of settlement. After three years' practice of the MHHIM project, till September 2012, 31% have been successfully resolved among the 78 petition cases in the 11 districts; 44% of which have not been fully resolved but showed a decreasing frequency of petition and turned to a more rational way of expression; and 25% have got connection with the PSWs despite of the failure in reaching consensus.[23]

Since most of the petition cases handled by PSWs are long-term and intractable ones, all the petitioners involved have developed a hostile and resentful attitude toward the local government. Meanwhile, many local officials also treat the petitioners as unruly, stubborn and unreasonable or even crazy guys after many years' reception of their complaints. However, an obvious outcome of hiring PSWs is that

[23]Data collected from the field work.

among all the 78 cases, no matter successfully settled or not, the petitioners' discontent toward the local officials has been greatly reduced and the relationship between the two parties largely improved. PSWs in the MHHIM project act as a bridge between the petitioners and the local government although social organizations are still under official supervision and have difficulty in coordinating local government agencies, judicial organs and the petitioners. It is a typical example of FG deployed by the local government to co-opt with social organizations in realizing stability maintenance with soft means rather than repression or physical coercion.[24]

Resolving Individual Petitioner's Protracted Dispute

Linhua, aged 57, was once a Stomatologist in the K District Center for Disease Control. In 2000, due to personnel changes in the District Health Bureau, she had to work in the Community Health Center. However, she was very unsatisfied with this arrangement and had complained to the District Health Bureau several times, requiring the recovery of her affiliation and compensation for her loss of the post allowance. At that time, according to the local policy of urban demolition project initiated by the K District Government, Linhua's family should move out from their original apartment in Y road. Unfortunately, her husband suddenly died of heart attack during their relocation in the fall of 2000 which led to her ascribing her husband's death to the demolition project caused by the local government.

These two incidents became the driving force for Linhua to take legal action against the District Health Bureau in 2003. She strongly requested the compensation for her loss caused by the personnel change and her husband's death. However, she failed the suit. Then she continued to sue the governmental agencies in the Second Intermediate Court and the High Court in 2005 in Shanghai. Given all the results went against her, Linhua turned to K District *Xinfang* Office in the same year.

Until 2013, Linhua has been petitioning for 8 years and developed deep hostility and distrust toward the local government. The local *Xinfang* Office replied to her that her demands were unreasonable and too excessive, requesting 150,000 yuan as compensation for her post allowance, 300,000 yuan for her husband's death and her litigation fee. It is impossible for the District Health Bureau or local government to pay for what she wants according to law. But Linhua insisted on her appeal and even went to the State *Xinfang* Bureau in Beijing in 2010.

In 2011, this case was referred to HX Social Workers Firm by the Street Women's Federation in K District. Mr. Pan and Ms. Ai are experienced social worker specialized in administrative law and psychological counseling. They got to know from the Street Office that Linhua had a 32-year-old daughter, Xiaoqing, who was unemployed and divorced three years ago and a 3-year-old granddaughter named Mimi. Mimi has been suffering from a congenital rare disease—muscular dystrophy—and is treated in the intensive care unit in the Shanghai Children' Hospital. Based on these

[24]Cai [1].

information, Mr. Pan tried to apply SWOT analysis to get connected with her and settle her disputes.[25] He focused on the "strengths and opportunities" to communicate, pacify and resolve her problems while overcoming the "weakness and threats" in the SWOT matrix.

Linhua has been very cautious attitude the social workers during their first half year's contact as she felt that Mr. Pan and Ms. Ai were dispatched by the local government to watch her and persuade her to stop petition and may even take coercive measures toward her. Mr. Pan tried several times to tell Linhua that they only worked as social workers and their professional ethic is to help others help themselves. Ms Ai also confirmed Linhua that their cooperation with local government is just for resource integration and quicker resolution of difficult cases. But this could hardly male Linhua accept them and still kept distance from them.

Then Mr. Pan focused on Linghua's life difficulties since it is the "weakness" drawn from the SWOT analysis. The stalemate was not broken until their fifth meeting when Mr. Pan succeeded in finding good doctors for Mimi and introducing Xiaoqing to work as a volunteer in a primary school's summer camp as she expressed strong desire in providing social service to students. Soon after this meeting, Xiaoqing started to change her attitude and proactively gave her QQ number to Ms. Ai and expressed her thanks and willingness to make friend with her. Unfortunately, Mimi's illness deteriorated and died on June 13. Linhua and Xiaoqing were in great sorrow but turned out more reliance and recognition to the social workers.

Succeeded in getting Linhua's acceptance and trust, Mr. Pan gradually communicated with her about the petition case and the demands she requested. However, in 2012, Linhua went again to the National Petition Bureau in Beijing with other petitioners from Shanghai but was intercepted by the local officials from Shanghai Petition Bureau and were drawn back to Shanghai immediately. At that moment, Linhua required the bureau to call Mr. Pan and Ms. Ai for help. As soon as the social workers got the information, they contacted the Shanghai *Xinfang* Bureau directly and met Linhua there. They not only explained the relevant law to Linhua, telling her that illegal petition and unreasonable demands were not allowed, but also told her that it was actually impossible for her to achieve her goals through this way. What she could do is to be rational and pursue her demands according to law.

Based upon her trust in the social workers, Linhua finally agreed to stop suing the local government and was willing to discuss about her compensation with the District Health Bureau. Mr. Pan and Ms. Ai immediately contacted the director of District Health Bureau and initiated negotiation between the two parties. Finally, Linhua got 50,000 yuan for her post allowance and 20,000 yuan as the compensation for the relocation. After she signed the agreement, the social workers helped to work in a community social organization as full-time staff.

[25]SWOT analysis aims to identify the key internal (the strengths and weaknesses internal to the organization) and external factors (the opportunities and threats presented by the environment external to the organization) important to achieving objectives before contacting the petitioners, see Hill and Westbrook [8].

Defusing Veterans' Collective Activism

Throughout the new century, the Chinese state has been roiled by contention launched by former military officers. Since 2009, there have been groups of military-transferred cadres from the state-owned enterprises (SOEs) protesting against the local governments, complaining about their unfair treatment by the Party-state. Among the 180 petitioners from various districts in Shanghai, all of them were born during 1930s and 1940, with 22% of whom have serious diseases and reply on basic living allowances. They also have enough time to make petitions and protest against the local and central government since they have retired.

There have been three key reasons for the veterans' organizing collective petition in Shanghai as in other places in China. Firstly, they encountered great interest loss as well as reputation damage caused by the restructure of SOE in the 1990s which led to their being laid off after leaving the military. Secondly, they felt frustrated and angry towards the underfunded and unevenly distributed social and medical benefits at local place. Thirdly, they have a righteous indignation when they attributed their life difficulties and poor living conditions to the local officials' corruption and the placement policies, which have discrepancy between the central document and the local implementations.

Similar ages/life experience and close ties of comradeship produced strong recognition and sense of collective identity among these veterans.[26] Unsatisfied with the poor status quo as military-transferred cadres, they took their grievances to the street and made moral claims for their basic survival rights. In contrast to other veterans, they stressed their contribution to the country but were discharged due to the historical factors and political arrangements by the PLA. Some of them even sent letters to the Shanghai Party Secretary Yu Zhengsheng in 2011, requesting for immediate medical benefits and same allowances as other places in China given their very poor living conditions.[27] The leader of this group, Mr. Shi, insisted on their petitions.

To relieve the veterans' contention and prevent them from large-scale collective activism, Shanghai Civil Affairs Bureau cooperated with Y Psychological Counseling Center, which is a professional social work institute specialized in psychological counseling, social work and petition mediation. Ten PSWs were dispatched to contact the veterans with their background information provided by the Civil Affairs Bureau. They applied a divide-and-rule strategy to pacify the ex-officers. However, different from Linhua's case, veterans in Shanghai were continually antagonistic to the PSWs.

The stalemate between the PSWs and retired officers is derived from their grievances toward the local authorities' failure in addressing their requests and providing enough allowances to them.[28] The PSWs' relationship with the local government, however, prevent them to win trust and acceptance from the veterans in that the veterans believed that they were trying to use control and surveillance in the

---

[26] Diamant and O'Brien [4].

[27] Veterans [28].

[28] Diamant and O'Brien [4].

name of care to them. However, apart from the tasks assigned by the government, social workers are sincerely helping the veterans improve their living conditions and address their problems. Ms. Wang, another experienced social worker, successfully contacted Mr. Shi with the help of her friends in the military. Concealing her real identity, Mr. Shi accepted to talk to her and thanked her for the care to them. Ms Wang brought many legal documents and explained to him that neither protest nor litigation could resolve their problems. Instead, they should be rational and try to talk frankly with the local government. Even if the Civil Affairs Bureau had difficulties in meeting all of their demands, communication and negotiation would be helpful for seeking a solution. Meanwhile, Ms Wang also showed her care to Mr. Shi's family about their health condition and living difficulties. Gradually Mr. Shi builds up friendship with Ms. Wang especially when she succeeded in applying for social relief subsidies to his wife, who was also a laid-off worker. From Shi, Ms. Wang got to know two other sub-leaders, Mr. Yan and Mr. Chen, who were in charge of mobilizing and organizing other protestors in M district. She then informed other social workers in the district to contact the sub-leaders and tried to make friends with them but still failed.

The PSWs find that veterans are suspicious and cautious toward them, questioning their relationship with the government. When seeing their poor living status, divorced, with severe disease, or receiving little poverty relief subsidy, the PSWs really wish to provide care and help to their family but was hindered by their dual-identity. After one year's contact and communication by Ms. Wang, Mr. Shi turned to be calmer and rational regarding their requests for the compensation and treated Ms. Wang as his friend. He agreed to meet the local officials with the company of Ms. Wang and other two sub-leaders. However, the veterans did not accept the amount of 300 yuan allowance per month stipulated by the government files since they felt that it was still too low and far from justice. And they insisted on the recovering of their military cadres' identity which was beyond the scope of current policy and the local government's capacity.

Discussion

With a stalled legal reform and lack of institutional means of addressing collective grievances in China, many petition cases, particularly the historically long-standing policy mistakes, can hardly be resolved through litigation or mediation. A coordinated network established by PSWs, Civil Affairs Bureau, Women's Federations and the *Xinfang* Bureaus integrate the administrative and social forces to resolve disputes more effectively. By pacifying the disgruntled petitioners with empathy and kind assistance, albeit not meeting their demands directly, PSWs' participation in dispute resolution represents a FG deployed by the local state aiming at relieving social grievances, preventing the escalation of social conflicts and maintaining social stability through emotional control, human sympathy and affection. Social work institutions also need to cooperate with local government in order to justify their legal status and continue their institutional development as well as to get financial support from the state. Moreover, cooperation with local governments can become a *quid pro quo* for the PSWs in collecting petitioners' personal information and their past petition experience and facilitating their contact with the petitioners. This kind of collaboration can even increase the chances of successful application for administrative resources to help the petitioners and build up mutual trust between the PSWs and the petitioners.[29] It is, in essence, a conflict resolution and legitimacy enhancement strategy as it helps to demobilize petitioners and defuse their resistance to the government. Since many of them have unreasonable requests and even become professional petitioners, FG deployed by the local state can effectively reduce the number of their petitions, stop them from complaining and change their attitude toward the local government especially when they accept to receive the compensation.

However, PSWs also encounter a dilemma of dual identity in the state outsourcing projects, i.e. act as social workers (helping petitioners help themselves) and government's employees (fulfilling the tasks of dispute resolution). This dilemma not only becomes a big obstacle for them to get recognition from the petitioners as shown in the cases but also undermines their reputation and integrity. The value of care and the pursuit for profit can hardly be balanced at this stage since the government holds strong political and financial control over social organizations and the latter also need to seek political support for its own development. Professional ethics have to give place to regime legitimacy and social stability if social organizations are unable to be independent and self-financed. What PSWs can offer while local officials cannot is *rationality* and *respect* to the petitioners, always responding with human sympathy, honor and dignity to the weak groups and helping them get subsidies and console them with affection. This very important value, to a large extent, becomes the key aspect that makes petitioners could recognize/accept the PSWs, mitigate the long-term hostility and tense relation with the local government, and settle the disputes in the end. Therefore, the approach of inviting PSWs in dispute resolution accords with the principles of right of relief for the weak group and stressed the psychological comfort/humane sympathy to the petitioners.

Despite the variations, all the mechanisms extensively practiced are characterized by a state-led mode that sidelines social forces in the dispute resolution. The collaborative relations between social workers and administrative agencies are proved to be helpful for the government in Shanghai as well as in other cities in China to achieve effective local governance in that social disputes could be controlled and relieved in time by flexible means (*linghuo shouduan*) as long as sufficient financial support from the local state. However, as the cases have shown, PSWs' role as a "third party" between the petitioners and governmental departments is distinguished by their relatively independent identity and their professional casework for individuals, families, and groups. With the increasing state control over social organizations and the PSWs' strong reliance on governments' support and resources, it is questionable whether this practice would lead to the de facto stronger control of the social organizations and damaging the rule-of-law development in the long run.

[29] Hsu and Hasmath [9].

Conclusion

Social conflicts and rampant corruption have become a double whammy for the CCP since the new millennium. The frequency of petition and the impact on Chinese society, consequently, are the result of the political arrangement and the local government's incapability of settling social conflicts. Meanwhile, petitions and social protests in recent years have urged the party-state to seek all possible means to maintain social stability and enhance regime legitimacy, even at the expense of rule of law. PSW, as a remedy for judicial deficiency and a rational choice for both local authorities and social organizations, as well as other multi-pronged means of dispute resolution, is in fact a FG devised by the party-state to use legitimate and nonthreatening ways of discontent containment and stability maintenance in the absence of a democratic system and rule of law.

This chapter argues that FG of dispute resolution and stability maintenance in authoritarian China actually reflects: (1) the state's incapability to provide legal or formal solutions to petitioners' grievances associated with their problems; (2) the discretion of resolving petitioners' demands have to go beyond law but within policy; and (3) a state-led cooperation between social organizations and local government. FG deployed by the local government can add political resilience to the regime in that it relieves long-term public contention and enhances citizens' recognition to the local state through addressing protractible and intractable disputes. Affective care, human sympathy and psychological comfort are paid special attention in establishing friendship with the aggrieved petitioners and PSWs. However, FG has several theoretical and empirical implications on social governance and dispute resolution in China.

Firstly, this concept reframes the currently diversified means of dispute resolution and stability maintenance with "either soft or hard" or "both soft and hard" means of addressing popular demands and defusing social contentions. "Soft" in affection and love to petitioners while "hard" in strong control over the outsourced social organizations, FG captures the feature of "relational repression" of O'Brien and Deng but extend it from strong ties in rural China to weak ties in urban China. It is proved to be effective to recover local petitioners' confidence in the *Xinfang* system and the local government when they finally made their long-term disputes settled albeit in a non-legal way. According to our field study, 38 petitioners among the 78 cases finally desisted from petition and 18 petitioners promised not to go to Beijing any more after their being contacted with PSWs. Particularly, most of the petitioners' negative feeling towards the local government has been obviously mitigated.

Secondly, PSWs' intervention in *Xinfang* demonstrates a state-led collaborative mode between the state and social organizations. The government's intention of inviting PSWs to manage *Xinfang* cases is to integrate the institutional way (judicial and administrative) and non-institutional way (social forces) to control petition activism and prevent challenges against the regime. Reflecting on the cases in Shanghai as well as in other places in China, it could, to a certain extent, reduce the number of petitions and solve intractable disputes at this moment. The incentive structure in

Chinese political system also pushes local innovative programs and helps to sustain and encourage more similar practices in dispute resolution and stability maintenance. Under the current cadre appraisal system, the number of petition cases resolved by the local government becomes a key indicator of the "effectiveness" in dispute resolution for the local officials. Therefore, the FG meets the double goals of the local authorities, i.e. fulfilling political tasks of stability maintenance and achieving good appraisals.

Thirdly, FG gains its rationality and popularity from the state authorities because political and administrative tactics often and routinely prevail over the rule of law in authoritarian states. Outsourcing projects actually display an ever-increasing social control by the party-state. The local state's selective rewards to the PSWs and the social work institutions turn out to be intrigues of recruiting and training its loyal defenders while sacrificing their professional ethics for achieving political goals since stability maintenance and regime legitimacy take precedence over PSWs' professional ethics during the dispute resolution process. Undoubtedly, to resolve petitioners' problems effectively calls for a real judicial reform to gradually transform political power structure with more focus on the rule of law. However, because of the far-lagged political reform and the unequal distribution/weak human rights protection in a booming society, the accumulated social risks have intensified and resulted in an explosive increase of visit-petitions, strikes, and mass disturbances of different types since the promotion of rule of law has always yielded to police guidelines.

Social workers, who have been paid more and more attention in China, have to survive and develop between their instrumental pursuit vis-à-vis value interest, i.e. to seek resources and political support from local government and to help the petitioners solve their problems and improve their life in local communities. However, given the state's domination over social organization and a stagnant political-legal development, the effectiveness of FG in addressing the root problems in China remains to been seen.

References

1. Cai, Y. (2008). Power structure and regime resilience: Contentious politics in China. *British Journal of Political Science, 38*(3), 411–432.
2. Chen, F., & Kang, Y. (2016). Disorganized popular contention and local Institutional Building in China: A case study in guangdong. *Journal of Contemporary China, 25*(100), 596–612.
3. Dahl, R. A. (1961). *Who governs? Democracy and power in an American city*. New Haven: Yale University Press.
4. Diamant, N. J., & O'Brien, K. (2015). Veteran's political activism in China. *Modern China, 41*(3), 278–312.
5. Diamond, L. (1994). Rethinking civil society: Toward democratic consolidation. *Journal of Democracy, 5*(3), 4–17.
6. Goldstone, J. A., & Tilly, C. (2001). Threat (and Opportunity): Popular action and state response in the dynamics of contentious action. In R. R. Aminzade, J. A. Goldstone, D. McAdam, E. J. Perry, W. H. Sewell Jr., S. Tarrow & C. Tilley (Eds.), *Silence and voice in the study of contentious politics* (179–194). New York: Cambridge University Press.

7. Government of the Republic of China. (2011). Ministry of Civil Affairs. Retrieved November 8, 2011, from http://www.mca.gov.cn/article/yw/shgzyzyfw/fgwj/201507/20150700850352.shtml and April 26, 2012. Retrieved March 9, 2018, from http://www.mca.gov.cn/article/zwgk/mzyw/201204/20120400302320.shtml.
8. Hill, T., & Westbrook, R. (1997). SWOT analysis: It's time for a product recall. *Long Range Planning, 30*(1), 46–52.
9. Hsu, J., & Hasmath, R. (2014). The local corporatist state and NGO relations in China. *Journal of Contemporary China, 23*(87), 516–534.
10. Hu, J. (2011). Grand mediation: Mechanism and application in China. *Asian Survey, 51*(6), 1065–1089.
11. Hu, J. (2016). *Shi Hexie Shequ Yunzhuan Qilai: Dangdai Zhongguo Chengshi Shequ Jiufen Huajie Yanjiu (Making Harmonious Community Work: A Study on Disputes Resolution in Urban Communities in Contemporary China)*. Shanghai: Shanghai People's Press.
12. Hu, J., & Zheng, Y. (2016). Breaking the dilemma between litigation and non-litigation: Diversified mechanism of dispute resolution' in China. *China Perspectives, 2,* 45–53.
13. K District Statistical Yearbook. (2009–2014).
14. Landry, P. (2008). *Decentralized authoritarianism in China: The communist party's control of local elites in the Post-Mao Era*. Cambridge: Cambridge University Press.
15. Lee, X., & Zhifen, L. (2016). Shegong Jieru Xinfang Gongzuo de Zhuanbian. (The Change of Involving Social Workers' in Petition Cases). *Zhongguo Shehui Gongzuo* (*China Social Work*), *24*, 32–33.
16. Manning, S. S. (1997). The social worker as moral citizen: Ethics in action. *Social Work, 42*(3), 223–230.
17. Migdal, J. S. (1988). *Strong societies and weak states—state-society relations and state capabilities in the third world.* Princeton: Princeton University Press.
18. Minzner, C. F. (2006). Xinfang: An alternative to formal chinese legal institutions. *Stanford Journal of International Law, 42*, 103–179.
19. Perry, E. J. (2008). Reclaiming the Chinese revolution. *The Journal of Asian Studies, 67*(4), 1147–1164.
20. Pratchett, L. (2004). Local autonomy, local democracy and the "new localism". *Political Studies, 52*(2), 358–375.
21. Reamer, F. (1998). *Ethical standards in social work: A critical review of the NASW code of ethics*. Washington, DC: NASW Press.
22. Reuschemeyer, D., & Evans P. B. (1985). The state and economic transformation: Toward an analysis of the conditions underlying effective intervention. (translated by Grigory Yudin). *Diagnostic & Interventional Imaging, 93*(4), 232–245.
23. Saich, T. (2000). Negotiating the state: The development of social organizations in China. *The China Quarterly, 161,* 124–141.
24. Schmitter, P. C. (1974). Still the century of corporatism? In F. B. Pike & T. Stritch (Eds.), *The new Corporatism*. London: University of Notre Dame Press.
25. Su, L. (2010). Nengdong Sifa. (Active Judiciary). *Falv Shiyong* (*Journal of Law Application*), *1*, 5–16.
26. Teets, J. C. (2014). *Civil society under authoritarianism: The China model.* Cambridge: Cambridge University Press.
27. Unger, J., & Chan, A. (1995). China, corporatism, and the East Asia model. *The Australian Journal of Chinese Affairs, 33,* 29–53.
28. Veterans. (2011). Shanghai Giye Junzhuan Ganbu gei Shanghai Shiwei Shizhengfu de Yifeng Gongkaixin, (An Open Letter from Military-transferred Cadres in Enterprises to Shanghai Municipal Government), August 4, 2011. Retrieved February 2, 2017, from http://blog.boxun.com/hero/201108/voiceofveteran/23_1.shtml.
29. You, Y., & Qianmin, C. (2013). Minzhengju Yinjin Zhuanye Shegong Fuwu Futui Junren. (Civil Affairs Bureau Introduces Professional Social Workers to Serve Retired Soldiers), November 21, 2013. Retrieved 8 June, 2017, from http://www.zsnews.cn/news/2013/11/25/2546153.shtml.

Jieren Hu is an assciate professor in Law School at Tongji University and a visiting professor in the Law and Sociology Faculty at Qinghai Normal University, China. Her researches focus on mediation, dispute resolution and social governance.

Tong Wu is an Associate Professor in the School of Social Development at East China Normal University. His research focuses on localization of social work, governance of urban community in China and relations between social organizations and state.

Jingyan Fei is a Ph.D. candidate in the School of International Relations and Public Affairs at Fudan University. Her research focuses on the politics of migration and immigration, community governance and dispute resolution in China.

Chapter 7
Christianity and Patriotism: An Inter-disciplinary and Contextual Reflection

Pan-chiu Lai

Abstract The tension between patriotism and religious identity is an acute issue for Chinese Christianity. This chapter reconsiders patriotism from an inter-disciplinary and contextual perspective. It starts with a survey of the academic studies of patriotism from the perspectives of biological and cultural evolution, with a contextual analysis of the problem of patriotism in contemporary China, particularly Hong Kong. Based on the above survey and analysis, together with a review of patriotism from a Christian theological perspective, this chapter concludes with several suggestions concerning whether and how a Chinese Christian may love his/her country. There are several characteristics to this love: free and resistant to hegemony; with criticism and forgiveness; participation in diaspora; universal rather than exclusive; and with proper order.

Introduction

Being 'patriotic' appears to be a rather distinctive and prominent feature of the Christian churches in China. The two foremost Christian organizations in Mainland China, namely the Chinese Patriotic Catholic Association and the National Committee of Three-Self Patriotic Movement of the Protestant Churches in China, include the term 'patriotic' (*ai guo*) in their official names, and publish teaching materials on patriotism. In one of these materials, it is explicitly proclaimed that every religion, including Christianity, has the duty to 'love the country, love the church' (*ai guo ai jiao*),[1] which assumes that patriotism is an inalienable moral obligation for Chinese Christians, and it is legitimate to put 'love the country' before 'love the church'. This proclamation of patriotism may sound odd for outsiders but is quite understandable in its historical and political contexts. In China, due to the historical background of

[1]Zhongguo Jidu jiao san zi ai guo yun dong wei yuan hui [41].

P. Lai (✉)
Department of Cultural & Religious Studies, The Chinese University of Hong Kong, Shatin, Hong Kong, P. R. China
e-mail: pclai@cuhk.edu.hk

Z. Xie et al. (eds.), *Human Dignity, Human Rights, and Social Justice*,
https://doi.org/10.1007/978-981-15-5081-2_7

Christian missionary activities, Christianity was considered a foreign religion and associated with the Western colonial powers. In order to disassociate themselves from the foreign powers, the official Christian churches had to declare their patriotism loud and clear. However, given the absolutist and uncritical patriotism promoted by the totalitarian Communist regime, which is atheistic and holds a negative view on religion, the relationship between Christianity and patriotism or nationalism is inevitably an important yet thorny issue facing Christianity in contemporary China.[2]

This chapter adopts an inter-disciplinary and contextual approach to the issue of patriotism. It starts with a survey of the academic studies of patriotism from the perspectives of biological evolution as well as the contemporary cultural, social and political developments. Then, based on a contextual analysis of the issue of patriotism in contemporary China, including particularly Hong Kong, and a review of the Christian responses to patriotism, this chapter concludes with several suggestions concerning whether and how Christians may articulate and practice their patriotism in the Chinese context.

Perspective of Biological Evolution

The abstract noun 'patriotism' emerged in the early eighteenth century and can be traced back to *patriota* in Latin and finally to *πατριώτης* in Greek. It generally refers to the emotional attachment and devotion to one's country.[3] According to Charles Darwin (1809–1882), patriotism can enhance the competitiveness and thus survival of the relevant species or tribes. He wrote:

> A tribe including many members who, from possessing in a high degree of patriotism, fidelity, obedience, courage, and sympathy, were always ready to aid one another, and to sacrifice themselves for the common good, would be victorious over other tribes; and this would be natural selection.[4]

In contemporary biological studies of human behaviours, patriotism is discussed usually under the category of altruism. Some biologists suggest that most of the altruistic behaviors of human beings and other species can be explained by kin selection, which is based on blood relationship or genetic affinities. Some other biologists attempt to explain the altruistic behaviors, especially those between different species, in terms of reciprocal altruism.[5] Edward O. Wilson even suggests that human beings can conquer the earth because they are basically eusocial, and tribalism is a basic trait of human beings.[6] One may perhaps infer that the altruistic tendency starts usually from families or with those who have blood-relationship, and is further extended

---

[2]For a recent discussion, see: Zhao and Edmond [40] (articles in Chinese with English abstract), especially He [10].

[3]*The Oxford English Dictionary*, 2nd ed. (1989), s.vv. 'patriot', 'patriotism'.

[4]Darwin [5].

[5]See: Heinrich and Heinrich [11]; also, Bowles and Gintis [3].

[6]See: Wilson [37].

to nations. In other words, the affection toward one's nation is, by and large, an extension of familial relationship.

Since the altruism within families, kinsmen, tribes or nations is based on blood-relation or reciprocity among members, it may reinforce in-group favoritism, and exclude or hostile to the outsiders. For instance, kin selection based on blood relationship may lead to nepotism, which puts the benefits to the family or clan, before the wellbeing of the nation, the rule of law, and social justice. In the same vein, patriotism based on nationalism may drive people to make self-sacrifices for those who are fellow citizens, but it also may induce hatred or even killing of people of other nations.[7] Given the discriminatory tendency of familialism, tribalism, and even patriotism, one may ask the question concerning the overcoming of the narrowness or restrictedness of patriotism. Based on Darwin's theory, Boyd and Richerson attempt to argue that it may be possible to replace narrow patriotism and to achieve the moral progress that transcends what natural selection could attain by means of enlarging the scope of empathy.[8] However, it is important to note that the biological studies of empathy affirm the possibility of cross-species empathy on the one hand and highlights the limitations of patriotism on the other. As Frans de Waal puts it, 'No matter how much brainwashing we engage in and patriotic songs we sing, we will always think of ourselves before we think of society. If anything good has come out of the Communist 'experiment,' it is this clarification of the limits of solidarity.'[9] In other words, although individual human beings may be very patriotic due to their inclination toward reciprocal altruism, they also have the tendency of self-preservation and protect their near and dear ones. The love of one's nation will be checked and balanced by one's love of oneself, their family, etc.

To summarize the above discussion, patriotism is a sort of common and ordinary human affection, rather than a necessary truth to be deduced by rational thinking. Furthermore, ordinary people's love has many dimensions, including loving oneself, one's family, and even animals. These different kinds of love in some ways constrain the inclination toward patriotic love. When these loves are in conflict, individual human beings may have to prioritize them or even give up some of them. For the progress of humankind, the restrictedness of patriotism should and can be overcome by enlarging the scope of human empathy, which involves both biological heredity and human culture.[10]

---

[7] Flescher and Worthen [8].

[8] Richerson and Boyd [29].

[9] de Waal [35].

[10] See: Boyd and Richerson [4], Richerson and Boyd [30].

Perspective of Cultural Evolution

According to Ernst Troeltsch (1865–1923), there are significant differences and also a rather complicated relationship between patriotism and politics. Patriotism referred primarily to the commitment to one's home, language and kindred. This was supposed to be peaceful and individual. Since the rise of modern states, patriotism referred usually to a monolithic state constituted by a group of people speaking the same language, connected by certain blood relationship, and sharing the same pride and loyalty. More often, politicians used this patriotic emotion as a major tool to centralize powers for the sake of their own ambitions.[11] As Chris Baker states:

> Modern nation-state is a relatively recent invention. Indeed, for most of the human species have never participated in any kind of state nor identified with one. The nation-state, nationalism and national identity are not "naturally" occurring phenomena but contingent historical-cultural formations. In particular, they are socially and culturally constructed as collective forms of organization and identification.[12]

When modern states arose, each state claimed to be constituted by one nation or ethnic group. The patriotism advocated was thus often entwined with nationalism. Under such circumstances, the promotion or nurturing of patriotism generally appealed to the unity of the nation, proclaiming that all the nationals belong to one monolithic ethnic group, based on a blood relationship among the people (or sharing one common ancestor), continue to live in the same territory, sharing the same language, culture, history and religion. As Bhikhu Parekh points out, since the emergence of modern state in the seventeenth century, a static and exclusive paradigm of nation has dominated political theory and practice. This paradigm includes the following interconnected beliefs. First, the whole world is divided into different political communities or states and each one is a legally, politically, and even morally self-contained entity. Every person is a citizen of an identifiable state, and each state has its exclusive responsibility for all its citizens and vice versa. Second, each state is a sovereign state. It means that every nation has its own right to handle its internal and, under certain circumstances, external affairs in the way it pleases without any responsibility for other nations. Third, the state derives its legitimacy from its citizens and its only mission is to safeguard their collective interests. Finally, the citizens have the moral accountability to follow the state. This accountability is higher than other duties, including the universal obligations that human beings may have to each other.[13] As we are going to see, this static and exclusive identity of a nation attracted many theoretical criticisms,[14] and met practical resistance and challenges in the subsequent development in history.

The first resistance to this paradigm came from the Christian churches, especially the Catholic Church's struggle for the control of education and culture in order to

---

[11] Troeltsch [34, pp. 161–163].

[12] Baker [1].

[13] Parekh [28].

[14] Parekh [28, p. 240].

reinforce their nationals' loyalty to the state.[15] In addition to the challenges from the ecclesiastical institutions, the resistance might also come from the intellectuals, especially the 'organic intellectuals' who identify with the oppressed and resist the government's hegemony.[16] After all, the most fundamental challenge to patriotism in modern nation-states might be constituted by the social and cultural developments in the last century or so. Due to various historical reasons, especially the rapid development in transportation and also the process of colonization, the mobility of transnational population increased dramatically. As the phenomenon of diaspora has been becoming increasingly more common, many ethnically monolithic nation-states have changed into multi-ethnic countries. More and more people live as aliens, having double or even multiple national identities or citizenships. Individual's national identity has been increasingly becoming blurred, mixed and fluid. One's nationality is no longer entirely determined by the place of birth and becomes more a matter of personal choice.[17] These developments took place in many countries at different paces, which have become part of global trends. Some people, especially the intellectuals, prefer to identify themselves as world or global citizens. In other words, in addition to the challenges brought by globalization in political and economic realms, contemporary states have to face also the challenges constituted by the emergence of transnational civil society and the cosmopolitan vision adopted by their citizens.[18] In line with this cosmopolitan vision, Martha C. Nussbaum proposes a 'world-citizen model' of liberal education, which is, in comparison with the more Western-centric Gentleman's model, emphasizes more on critical thinking and the perspectives of the minority groups, and is thus more appropriate to our globalizing and pluralistic world.[19] This 'world-citizen' model does not exclude patriotic education, but tends to advocate a critical patriotism.[20]

From the above survey, it is obvious that since the emergence of modern nation-states, different governments or political parties endeavored to use or abuse patriotic love, which is actually a common and ordinary human emotion, and turn it into the love of the ruling political party or the government by enmeshing the nation, people, and the ruling party in order to reinforce the people's support to the ruling power. It is expected that such abuse will bring forth protests from some citizens, including the intellectuals. Hence, in contemporary societies, no matter whether it is about national identity in modern sense or citizenship in the global age, politics of identity is inevitable.[21] In other words, the question is not merely whether and how a person should be patriotic. Rather, it is necessary to realize that behind the various discourses on patriotism and patriotic education, there are power struggles involving different cultural politics.

---

[15] Maclear [22].

[16] Jenks [13].

[17] Baker [1, pp. 252–288].

[18] See: Beck [2].

[19] Nussbaum [24].

[20] Nussbaum [25].

[21] See: Parekh [28, pp. 56–79, 239–258].

Contemporary China/Hong Kong Context

The aforementioned influences of cultural evolution on patriotism, as we will see, took place in China as well, though it has certain distinctive features and regional differences between Mainland China and the other parts of China, especially Hong Kong.

From the collapse of the Manchurian Qing Dynasty to the establishment of the Republic of China, this political revolution was initially marked by exclusivist nationalism. For example, the original slogan raised by Sun Yat-sen (1866–1925) and other advocates of revolution was 'expelling Manchurians, restoring China.' This slogan regarded Manchurians as aliens, if not enemies, to China and had to be eradicated. Similar to the rise of nation-states in Europe in a few centuries ago, the overt purpose of the revolution was to establish a country or nation-state based on a monolithic ethnic group. However, the agenda proposed by the revolutionists was then changed into forming a multi-ethnic republic by uniting the five ethnic groups, namely Han, Manchurian, Mongolian, Hui, and Tibetan. Nowadays the People's Republic of China proclaims straightforwardly that China is a multi-ethnic country with at least fifty-six ethnic groups - including the majority Han. However, in the political propaganda launched by the government, there is a concept called *Zhong hua min zu* (the Chinese ethnic/nation), which includes all these fifty-six tribes. It is important to note that this concept is basically a construction of identity based on political considerations and does not comply with the strict academic definition of ethnicity. It is because the so-called '*Zhong hua min zu*' is a combination of many ethnic groups, rather than itself a monolithic ethnic group with a unique and unifying language, culture, or biological traits.

Although the political propaganda and/or the discourses made by the majority Han group tend to recognize China as an ethnically monolithic nation, some of the ethnic minority in the People's Republic of China are very aware of their ethnic, religious and cultural identities, which may be very different from those of the mainstream represented by the Hans. It is difficult for them to develop patriotic love from the concept of family or blood relationship. Furthermore, following the precedents and principle of nation-state, these ethnic groups, especially the Tibetans and the Uyghurs, may argue and even fight for the establishment of their own nation-states constituted by respective ethnic groups. In response, besides resorting to military suppression, the Chinese government also provides tangible benefits to these ethnic groups in order to highlight that these minorities' survival and livelihood (including their cultures and religions) will receive due protection and have good prospect of development in the Republic. Therefore, in its propaganda for patriotism, the Chinese government, on the one hand, upholds the flag of '*Zhong hua min zu*' in order to enhance the solidarity or national identity of the people. On the other hand, it also emphasizes that China as a multi-ethnic country respects the ethnic minorities and endeavours to enhance harmony among different ethnic groups.

The issue of patriotism is even more complicated in Hong Kong than in Mainland China. The national identification of Hong Kong people, both objectively and subjectively, is very diffused or even full of tension. Hong Kong was a British colony until 1997, and the citizens of Hong Kong enjoyed a high degree of individual freedom without democracy in a formal way. Before 1997, the ethnic 'Chinese' (no matter how it was defined) who had been born in Hong Kong were offered the choice to declare themselves to be either British or Chinese as their nationality when they applied for their identity cards. Patriotism was basically absent in the colony's education system.

Disregarding those who live in Hong Kong temporarily for studying (mainly from Mainland China) or working as domestic helpers (mainly from the Philippines and Indonesia), the 'permanent residents' of Hong Kong include a significant number of ethnic minority groups who are not recognized as ethnic Chinese. In addition to the ethnic groups from India, Pakistan, Nepal, etc., who settled in Hong Kong for several generations, there are also some 'foreigners' who had worked in Hong Kong for many years, and became permanent residents of Hong Kong while holding passports of their home countries. Among the ethnic Chinese living in Hong Kong, many of them escaped from Mainland China before or after 1949. Some of them and probably also their descendants might subjectively prefer to identify themselves with the Republic of China rather than the People's Republic of China. During the 1980s and 1990s, many people of Hong Kong immigrated to Canada, United Kingdom, Australia, USA, etc. and some of them returned to Hong Kong with foreign passports. No matter whether legally they have dual citizenship or even multiple nationality, the problem remains which country they subjectively love more - the People's Republic of China or, say, Canada?

Other than these factors, the promotion of patriotism in Hong Kong may meet some other difficulties. For example, some political incidents in Mainland China, such as the June Fourth movement in 1989, and the reports concerning the corruptions of government officials or violations of human rights in China may also affect the patriotic sentiment of the people of Hong Kong. In fact, many intellectuals in Hong Kong continue to criticize the Chinese government before and after 1997. It is noteworthy that many Chinese students, including those in Hong Kong, are resistant to the political education to be imposed by the Chinese government, and incline towards some sort of critical patriotism.[22] In recent years, the younger generation of Hong Kong, including particularly those born after 1997, became even more critical towards the Chinese government. Many of them prefer to identify themselves as 'Hongkongers' rather than Chinese. Many of them played important roles in the campaign/demonstration in 2012 against the imposition of patriotic education on secondary schools, as well as the Umbrella Movement in 2014 against the Chinese government's decision on the regulations concerning the election of the Chief Executive to be held in Hong Kong in 2017 and the ongoing Anti-Extradition Law Amendment Bill Movement in 2019.

Due to various reasons, in comparison with mainland China, the Hong Kong population is highly pluralistic, and the national identification is more diffused and

[22] See: Fairbrother [7].

fluid. Many people of Hong Kong have certain experience of diaspora; and they long for freedom and resist hegemony. Relatively speaking, the citizens of Hong Kong in general may have a more cosmopolitan perspective and open to universal values. Hence, it is difficult to adopt a static and exclusive national identity as a basis for the promotion of patriotism.

Christianity and Patriotism

The unequivocal affirmation of patriotism made by the Chinese Christian churches in Mainland China mentioned above is not only unwarranted from the perspectives of biological and cultural evolution, it is also dubious from the perspective of the Christian tradition, which may have much counter evidence challenging this uncritical patriotic position.

It is obvious that the Biblical narrative might query the Chinese saying ‘there is no family without the nation’ by indicating that nation was human construction after the flood (Gen. 10:5, 20, 32) rather than part of the original created order. Furthermore, God’s response to the Israelites’ demand for a human king was basically negative (1 Sam. 8). Though the coming kingship of God remained an important part of hope in the Old Testament, and there were many Israelites/Jews who hoped for the revival of Israel as a nation or political entity, early Christians seemed to keep a distance from this revivalist hope (Acts 1:1–6). If engagement in political movements reviving Israel or countering the Roman regime is a criterion for patriotism, the Jewish Christians were not patriotic for the Israelite nation. However, it does not mean that they had any patriotic love to the Roman Empire.

In terms of ethnicity, Paul the Apostle was Jewish, whereas in terms of citizenship or nationality, he was a Roman citizen. He had a strong affection to his fellow kinsmen (Rom., 9:1–3), but with respect to the Roman Empire, Paul only asked Christians in Rome (including Jewish and non-Jewish) to submit to the rulers by paying them due respect and taxes (Rom. 13:1–7). Note that the motivation for the submission is not patriotism to the Roman Empire but fear of punishment; conscience is involved at its best. Simply put, what Paul demands is just a duty or responsibility of citizenship. It does not necessarily involve any subjective emotion or engaging love. Actually, what Paul emphasizes more is heavenly citizenship (Phil. 3:20) and submission to Christ (2 Cor. 5:20), rather than submission to the Roman Empire or the emperor. In some other epistles attributed to Paul, there are teachings exhorting believers to pray for those who are in high positions. However, these are for the sake of living a quiet and peaceful life (1Tim. 2:1–2). It is in line with the Old Testament teaching ‘seek the peace of the city,’ which is also for self-preservation - ‘for in the peace thereof shall ye have peace’ (Jeremiah 29:7). What is reflected here is a very functional, pragmatic, or utilitarian attitude towards the political authority, without any patriotic feeling or emotion.

The attitude of Jesus of Nazareth regarding the Roman Empire would need no further elaboration. The often-cited texts on paying tax to Caesar (Mt. 22:15-22, Lk.

20:19–26) reflect a rather indifferent attitude toward the Roman regime: since the coin has the impression of Caesar, then by paying tax it was just returning it to him. Jesus finished his teaching by saying 'to God the things that are God's' to remind the people that one's loyalty to God should be more ultimate than that to Caesar.

In the New Testament era, there were many believers in the *diaspora*. For example, 1 Peter was written for the 'resident aliens' (παρεπιδήμοις διασπορα), who might be Jewish Christians living in different places (1 Pet. 1:1). The book highlights their identity as 'sojourners' (1 Pet. 2:11) and 'resident aliens' (1 Pet. 2:13–17), and advises them to submit to emperors, governors, and even all human institutions, including 'honor everyone, love the family of believers, fear God, and honor the emperor.' (1 Pet. 2:17) However, it is important to note that this submission is not due to patriotism, but for the sake of the Lord and for glorifying God (1 Pet. 2:13). Furthermore, honoring the emperor is just one of the various duties of the Christians. Moreover, different attitudes are adopted toward different recipients: to God, fear (φοβεισθε); to fellow believers, love (αγαπατε); to non-believers, respect (τιμήσατε); to emperors, respect (τιματε), which shares the same root. Put another way, neither it means to fear emperors as one should fear God, nor to love emperors as if they were brothers in Christ. In a nutshell, just respect emperors like respecting people outside the church.

Other than the Jewish Christians, the non-Jewish Christians might also become distant from the local people because of their faith and had to live in their homeland as if they were in foreign lands. As a document of early Christianity states:

> They live in their own countries, but only as aliens. They have a share in everything as citizens and endure everything as foreigners. Every foreign land is their fatherland, yet for them every fatherland is a foreign land. They busy themselves on earth, but their citizenship is in heaven.[23]

Certainly, it does not mean that Christians must be aloof to the world. Rather, as Bruce W. Winter's study of early Christianity points out, though the early Christians might regard themselves as resident aliens, they still sought for peace of the cities where they lived.[24]

From the above brief review, the most important concern is the identity of being a citizen of God's Kingdom. The issue of belonging to which particular nation on earth is secondary. Christians do not deny their moral responsibilities to the cities or countries they live, but this concern or responsibility is subordinate to the love of or loyalty to God.

It is undeniable that the Protestant Reformation was related to the rise of nation-states and patriotism in various ways. For example, the Reformers' proposals of using vernacular languages in worship and the translation of the Bible might have induced the rise of nationalism. Some of the reformation was backed by feudal lords, city councils, or the emperors. The success of the reformation further reinforced the roles of states and even their influences on local churches. Some reformers, for

---

[23] *Epistula ad Diognetum* 5.5 [6].

[24] Winter [39].

example Martin Luther (1483–1546), were unknowingly or even reluctantly exalted to be national heroes.[25] In addition, there were other reformers who were full of patriotic love. One example is Huldrych Zwingli (1484–1531), whose patriotism is vivid in his theological discourses regarding the government.[26] However, there are also some Protestants, e.g. the non-Conformists, who might put their religion before their national identity, and preferred to leave their home country in order to practice their own religion instead of the state religion imposed by the government.

There are some modern Christian intellectuals offering their critical reflections on patriotism, and some of their views echo the aforementioned views from the perspectives of biological and cultural evolutions. For example, in his *The Four Loves*, C. S. Lewis (1898–1963) discusses patriotism in length. Besides the distinction between healthy and wicked patriotism, Lewis also differentiates several models of patriotism. The first one is the love of home. This helps us go beyond self-love and family-centeredness, though it is still not pure charity and may become hindrance to spiritual love. The second kind of patriotism is basically national pride regarding the past of one's country. This kind of love can make people become cynical or blind voluntarily, when the dark sides of a nation's history are exposed. The third one is not a love but belief, which may bring forth racism. It is thus better to keep patriotism at the affective level without turning it into a belief, which believes that one's own nation (or people) is more superior to other countries (or peoples).[27] Lewis particularly warns: 'When the natural loves become lawless they do not merely do harm to other loves; they themselves cease to be the loves they were.'[28] The paradoxical nature of patriotism mentioned by Lewis was also noticed by Reinhold Niebuhr (1892–1971), who suggests that each individual person can have sympathy and righteousness to the extent that self-sacrificing is possible, but the communities formed by these individuals can transform such personal selflessness into collective egoism.[29]

After the 9/11 event, when Americans' patriotism roared, a group of American theologians had a focused discussion on patriotism and published a book expressing their critical theological reflections on patriotism.[30] As the editor writes in the introduction of the volume:

> for those of us who identify ourselves not merely as U.S. citizens but also as "resident aliens"—Christians who want to embrace community life without pledging ultimate allegiance to any political authority, civil society, or form of government, no matter how virtuous it may be. As *resident aliens*, we can neither escape the recent wave of U.S. patriotism nor avoid hearing the rhetoric of the partisan strife between conservatives and liberals.[31]

It is noteworthy that the expression 'resident aliens' adopted here indicates their priority of identifying themselves as Christians or heavenly subjects, rather than

[25]Oberman [26].

[26]See: Stephens [32], Gäbler [9].

[27]Lewis [15].

[28]Ibid., p. 28.

[29]Niebuhr [23].

[30]Long and Sadd [21].

[31]Long and Sadd [20, p. 3].

American citizens. As the subtitle of this book entails, it offers diverse perspectives rather than a single perspective on patriotism. For instance, Robert Jenson, whose position is relatively more radical, argues that patriotism means to happily accept death for a fatherland (*patria*). This sweet acceptance of death can be extended to a *res publica* where we can enjoy our shared public possessions. In this sense, there is only one polity that Christians would die willingly for—the Church.[32] In a relatively milder tone, Theodore R. Weber mentions that though we are resident aliens, we still have the theological grounded responsibility to seek welfare for that city we live in (Jeremiah 29:7).

> Patriotism in the ordinary sense of the word is not a primary claim on Christians. Our primary loyalty is to God above all other things or relationships. ..... Patriotism in the context of grace never rightly can be a definer or identity that overrides loyalty to God in Christ and separates us in some final and qualitative sense from the other peoples of the world. On the other hand, the loyalty generated in the divine-human encounter does not excuse us from fulfilling the relative obligations of temporal patriotism in seeking the welfare of the city where we live.[33]

Referring to nationalism rather than patriotism, Walter Wink puts it in a more positive way: 'We must be international and transnational, but not antinational. The only cure for the evils of nationalism, paradoxically, is genuine love for one's nation as a creature of God.'[34] Wink's approach to nationalism is basically in line with the inter-disciplinary perspectives mentioned above, excepting the expression 'a creature of God.' This is because both the biblical narratives and the secular theories mentioned above would prefer to take nation as a human construction rather than a creature of God created by God directly. The alternative view of taking nation as a human construction, rather than God's creation, may offer a more proper attitude to the nation or state. As Paul Tillich (1886–1965) says:

> Nationalism is ultimately rooted in the natural and necessary self-affirmation of every social group, analogous to that of every living being. This self-affirmation has nothing to do with selfishness (though it may be distorted into selfishness). It is the "one of oneself" in the sense of the words of Jesus about loving one's neighbor.[35]

Accordingly, nationalism per se is nothing right or wrong. It is based on a sort of natural self-affirmation. If this self-affirmation becomes a will to power or even a quasi-religious claim, forgetting or neglecting one's own limitations, or even absolutizing oneself, then it will become demonic or even self-destructive. However, if the national consciousness is humanized, being aware of its own limited validity, and has vocational consciousness which realizes that itself can show an ambiguous but yet infinite significance, a nation can become the supranational unity of humankind or the Kingdom of God in religious terminology.[36] In accordance with this point of view, a nation as a finite construction should not be regarded as the ultimate concern,

---

[32] Jenson [14, pp. 147–148].

[33] Weber [36, pp. 238–239].

[34] Wink [38, p. 22].

[35] Tillich [33].

[36] Tillich [33, p. 17].

let alone to worship it. This is not to deny its value and the active role played in the unity of humanity, but Christians should not blindly worship and accept everything of the nation uncritically, and they do not necessarily reject everything from the nation either. Instead, Christians can adopt an attitude of dialectical union of rejection and acceptance. This is precisely the attitude that Christianity should embrace when they face other religions and quasi-religions.[37]

Contextual Reflection

According to the above theological reflections, for Hong Kong Christians, the love of the country or patriotism, which is not only congruent with Christian beliefs, including the priority of the Christian identity vis-à-vis the national identity, but also more practical in Hong Kong context, appear to have the following characteristics.

Free from Coercion and Resistant to Hegemony

From the above discussion, one may find that patriotism as a human sentiment or emotion is natural, common, and innocent. Therefore, it should not be forbidden, and should not be commanded either. This is because love should be love in freedom and cannot be enforced. Hence, the most important issue is not about which nation we should love or love most, but how to love. Facing national or patriotic education, especially the cultural politics involved, Christian theologians have to seriously consider whether they would choose to be 'organic intellectuals' or supporters of cultural hegemony choreographed by the government.

Both Critical and Forgiving

The love upheld by Christianity contains criticism and judgement, but it also includes forgiveness. Genuine and enduring love should be able to face the dark sides of the beloved ones. Of course, this does not mean an uncritical acceptance of whatever they do. If this critical and forgiving love is applied to one's nation or country, it may be easier to develop sort of critical patriotism, which may face positively the dark sides of a nation and its past mistakes. It is because Christianity believes that God loves sinners but hates sin. The assumption here is that sin is not an inherent and inalienable part of human nature. In principle, human nature and sin are separable, and sins or mistakes are corrigible or removable without damaging human nature.[38]

---

[37] Tillich [33, pp. 27–51].

[38] Lai [16].

If this understanding is applied to patriotism, we can acknowledge a nation's past mistakes and yet love it at the same time. One's love of one's own country or people does not necessarily imply one's wholehearted support to the ruling party, which is removable in principle. As far as the long-term benefits of the country are concerned, critical patriotism may be far better than uncritical patriotism.

Advocating Participation in Diaspora

As for Hong Kong Christians, their sense of national identity is relatively blurred. However, they are not unfamiliar with the situation and feeling of *diaspora*. 'Seek welfare of the city' was once a popular slogan in Hong Kong churches and widely accepted by Christians of different political positions. If we identify ourselves as resident aliens and practice the principle of seeking welfare for the city where we live, our participation in society and responsibilities to the countries we live are affirmed. There is no need to resolve to the grand narrative of nationalism or patriotism promoted by the government. At first glance, it appears to be not very patriotic, but it fits better the phenomenal fluidity of national identity of contemporary people, especially the diaspora experience or feeling shared by many of the people of Hong Kong. It is thus more plausible and practical in the Hong Kong context.

Inclusive and Universal Rather Than Exclusive

As a 'global religion' or 'world religion', Christianity is different from patriotism in its cosmopolitan vision. Christianity's cosmopolitanism is exemplified by not only its insistence on the ecumenical ideal, but also its practice in missions, especially the commissioning of missionaries overseas. Though some of the activities of the missionaries openly or quietly, directly or indirectly, support the interests of their own countries or peoples, their missionary works usually serve more the 'foreigners' rather than their 'nationals'. It is interesting to note that many of the foreign missionaries to China are appreciated by Christians from China as well as their respective homelands, without being criticized as 'un-patriotic' to their own countries. These might reflect that Christianity upholds a universal love which transcends national boundaries, and regards it nobler than the love of one's own nation. After all, this Christian cosmopolitanism may transcend but not necessarily deny patriotism. In light of evolutionary theory, this inclusive and universal love may overcome narrow patriotism, perfect patriotism, and facilitate the moral progress of humankind.

Orderly Rather Than Disorderly

Christianity affirms that love has different forms referring to different kinds of recipients. How to prioritize different forms of love is an important issue for Christian ethics.[39] This issue is certainly important to Christians who live in liberal societies which emphasize individual freedom and rights.[40] This is also crucial for believers who live in totalitarian states upholding nationalism and/or collectivism. Since nation relates to just a part of life or daily living rather than the whole, patriotic love should be placed among different kinds of love for moderation and balance. For example, St. Thomas Aquinas (1225–1274) affirms the order of love, meaning that besides loving God, oneself and family (especially parents), one should also love one's own clan, tribe, and even fellow creatures in nature.[41] Regarding the priority, the love of nation should be placed after the love of parents because this fits better the nature of humanity, and the love of parents should follow after that of God. According to St. Thomas' basic position regarding grace and nature, God's supernatural love does not deny but perfect what is in human nature, including the love of oneself, parents, kindred, and nation.[42] This position can be taken as the origin of the affirmation of patriotism in the Catholic theology. Still, this kind of patriotic love is affirmed through the affirmation of common good.[43] As such, Christianity can provide a broader framework to handle different kinds of love, including the proper relationship between patriotism and other kinds of love. In this way, patriotism can proceed properly, and will be beneficial to the relevant nations and perhaps to humankind as a whole.[44]

References

1. Baker, C. (2012). *Cultural studies: Theory and practice* (4th ed., p. 259). Los Angeles: Sage.
2. Beck, U. (2000). *What is globalization? Translated by Patrick Camiller* (pp. 64–86) Cambridge: Polity Press; Malden, MA: Blackwell.
3. Bowles, S., & Gintis, H. (2011). *A cooperative species: Human reciprocity and its evolution*. Princeton: Princeton University Press.
4. Boyd, R., & Richerson, P. J. (2005). *The origin and evolution of cultures*. Oxford: Oxford University Press.
5. Darwin, C. (1874). *The descent of man and selection in relation to sex* (2nd ed., Vol. 2, pp. 178–1789). New York: American Home Library.
6. *Epistula ad Diognetum*. (1953). In E. R. Fairweather & C. C. Richardson et al., (Eds.), The so-called letter to diognetus. Translated by Cyril C. Richardson et al. (p. 217). London: SCM Press.

[39] See further: Oord [27].

[40] See: Schindler [31].

[41] Lai and Tao [18] (in Chinese with abstract in English).

[42] See: Lai and Tao [17, pp. 183–214 at 197–205] (in Chinese with abstract in English).

[43] Hinze [12, p. 134].

[44] This essay is a substantially abridged and revised English version of a chapter of my book in Chinese: Lai [19].

7. Fairbrother, G. P. (2003). *Toward critical patriotism: Student resistance of political education*. Hong Kong: Hong Kong University Press.
8. Flescher, A. M., & D. L. Worthen. (2007). *Altruistic species: Scientific, philosophical, and religious perspectives of human benevolence* (pp. 144–148). Philadelphia: Templeton Foundation Press.
9. Gäbler, U. (1986). *Huldrych Zwingli: His life and work*. Translated by Ruth C. L. Gritsch. Edinburgh: T & T Clark.
10. He, G. (2011). The dragon and the dove: Nationalism, state power and christianity in China." *Logos & Pneuma, 35*, (Autumn 2011), 129–46.
11. Heinrich, N., & Heinrich, J. (2007). *Why human cooperate: A cultural and evolutionary explanation*. Oxford: Oxford University Press.
12. Hinze, C. F. (2007). A distinctively Catholic patriotism? In M. G. Long & T. W. Sadd (Eds.), *God and country?* (pp. 129–146). New York: Palgrave Macmillan.
13. Jenks, C. (1993). *Culture* (pp. 80–84). London: Routledge.
14. Jenson, R. (2007). Is patriotism a virtue? In M. G. Long & T. W. Sadd (Eds.), *God and Country?* (pp. 147–154). New York: Palgrave Macmillan.
15. Lewis, C. S. (1988). *The four loves* (pp. 22–30). New York: Harcourt.
16. Lai, P.-C. (2006). Barth's doctrines of sin and humanity in Buddhist perspective. *Studies in Interreligious Studies, 16*(1), 41–58.
17. Lai, P.-C., & Tao, W. (2013). Altruism in Christian, Confucian and evolutionary perspectives. *Sino-Christian Studies, 15*, 183–214.
18. Lai, P.-C., & Tao, W. (2010). Reconsidering St. Thomas's ecological ethics. *Universitas, 37*(11), 155–173.
19. Lai, P. (2014). (= Lai Pan-chiu), *Guang chang shang de han yu shen xue* [Sino-Christian Theology in the Public Square] (pp. 263–309). Hong Kong: Logos & Pneuma.
20. Long, M. G., & Sadd, T. W. (2007). Introduction: Why rethink Christianity and patriotism. In M. G. Long & T. W. Sadd (Eds.), *God and country?* (pp. 1–6). New York: Palgrave Macmillan.
21. Long, M. G., & Sadd, T. W. (Eds.). (2007). *God and country? Diverse perspectives on Christianity and patriotism*. New York: Palgrave Macmillan.
22. Maclear, J. F. (Ed.). (1985). *Church and state in the modern age: A documentary history* (pp. 253–256, 261–264, 267–270, 275–278). Oxford: Oxford University Press.
23. Niebuhr, R. (1932). *Moral man and immoral society* (pp. 90–91) New York: Charles Scribner's Sons.
24. Nussbaum, M. (1997). *Cultivating humanity: A classical defense of reform in liberal education* (pp. 293–301). Cambridge, MA: Harvard University Press.
25. Nussbaum, M. (2013). *Political emotions: Why love matters for justice* (pp. 204–56). Cambridge, MA: Belknap Press of Harvard University Press.
26. Oberman, H. A. (1994). *The impact of the reformation* (pp. 69–78). Edinburgh: T & T Clark.
27. Oord, T. J. (2010). *Defining love: A philosophical, scientific, and theological engagement* (pp. 31–63). Grand Rapids, MI: Brazos.
28. Parekh, B. (2008). *A new politics of identity: Political principles for an independent world* (pp. 239–240). Basingstoke, UK: Palgrave Macmillan.
29. Richerson, P. J., & Boyd, R. (2004). Darwinian evolutionary ethics: Between patriotism and sympathy. In Philip Clayton & J. Schloss (Eds.), *Evolution and ethics: Human morality in biological and religious perspective* (pp. 50–76). Grand Rapids, MI: William B. Eerdmans.
30. Richerson, P. J., & Boyd, R. (2005). *Not by genes alone: How culture transformed human evolution*. Chicago: University of Chicago Press.
31. Schindler, D. L., & Love, O. (2011). *Liberal societies and the memory of god*. Grand Rapids, MI: Eerdmans.
32. Stephens, W. P. (1986). *The theology of Huldrych Zwingli* (pp. 7–8, 282–310). Oxford: Clarendon.
33. Tillich, P. (1964). *Christianity and the encounter of the world religions* (pp. 14–15). New York: Columbia University Press.

34. Troeltsch, E. (1932). Politics, patriotism, religion. In *Christian thought: Its history and application*, Translated by B. F. von Hügel (Ed.) 131–67. London: University of London Press.
35. de Waal, F. (2009). *The age of empathy: Nature's lessons for a kinder society* (p. 36). New York: Three Rivers.
36. Weber, T. R. (2007). Patriotic legislating in the context of grace?" In M. G. Long & T. W. Sadd (Eds.), *God and country?* (pp 225–240). New York: Palgrave Macmillan.
37. Wilson, E. O. (2012). *The social conquest of earth*. London: Liveright.
38. Wink, W. (2007). Angels of the nations? In M. G. Long & T. W. Sadd (Eds.), *God and country?* (pp. 9–22). New York: Palgrave Macmillan.
39. Winter, B. W. (1994). *Seek the welfare of the city: Christians as benefactors and citizens*. Grand Rapids, MI: Wm. B. Eerdmans.
40. Zhao, L., & Tang, E. (Eds.). (2011). Christianity and nationalism. Special issue. *Logos & Pneuma, 35*(Autumn 2011), 19–146.
41. Zhongguo Jidu jiao san zi ai guo yun dong wei yuan hui. [National Committee of Three-Self Patriotic Movement of the Protestant Churches in China] and Zhongguo Jidu jiao xie hui [China Christian Council] (Eds.). (2006). *Jidu jiao ai guo zhu yi jiao cai (shi yong ban)* [Christian Patriotism Teaching Materials (Trial Version)]. Beijing: Zong jiao weh hua chu ban she.

Pan-chiu Lai is Professor of Religious Studies, The Chinese University of Hong Kong. He was the speaker for the Heidelberger Ecumenical Forum (Heidelberg University, 2002) and Edward Cadbury Lectures (University of Birmingham, 2006). His publications include Towards a Trinitarian Theology of Religions: A Study of Paul Tillich's Thought (1994); Confucian-Christian Dialogue and Ecological Concern (2006, in Chinese, co-authored with Lin Hongxing); Sino-Christian Theology: A Theological Qua Cultural Movement in Contemporary China (co-edited with Jason Lam, 2010); Mahayana Christian Theology (in Chinese, 2011); Sino-Christian Theology in the Public Square (in Chinese, 2014). He has also published over two hundred journal articles and book chapters in Chinese or English.

Chapter 8
How Love Is Possible: A Christian Approach to the Problem of Social Justice in China

Zhibin Xie

Abstract The issue of love and justice has become increasingly an outstanding moral and social problem in contemporary China. The marginalized group of people in the areas of education, job market, and social welfare in China raises various problems of conflict and inequality, which demand justice in those areas. Regarding just settlement for this group, some relevant studies in disciplines such as political science, law and sociology have attended more to institutional, distributive arrangements and economic factors. This chapter aims to understand the moral identity of this marginalized group from Christian theological perspective of love and explore its implications to the problem of social justice in China. Drawing from and attempting to integrate both Reinhold Niebuhr and Nicholas Wolterstorff's distinctive positions on love and justice, this chapter points out the possibilities and limitations of applying Christian love in its relationship to social justice in Chinese society. It proposes that if justice is embedded into the ideal of love, justice will not become a pure and mechanic political concept, on the one hand, and the ideas of "justice in love" and "love complementing justice" will enrich and enhance the discourse on social justice in the Chinese context on the other.

Introduction

In contemporary academia, the problem of social justice has been an important issue in social studies; in particular the concept of the just social institution in political philosophy. In international bodies, this issue also receives wide attention. In 2007, the General Assembly of United Nations proclaimed February 20 as World Day of Social Justice for the purpose of poverty eradication, the promotion of full employment and decent work, gender equality and access to social well-being and justice for

[1] United Nations [20].

Z. Xie (✉)
School of Humanities, Tongji University, 1239 Siping Road, Shanghai, P. R. China
e-mail: xiezhibin@hotmail.com

Z. Xie et al. (eds.), *Human Dignity, Human Rights, and Social Justice*,
https://doi.org/10.1007/978-981-15-5081-2_8

all. Particularly it aims to foster the vulnerable group's fuller engagement in social and economic life.[1]

The Chinese government regard the principle of social justice as one of the core socialist values and the basic condition of social harmony. However, the marginalized group of people in the areas of education, job market, and social welfare in China can be neglected or not treated equally with others. This raises problems of conflict and inequality, which demand justice to be addressed. Regarding just settlement for this group, some relevant studies in disciplines such as philosophy, political science, law and sociology have paid much attention to institutional, distributive arrangements, economic factors, the rule of law, from such principles as rights, duty, obligations, interests, just distribution, and equal opportunities. In general, regarding the problem of social justice, the aspect of institution is much emphasized either from government or academia. As a Chinese legal scholar Zhiping Liang points out, 'Social justice is related to institutions. The realization of social justice ought to rely on the establishment and improvement of institutions, as the absence of social justice emerges from the institution'.[2]

However, we may still ask the following questions: besides the rationale institutional arrangement, what else do we need to address concerning the problem of social justice? What is the foundation of human dignity in engaging the issues of social justice? What moral values in the vulnerable group are deserved to be taken into institutional consideration? For these questions, this chapter attempts to introduce the core idea of love in Christianity to explore its relevance to the issues of social justice. According to Gene Outka in his *Agage: An Ethical Analysis*, the ethical implication of Agape includes equal regard, self-sacrifice and mutuality.[3] In my view, this understanding provides a good framework for approaching the relevance of Christian love to social justice, even though various thinkers may give distinctive focus on the meaning of love when they elaborate its ethical and social implications.

This study is based on the flowing considerations: first, the idea of Christian love, as an ideal of individual Christian life, which can be extended to the issues of social, economic and political issues (such as justice); second, both the values of social justice and fraternity (love, in general) are regarded as common values in contemporary China and yet there is a lack of understanding and attention to the internal relationship between those two concepts but diverse sources on the concept of love such as found in the rich traditions of Confucianism and Buddhism show the internal relationship between love and justice as found in Christianity. While bringing Christian perspectives into the discussion on public issues such as social justice, I bear a burden to invoke the use of distinctive Christian resources (alongside with other resources) in its relation to social justice in engaging public discourse in China.

For this purpose, this chapter aims to understand the moral identity of the marginalized group from a Christian theological perspective of love and explore its implications to the problem of social justice in China. Drawing from and attempting to

[2]Liang [8].

[3]Outka [14].

integrate both Reinhold Niebuhr and Nicholas Wolterstorff's distinctive positions on love and justice, this chapter points out the possibilities and limitations of applying Christian love in its relationship to social justice in Chinese society. It proposes that if justice is penetrated into the ideal of love, justice will not become pure and mechanic political concept, on the one hand, and the ideas of "justice in love" and "love complementing justice" will enrich and enhance the discourse on social justice in the Chinese context, on the other.

Reinhold Niebuhr and Nicholas Wolterstorff on Love and Justice: How Love Is Possible

For Niebuhr, the issue of love and justice is one of the key themes in his Christian ethics. In recognition of the imperfect world and the reality of sin and evil, Niebuhr emphasizes that the perfect love ("agape") exemplified by Jesus is a kind of ideal and absoluteness of spirituality and morality. Love is the moral norm of Christian life as it is the ultimate and highest possibility between intermediate persons. For Niebuhr, the ideal of Christian love implies that sacrificial love of Jesus is inclusive and absolute love, which includes forgiveness. Yet, love as forgiveness is the most difficult thing to be realized in all human moral achievements. Indeed, as moral ideals, sacrificial love and forgiving love are the essence of Christian ethics and can only serve as "highest religious imagination" or "highest virtue." Christian love in the sense of self-sacrifice and forgiveness can only be realized in such conditions as intimate relationship and religious communities, but not in complex social relationships. In other words, "'pure love' cannot be a possible foundation for an adequate social ethic because of man's sin, which an adequate ethic must take into account."[4] This reflects Niebuhr's distinction between religious ethics and rational (social) ethics: 'A rational ethic aims at justice, and a religious ethic makes love the ideal'.[5] Niebuhr makes his statement about religious force particularly the ideal of love in individual, religious communities and society in this way:

> Yet the full force of religious faith will never be available for the building of a just society, because its highest visions are those which proceed from the insights of a sensitive individual conscience. If they are realized at all, they will be realized in intimate religious communities, in which individual ideas achieve social realization but do not conquer society.[6]

Based on these understandings, Niebuhr brings his vision of wider society in terms of justice: 'The ordinary affairs of the community, the structure of politics and economics, must be governed by the spirit of justice and by specific and detailed definitions of rights and duties'.[7] Just institutions locate different persons and groups'

---

[4]Robertson [19].

[5]Niebuhr [13].

[6]Ibid., p. 81.

[7]Niebuhr [12].

needs, interests and potential conflicts from within. For Niebuhr, 'The problem of politics and economics is the problem of justice. The question of politics is how to coerce the anarchy of conflicting human interests into some kind of order, offering human beings the greatest possible opportunity for mutual support'.[8]

In his "Introduction" to Niebuhr's *The Children of Light and the Children of Darkness*, Gary Dorrien provides a careful analysis on the development of Niebhur's understanding of love and justice: 'In the 1930s Niebuhr equated justice with equality, or an equal balance of power, and he blasted everyone who tried to get a social ethic out of Jesus. Always he admonished that Jesus was no help with problems of proximate means and ends, necessary violence, and calculated consequences.'[9] Later on, Niebuhr gradually recognized the problem of "dichotomizing between love and justice" and tends to underline the "social relevance" of the love ethic: 'Love is not merely the content of an impossible ethical ideal. It is the motive force of the struggle for justice'.[10] In other words, 'Social justice is an application of the law of love to the sociopolitical sphere, and love is the motivating energy of the struggle for justice'.[11]

It is now clear that Niebuhr's approach to the problem of love and justice moves further from the distinction to its internal connection, that is, how the law of love is essential to the spirit of justice: 'In so far as justice admits the claims of the self, it is something less than love. Yet it cannot exist without love and remain justice. For without the "grace" of love, justice always degenerates into something less than justice'.[12] From this perspective, he even expects that justice works towards the relative realization of love in the world: 'Yet the law of love is involved in all approximations of justice, not only as the source of the norms of justice, but as an ultimate perspective by which their limitations are discovered'.[13] How does love serve as the source of justice? Niebuhr explains: 'equality is always the regulative principle of justice; and in the ideal of equality there is an echo of the law of love'.[14] In other words, 'Love is the ground, source, and basis of these proximate principles (freedom, equality, equal justice), These proximate principles point toward love as their end and fulfillment as well as critical standard'.[15] This is what Niebuhr regards love as "impossible possibility": impossible in its immediate implications in concrete complex social and political conditions, possible in its ultimate and guiding principles.

In Paul Ramsey's words, Niebuhr's basic understanding of love and justice (justice "points toward" and finds "fulfilment" in love) shows their dynamic relationship, 'While establishing the transcendence of love', he also seeks to point out the relevance of the transcendent as 'both the ground and the fulfilment of existence,' as 'a basis of

[8]Niebuhr [10].

[9]Dorrien [4].

[10]Ibid.

[11]Ibid., xxiii.

[12]Niebuhr [12, p. 28].

[13]Niebuhr [10].

[14]Ibid., p. 108.

[15]Ramsey [17].

even the most minimal social standards,' and 'not only as the source of all norms of justice, but as an ultimate perspective by which their limitations are discovered.'[16] Robin Lovin describes it this way: 'Love draws our understanding of what justice requires in a more and more inclusive and generous direction, rather than allowing us to settle into a mutually disinterested, minimalist definition of justice.'[17] John C. Bennett also emphasizes this by saying:

> …justice must always be thought of in dynamic terms, love can always raise justice to new heights. There is an indeterminateness about the possibilities of transforming justice by love. Love makes our consciences more sensitive to the needs of others, especially to the needs of those who have been neglected or exploited. …love never takes the place of justice even under the best possible human conditions.[18]

The dynamic between love and justice points to the source, limitation and fulfillment of justice in terms of love while recognizing sharply the distance between two.

For Niebuhr, in general human and social conditions, in face of cruel and conflicting social realities, Christian love is a kind of ultimate possibility but not of possiblity in reality; the ideal of love can act as corrective power in reality, but not operative principles in political life. As Dorrien explains, 'The meaning of justice cannot be taken directly from the principles. It is determined only in the interaction of love and situation, through the mediation of the principles of equality, freedom, and order'.[19] In Wolterstorff's understanding, for Niebuhr, 'What's called for in cases of conflict is justice, not agapic love'.[20] The full realization of love is only possible under non-conflict conditions, 'Justice is relevant where the self-interest of different parties is in conflict; it consists of the just resolution of those conflicts'.[21] Moreover, Niebuhr concedes that we will also never fully succeed in fulfilling the demands of justice:

> What needs to be added is that Jesus' ethic of love is incapable of being fulfilled in this present age *without perpetrating or abetting injustice or inviting victimization*. The impossibility of fulfilling the ethic without violating justice is what shows that it was never meant as a universal ethic for life in this present age.[22]

In general, Niebuhr emphasizes the "conceptual incompatibility" between love and justice:

> A fundamental assumption in both Nygren and Niebuhr is that love may conflict with justice and nonetheless be *well-informed*. Nygren instructs us to remain faithful to love in such situations of conflict at the cost of perpetrating injustice; Niebuhr instructs us to remain faithful to justice in situations of conflict at the cost of love.[23]

---

[16]Ibid., p. 94.

[17]Lovin [9].

[18]Bennett [2].

[19]Dorrien [4, xxiii].

[20]Wolterstorff [21].

[21]Ibid., p. 67.

[22]Ibid., p. 63.

[23]Ibid., p. 71.

Departing from Anders Nygren and Niebuhr, Wolterstorff attempts to develop the idea of "love incorporating justice" by suggesting that even in non-conflictual situations it does not mean that justice is irrelevant. Justice in conflict does not represent the whole of justice, 'I may treat you justly even though there is no conflict between two of us and even though neither of us has wronged the other. I may treat you justly in a situation of 'frictionless harmony'. I do so if I treat you in such a way as befits your worth'.[24] For Wolterstorff, respect for the other's worth and just treatment to the other demonstrate love itself, without conflicting with the law of love, nor restraining or complementing the law of love. He says, 'treating the neighbor justly is not viewed as incompatible with loving the neighbor, nor is it viewed as an alternative to loving him. Treating the neighbor justly is an example of loving him, a way of loving him. Love is not justice-indifferent benevolence'.[25]

Wolterstorff's understanding of the meaning of love and its relevance to justice derives from the teaching of Jesus: "You shall love your neighbor as yourself." He places much emphasis on acknowledgement of human worth and dignity and regards neighbor and other members of the human community as our "moral counterpart". For him, Christian love has significant implications for "care" for others. In this sense, even in non-conflicting situations, human beings should learn respect for the other and just treatment with the other. It is that justice generated by love, which distinguishes itself from Niebuhr's position of the incompatibility of love and justice.

Even though Niebuhr and Wolterstoff have distinctive understanding of love and justice: the distance between them, on the one hand, and a justice in love with a focus on human fellowship as "moral counterpart" and the requirement of justice in harmonious situation, on the other. I consider there to be a central problem. How is it possible for Christian love to engage social justice? Does love only serve an ideal and one kind of corrective power for justice? Or, how far can it be applied and embodied in complex social, economic and political issues? In the following sections, I shall explore the possible implication of Christian love in approaching the problem of social justice in China.

Christian Love and Social Justice in China: How to Express Love

1. *The ideal and limitation of love in the Chinese context*

As Niebuhr understands, the spirit of sacrifice, unselfishness, and forgiveness from Christian love has board implications for wide Christian communities. In Chinese society, it is observed that a large number of Christians practice well the moral norms (including Christian love) in their personal life, family, church community, civil life, and professional life. Yet as Niebuhr suggests, 'the full force of religious faith will

[24]Ibid., p. 90.

[25]Ibid., p. 83.

never be available for the building of a just society…but do not conquer society'.[26] Despite these, we cannot deny that the idea of love initiated by religious believers and communities can enhance individual moral life as well as bestow healthy components to intimate social relationships and even give a guide to resolve conflict and inequality in society. Even though Niebuhr insists that with respect to conflict realities in social, political, and economic life, religious ideals (such as love) and power cannot be applied directly to construct social justice, but he thinks that if the ideal of justice is penetrated by the ideal of love, it will not become a purely political idea, as he claims, 'Every genuine passion for social justice will always contain a religious element within it. Religion will always leaven the idea of justice with the ideal of love. It will prevent the idea of justice, which is political-ethical ideal, from becoming a purely political one, with the ethical element washed out'.[27] This point can be relevant in the Chinese context.

Chinese society, in its pursuit of social justice in various areas, many considerations are given to the relationship of rights and duties, institutional arrangement and rational measures on various issues such as education and medical policy. In these circumstances, it will make some differences if we have an eye on the moral ideal deriving from the religious and ethical system in order that the idea of justice does not collapse into pure political idea, without the direction of moral sensitivity and without recognizing the relative limitation of institutions and justice. It is a certain moral power that directs, criticizes, corrects and then lead to perfect justice, in Niebuhr's term, to 'bear our Christian witness in the cause of justice'.[28]

This support of moral ideal and conscience, according to Niebuhr, rooted in religious communities. However, in contemporary China, in the case of Christianity, Christian faith and practice and the formation of Christian communities faces certain constraints and challenge. Culturally, Christians are still a minority among the practice of variety of religions in China.[29] Politically, with regard to Christianity in China, there is a general structure of both churches with registration with government under the umbrella of China Christian Council and Three-Self Patriotic Movement and churches without registration with government in terms of church governance—used to be called "house church." It is often the latter (even some cases of the former) which has to encounter the pressures such as splitting groups, closing churches, and demolishing of church buildings. The expression of Christian love (like forgiveness) experiences limitation under these cultural and political conditions. It will be a far

[26]Niebuhr [11].

[27]Niebuhr [11, pp. 80–81].

[28]Rasmussen [18].

[29]At this point, I have been aware of the fact of religious diversity in China. In 2014 Pew Research Center produced an index that ranks each country by its level of religious diversity, in which Singapore is listed the first, Taiwan the second, mainland China the ninth, and Hong Kong the tenth. Here we see the Chinese societies has high level of religious diversity and the Asia-Pacific region has the highest level of religious diversity. In more details, in mainland China, the percentage of the followers of major religions is: Christian 5.1%, Muslim 1.8%, Buddhist 18.2%, Folk religion 21.9%, and particularly 52.2% (more than half) identified "unaffiliated." See Pew Research Centre [15].

and hard process for maintaining this moral ideal in supporting and directing social justice from a long-term perspective.

2. *Compatibility of love and justice in the Chinese context*

By contrast, Wolterstorff's account of compatibility of love and justice, which means justice as expression of love in non-conflicting situations towards respect for human worth and just treatment for the other, may have certain implications in the Chinese context. Justice ought to be indispensable in society; furthermore, to bind love and justice together even that in harmonious situation justice is indeed an action of love. This understanding gives us a more general picture of what justice really is. In contemporary China, greater concern with social justice arises only when some unjust issues (such as corruption, rich-poor gap, unequal competition in economics, unequal treatment in education, and ecological problem) take place. It is supposed in Chinese society that the needs and circumstances of the others should be taken into account in certain political considerations and the distribution of resources and opportunities such as education, employment, and medical care. This consideration would help minimize the opportunities of inequality and of harm to some special groups particularly the marginalized ones, who are deserved equal regard when political power is operated, and certain laws and public policies are exercised towards the resolution of these social problems. It is a basic requirement for a just institution. Here I would suggest that any social and political arrangements be guided by the principles of justice supported by the spirit of certain religious and moral ideas such as love in its concern with the moral worth of fellow human being in various situations.

In this regard, Catholic teaching on love and justice agrees with Woltertorff's idea in its precept of "love entails justice" on the one hand, and complements this point by suggesting that love transcends justice, on the other: our society not only needs justice at its "cold face" but also warmness and care[30]; love deriving from religious resources provides one kind of special care and hope, so as to smooth social conflict. Love demands justice, which is not the whole of society. A society maintained by the principles of devotion, forgiveness and care complement what might be missing such requirements as retributive justice. It also encourages an ideal of a "civilization of love" or "love in political, economic, and social life": love should be embodied in each social relationship, resulting in engaging service in various spheres of social life.[31]

It seems that the ideal of "justice in love" either in Wolterstoff's version or in Catholic teaching (in their different tones) is consistent with Chinese church leader, Bishop Guangxun Ding's understanding. Starting from the idea of "cosmic love of Christ," he insists the compatibility of love and justice: '…justice, fairness—those are not the opposite of love, rather, they are entailed in love; when we practice love beyond one small scale and when we distribute love to the mass rationally, love attains its form of justice and fairness'.[32]

[30] See Benedict [1].

[31] See Pontifical Council for Justice and Peace [16].

[32] Ding [3].

So, then, in practice, how can love be incorporated into the problem of social justice in China? Here I will refer to two cases in Chinese society. First, a case relevant to education justice. During the urbanization, some children in some rural areas whose parents, for economic reasons, have to leave their children and take jobs in cities, were under the Chinese educational system not allowed and encouraged to take full schooling in cities so that they could live together with their parents. These children have to be raised by and live with their grandparents or other relatives at their home town. Some problems emerged from this group in terms of living and studying: the lack of social care and longing for parents' love which resulted in some psychological problems such as rebellious mentality. In response to these problems some institutional adjustments need to be done such as "registered residence" (*Hu Kou 户口*) difference between rural and urban areas, the adjustments which point to relatively equal educational opportunities of those children, equal treatment between those people from the rural and the urban, and educational support to those children from their local government. Besides those institutional considerations, the children's emotional and psychological needs as well as character development are a significant component in resolving those problems. It is important to recognize that institutional aspect is not enough towards helping the group. Furthermore, some policy and services towards the group would work well if they accommodate the groups' emotional and psychological needs besides providing educational opportunities.

Similarly, "Sun Zhigang Event" took place in Guangzhou in 2003 (one college graduate was detained and attacked to death due to the absence of a temporary resident certificate) also shows the different treatment between urban citizens and those moving to cities without receiving formal residency and discloses the problem of "identity politics" of Chinese farmers who are living in the cities: 'In cities, they are regarded as foreigners, facing discrimination in terms of residency, employment, education and psychology, thus live in the margin of society; even though they live a city for long period, they are not likely receive the identity of urban residency'.[33] Discussions of this event eventually resulted in the abolition of two unconstitutional detention regulations regarding 'non-identity' people in a city, but the questions raised about "registered residence," urban-rural gap, the identity of a farmer in city and equal citizenship are still there.

As I see it, these two cases among others reflect the experience of marginalized people, such as the identity and rights of farmers and other people moving to cities (including their children's education opportunities). Some local governments do not systematically include the children who do not receive the local residency in the equal education system. Some employees from the rural areas moving to a city do not have equal rights with those originally from that city. Besides, there are some groups who are not able to afford themselves schooling. These groups deserve constant respect and care in the moral sense, which affects the issue whether they may be treated

---

[33]Zhiping Liang, 'The Death of a Detained: The Dilemma and Way-out of Identity Politics in Contemporary China', [Bei Shourong Zhe Zhisi: Dangdai Zhongguo Shenfen Zhengzhi de Kunjing Yu Chulu "被收容者之死: 当代中国身份政治的困境与出路"], in Zhiping Zhang, *Social Justice in Transformative Period*, p. 188.

justly or not. I believe if this aspect is introduced into the process of governmental policy, it will contribute to the absence of "pure just legal institutions," which might contain some risk such as discrimination and inequality. From this point of view, when we take into account moral status of the vulnerable and marginalized, it is our hope that charity, love and justice could function together leaning towards a caring and just society. As Robert E. Goodin urges, we should, 'make duties of justice morally binding—considerations relating to the particular vulnerability of one person to another—also give rise to far more extensive duties of charity or humanity. The effect of that is to put duties like charity or humanity morally on a par with those of justice and to say that (depending on the circumstances) charity can be every bit as compelling as justice, narrowly construed'.[34] In my view, this approach stands in the line of "compatibility between love and justice" proposed by some Christian thinkers.

Conclusion: The Ideal of Love and Its Just Expression

Indeed, as Lauretta Conklin Frederking suggests, 'social justice is also a place where religions can come together and must come together to sort out agreements and disagreements'.[35] Especially for Christianity, its tradition gets involved in the understanding of truth, justice and charity and bears the burden of these matters. Christian theologians "speak from a community of faith which includes world-wide a multitude of the victims of injustice and oppression, whose cry it is part of the theologian's task to articulate. They claim to have insights into the nature and the demands of justice which are true, and are sometimes recognized as such in a broader arena than the church."[36] Standing along with this tradition, in this Chapter I examined Niebuhr and Wolterstorff's distinctive positions on love's engagement with social justice while I referred to Catholic doctrine on this topic so far. A crucial theme arising within their discussions is: to what degree does love give impact to justice? It seems to me they all agree that love acts as the spirit of justice even though the ways of its impacts are different. In the Chinese context, the relevance of Christian love to social justice cannot be simply interpreted from any defined version of that relationship. Current discussions on social justice in contemporary China are much concerned with rational institutional aspects and here I propose to introduce the distinctive aspect of love—in its religious sense in particular—to understand better the problem of social justice in China. In China, we need a kind of Niebuhrian's religious passion for an ideal conferred on justice in order to direct, guarantee and correct the principles and practice of justice; we also need to go further to put into effect the idea of "compatibility of love and justice". The ideal and implication of Christian love,

---

[34]Goodin [7].

[35]Frederking [5].

[36]Forrester [6].

in its specific moral resources, will enrich and advance the view of social justice in the Chinese context.

References

1. Benedict XVI. (2019). *Encyclical Letter Caritas in Veritate of the Supreme Pontiff.* Retrieved October 30, 2019, from http://w2.vatican.va/content/benedict-xvi/en/encyclicals/documents/hf_ben-xvi_enc_20090629_caritas-in-veritate.html.
2. Bennett, J. C. (1956). Reinhold Niebuhr's social ethics. In W. K. Charles & Bretall R. W. (Eds.), *Reinhold Niebuhr: His religious, social, and political thought* (p. 59).
3. Ding, G. X. (1997). Learning from theology of liberation, theology of Pierre Teilhard de Chardi and process theology. In G. X. Ding (Ed.), *Collected works of Guangxun Ding* (p. 214). Nanjing: Translation Press.
4. Dorrien, G. (2011). Introduction to Reinhold Niebuhr. In *The children of light and the children of darkness* (p. xxii). Chicago and London: The University of Chicago Press.
5. Frederking, L. C. (2014). *Reconstructing social justice* (p. 97). New York, NY: Routledge.
6. Forrester, D. B. (2010). *Forrester on Christian ethics and practical theology: Collected writings on Christianity, India, and the social order* (p. 252). Surrey, England: Ashgate.
7. Goodin, R. E. (1985). *Protecting the vulnerable: A reanalysis of our social responsibility* (pp. 26–27). Chicago: The University of Chicago Press.
8. Liang, Z. (2010). Introduction. In Z. Liang (Ed.) *Social justice in transformative period: Problem and prospect* [Zhuanxingqi de Shehui Gongzheng: Wenti yu Qianjing 转型期的社会公正:问题与前景] (p. 5). Beijing: Three Joint Publishing House.
9. Lovin, R. (1995). *Reinhold Niebuhr and Christian realism* (p. 199). Cambridge University Press.
10. Niebuhr, R. (1935). *An interpretation of Christian ethics* (p. 140). New York, London: Harper Brothers Publishers.
11. Niebuhr, R. (1947). *Moral man and immoral society: A study in ethics and politics* (p. 81). New York: Charles Scribner's Sons.
12. Niebuhr, R. (1992). *Love and justice: Selections from the shorter writings* (p. 25). Louisville, KY: Westminster/John Knox Press.
13. Niebuhr, R. (1998). *Moral man and immoral society: A study in ethics and politics* (p. 57). Eugene: Wipf and Stock Publishers.
14. Outka, G. (1972). *Agape: An ethical analysis* (pp. 7–54). New Haven and London: Yale University Press (1972).
15. Pew Research Centre. (2017). Religious Diversity Index Scores by Country. Retrieved June 7, 2017, http://www.pewforum.org/2014/04/04/religious-diversity-index-scores-by-country/.
16. Pontifical Council for Justice and Peace. (2005). *Compendium of the social doctrine of the church* (pp. 294–295). London: Burns & Oates.
17. Ramsey, P. (1956). Love and law. In C. W. Kegley & R. W. Bretall, (Eds.), *Reinhold Niebuhr: His religious, social, and political thought*, (p. 95). New York: The Macmillan Company
18. Rasmussen, L. (Ed.). (1989). *Reinhold Niebuhr: Theologian of public life* (p. 127) London: Collins.
19. Robertson, D.B. (1992). "Introduction" to Reinhold Niebuhr. *Love and justice: Selections from the shorter writings* (p. 12). Louisville, KY: Westminster/John Knox Press.
20. United Nations. (2019). If you want peace & development, work for social justice. Retrieved May 30, 2019, from http://www.un.org/zh/events/socialjusticeday/index.shtml.
21. Wolterstorff, N. (2011). *Justice in love* (p. 66). Grand Rapids, MI: Eerdamans.

Zhibin Xie received his doctorate from The University of Hong Kong, and is Professor of Philosophy at Tongji University, Shanghai, P. R. China. He is a research fellow of the Institute of Sino-Christian Studies (Hong Kong) and a member of the Center of Theological Inquiry in Princeton. His research interests include Christian philosophy and ethics, public theology, religion and politics in China. His major publications include *Religious Diversity and Public Religion in China* (in English, 2006), *Public Theology and Globalization: A Study in Max Stackhouse's Christian Ethics* (in Chinese, 2008), and *Why Public? How Theological? A Retrospect and Prospect for Sino-Christian Public Theology* (in Chinese, 2016). He has also published articles in a number of journals including *Asian Journal of Theology*, *International Journal of Public Theology*, *Political Theology*, and *Journal of Church and State*.

Part II
Human Dignity, Human Rights, and Social Justice: Global Perspectives on Theory and Practice

Chapter 9
Social Justice, Political Science, and Christian Thought

James W. Skillen

Abstract The challenge of developing a philosophy of social diversity and political pluralism confronts people throughout the world today at all stages of social, economic, and political development, whether from a Christian or any other standpoint. The words in the title of this chapter can be interpreted in many ways. My aim is to offer an historical-critical interpretation of their meaning in the West from the time of early Christianity to the present day.

The expansion of Christianity in the first centuries after Christ came chiefly from the conversion of Gentiles—non-Jewish peoples—whose political, intellectual, and social experiences were predominantly Roman and Greek rather than Jewish. The biblical story of God's rule over the nations and special covenants made with Noah, Abraham, Israel, and David, leading to the revelation of Jesus Christ, had not shaped gentile culture. F. Edward Cranz makes this point, in particular to the great church father and bishop Aurelius Augustine, by saying, 'Paul is engaged in a Christian transformation of an earlier Judaism; Augustine is primarily engaged in a Christian transformation of an earlier Hellenism.'[1] It was also the case, as Walter Ullmann points out, that the 'state' as we know it today did not exist in that era, and the word 'political', which was derived from *polis* (the Greek city-state), dropped out of use in the early Christian period. It came back into use only after recovery of the work of Aristotle in the thirteenth century after Christ. The term used in the Roman world was 'government' (*gubernatio* or *gubernator*), often in conjunction with the word 'jurisdiction' (*jus dicere*), which means the right to lay down the law.[2]

In the Roman Empire the emperor was responsible to establish and enforce law in the early Christian period. The growing church did not, by and large, call into question the Roman imperial system of governance. The figure who most significantly influenced the church's life and thought in the centuries that followed was Augustine

[1] Cranz [9].
[2] Ullmann [29, p. 17].

J. W. Skillen (✉)
Center for Public Justice, 1817 Parkside Circle, Birmingham, AL 35209, USA
e-mail: jwskillen@gmail.com

Z. Xie et al. (eds.), *Human Dignity, Human Rights, and Social Justice*,
https://doi.org/10.1007/978-981-15-5081-2_9

(354–430). After his conversion to Christianity he became the Bishop of Hippo in North Africa. Influenced by Neoplatonism and other Greco-Roman philosophies and religions, he worked the rest of his life to rethink the meaning of life from a Christian point of view.[3] He concluded that true justice can never be found or realized on earth due to human sinfulness but will be realized only in the city of God when it is fulfilled after the final appearance of Christ. For him, earthly government and private property were instituted (or permitted) by God in response to sin; they are not natural for human creatures. Government exists primarily to restrain and punish evil. However, at a crucial stage in his life Augustine came to believe that some use of force on the part of government may contribute to the well-being of the church, which partially embodies and looks ahead to the city of God. The contrasting ideas that Augustine developed on the relation of the church to society and government were not entirely compatible with one another. Perhaps that is why Christians took political life and thought in a variety of incompatible directions in the centuries to come.

By the time of Pope Gelasius I in the fifth century, the primary line of Augustinian thought that had been adopted was that of government serving the church. The battle lines between pope and emperor were being drawn over the relative positions of authority that each should hold in the empire. Gelasius, who argued that papal authority was superior to the emperor's, spoke of the pope's *auctoritas* (authority) and of the emperors mere *regia potestas* (ruling power).[4] The emperor did not accept such a subordination of his authority to that of the church, though eventually that is what took hold in the West because the emperors lost control of the city of Rome and much of what we now call Western Europe. The Gelasian argument was that Christ delegated to the church both a spiritual sword and an earthly sword; the pope retained the sword of spiritual authority and delegated the sword of earthly power to those authorized to govern under papal oversight. Oliver and Joan Lockwood O'Donovan write that Pope Gelasius' assertion of papal supremacy 'defined the relation of ecclesiastical and secular authority in a form which would prove decisive within the Western Church for subsequent centuries'.[5]

When Justinian (483–565) became emperor a few decades after Pope Gelasius had articulated his two-swords doctrine, he set out to reestablish the glory of the empire and the preeminence of its Caesar. He began by collecting and codifying the whole of Roman law—collections that became the famous and highly influential *Corpus Juris Civilis*, the *Digest*, and the *Institutes*. These, Justinian believed, would demonstrate the legitimacy and true greatness of imperial Rome. Among other things, the treatises offered a detailed legal argument that the Roman Caesar was the rightful sovereign of Christendom and superior to the church, the one 'who directed and ruled the empire in accordance with Christian principles emanating from the fount of all Christianity, the divine majesty of the emperor himself'.[6] For the next five

[3]On Augustine's life and thought see, for example, Fox [10], Augustine [3–5].

[4]Ullmann, *Political Thought*, p. 41.

[5]O'Donovan and O'Donovan [22, p. 177].

[6]Ullmann, *Political Thought*, p. 47.

centuries the competition for supremacy between emperor and pope continued as Roman imperial power declined in the West and the Roman Catholic Church gained strength under papal authority.

The Roman emperor did, however, retain his supremacy in the East, which became the Byzantine Empire, with headquarters in Constantinople (founded by Constantine in 330 as a second Rome). And the eastern branch of the church (eventually to be called the Orthodox Church, or Eastern Orthodox Church) continued to uphold the principle of imperial supremacy over the Christian empire. That system came to be described as Caesaropapism. The western branch of the church, on the other hand, gradually and slowly built 'Christendom' under ecclesiastical supremacy with headquarters in Rome.[7]

From the fourth century onward, the Western church increasingly took on the identity of an earthly governing *institution* led by the pope. The church institution became more and more identified with its full-time clergy. Ordinary members of the church were referred to as laypeople who were connected to the institutional church by participation in its sacraments and worship. The older biblical idea of the church as a community of all the faithful—the body of Christ—became subordinated to the doctrine that the sacrament of bread and wine were Christ's body and blood. There were at least two reasons for this. The first was that a hierarchy of governance—spiritual above temporal—became the defining characteristic of the society of *Christendom*. The second was that by the time of the High Middle Ages almost everyone in Christendom was baptized as an infant. Consequently, the church as a community of faith was no longer distinguishable from the society at large. Everyone was part of Christendom and thus under the moral authority of the church.

In 1075, a great Papal Revolution began. The highly influential Archdeacon Hildebrand, not yet an ordained priest, much less a bishop, was elected Pope Gregory VII.[8] The new pope wanted to settle the question of supreme authority once and for all. He believed this was not only a spiritual matter but also something 'required by the justice (*justitia*) and the law (*ius*) of Christ'.[9] Much like Emperor Justinian had done nearly 500 years earlier, Gregory set out to establish the truth of his supreme position on a comprehensive legal basis. He appointed experts in theology and law to develop what became the Roman Catholic Church's *canon law*. He and his successors composed what the O'Donovans describe as an elaborate legal brief in support of St. Peter's authority as the Vicar of Christ, 'the structure and unity of the *corpus Christianum*', and 'Christ's earthly kingship'.[10] Gregory declared that the Bishop of Rome should henceforth be recognized as the supreme authority over the whole church, including the eastern branch. Papal authority was to stand above all lower ranks of clergy and laity and over the entire empire and all governmental powers throughout Christendom. His pronouncement sealed the 1054 division between the western and eastern branches of the church because the bishops of the eastern church refused

---

[7]For more on the two systems, see Ullmann, *Political Thought*, pp. 19–44.

[8]Berman [6, p. 206].

[9]O'Donovan and O'Donovan, *Sourcebook*, p. 232.

[10]Ibid.

to bow to the supremacy of the Bishop of Rome. Gregory's pronouncement also heightened the conflict between pope and emperor until a settlement was reached in 1122 that confirmed the supremacy of papal authority in the West. After that, writes historian Johan Huizinga, a second metaphor became prominent alongside the two-swords imagery to symbolize the church's preeminent authority, namely, the image of two heavenly bodies with the sun having primacy above the moon.[11]

One can see from this brief overview of the church's first millenium that *social justice* meant conformity to the decrees of the emperor or the pope and to the laws and customs promulgated under their authority. Also crucial to the western idea of justice from about 400 to 1600 was the proper subordination of the emperor and all other forms of government to the pope. The reason for this idea of justice was that social order and harmony were believed to be dependent on a hierarchy from highest authority down to the lowest levels of human subjection within the single realm of Roman Christendom.

During that time as well, there was no *science of politics* in either the classical or the modern sense. Political knowledge and theories were derived primarily from interpreting the exercise of hierarchical authority and then either adapting to it or challenging it. *Christian political thought*, therefore, consisted of a growing body of legal and governing doctrines as exemplified by the canon law of the church that was formulated during the Papal Revolution begun in 1075.

One of the consequences of the long struggle between emperor and pope for supreme authority was the development of two dominant institutions that each claimed comprehensive jurisdiction. In the West this led to the need to distinguish the different kinds of responsibilities, social bodies, and functions that were seen as subordinate to the church. Not only governing authorities but also familial, academic, and economic organizations were identified as *not* religious since they were not part of the church's institutional organizations but were identified as authorities for so-called 'secular' capacities, though at that time the word 'secular' did not mean unrelated to God. 'Secular' meant 'of or pertaining to life in *this* world'—the Latin '*saeculum*'. In making this distinction the church was engaged in distinguishing its superior spiritual authority from subordinate secular authorities. However, that effort pushed those in positions of governing authority to seek clarity about the kind of authority they held. Consequently, over a period of about six or seven centuries, important steps were taken to recognize the diversity of types of institutions and responsibilities that existed, including universities, independent cities, crafts and guilds, various courts of law, and more.

In keeping with the sacred-secular hierarchy of western Christendom, two different levels of ethical norms were developed. The higher level of ethical norms held for those in church offices, entailing vows of poverty, celibacy, and obedience to superior ecclesiastical authorities. The lower level of ethical norms held for laypeople who married, accumulated property, income, and debts, fought in wars, and operated by natural reason in this world. That order of ethics and law continued for as long as Christendom maintained its hierarchical unity. But institutional developments and

[11]Huizinga [14, p. 247].

social behavior were changing in ways that would lead eventually to the independence of non-ecclesiastical (secular) institutions from the church.

In fact, the first resort of kings in the later Middle Ages and early modern period was to claim *direct* (rather than indirect) ordination by God. This was the claim of a 'divine right' of monarchical authority instead of an ecclesiastically mediated authority. That, in turn, led to the recovery and modification of older imperial and Frankish ideas of monarchical superiority over the church within the splintering political territories of Europe. Yet that change did not come quickly. Even John of Salisbury (c. 1120–80), who supported this idea argued that to become a prince 'one must have the approval of the ecclesiastical authority. Since the prince is subject to God, he is subject also to the priesthood, 'who represent God on earth'.[12]

At the heart of the centuries-long jurisdictional dispute between church and temporal governments there was a problem that could not be resolved by insisting on a hierarchical view of authority. On the one hand, it might be possible to recognize that church and state are different in kind and exercise different types of responsibility. But on the other hand, the dispute between pope and emperor over supremacy could not by itself clarify the specific kinds of responsibilities and jurisdictions that belong to each of them. Neither would a settlement of the proper hierarchy of church and state answer questions about the responsibilities and jurisdictions that belong to academic and economic institutions and organizations. Placing church or government at the top of the social hierarchy does not address that question. Moreover, if the church (in the biblicalsense—the people of God in Chirst is a community of faith that embraces all Christians in all aspects of their lives, then the diversity of responsibilities on earth cannot be adequately identified, distinguished, and interrelated simply by an agreement that the pope or the emperor (or king) is Christ's vicar (sole representative) on earth. Social justice, therefore, becomes a more complicated matter than envisioned in early and medieval Christianity.

The most sophisticated intellectual attempt to comprehend these complexities in a rounded philosophical and theological system was made by Thomas Aquinas (1225–1274), the greatest theologian and philosopher of the church after Augustine. Aquinas drew on all strands of Christian practice and thinking up to his day and he also made use of the ancient Greek philosopher Aristotle, whose writings had recently been recovered, translated, and reintroduced into the West by Muslim philosophers.[13] Among Aquinas's many achievements was his interpretation of political life as a *natural* community, part of human life by nature. Unlike Augustine who believed that God established government because of sin to restrain and punish evildoers and to uphold a modicum of order in a sinful world, Aquinas drew on Aristotle's idea of the polis as a perfect or complete natural community. Political community is the

[12]Berman, *Law and Revolution*, p. 285.

[13]On the contribution of Aquinas [1], see also Copleston [8], Colish [7, pp. 265–302, 335–359], O'Donovans, *Sourcebook*, with selected texts and an introduction by the editors, pp. 320–361.

most complete *natural* expression of human sociability and the *whole* of which all other social relations are *parts*.[14]

The Thomistic philosophical and theological synthesis reflected the structure and spirit of Christendom in that day. On the one hand, Aquinas worked to secure a firmer place and identity for human life in this world, including politics, as something that expresses the rational nature of human beings created by God. On the other hand, he was also giving support to the conviction that what is natural, philosophical, and political is not sufficient to bring about the highest fulfillment of life. He firmly located the ultimate end and perfection of life beyond the natural world. The experience of God's supernatural grace by faith through the church's sacramental communion opens believers to eternal life. That is what will bring about the greatest human happiness, the true fulfillment of life. Grace perfects nature rather than annulling it. Life in political community has its place, but it is not the highest place. The church is superior to earthly governments.

After the breakdown of the grand medieval synthesis in the centuries following Aquinas, the so-called 'secular' or natural world began to be understood in a very different way. Under the influence of a new humanistic spirit, people began to aspire to freedom and autonomy on earth. What had been called the 'secular' world was breaking free from the church rather than remaining subordinate to it. Humans in their natural lives in this world were less and less willing to subject their science, philosophy, arts, trade, and local governments to church authority. The grand hierarchy of a unified Christendom was coming undone. From the new modern point of view, the secular world was becoming independent and self-sufficient, *no longer* in need of religious supervision. That is not what Aquinas intended or expected would happen, but looking back from our day we can see how the modern humanist could find an opening in the philosophy of Aquinas (and in the medieval, hierarchical social order in general) that would lead to the detachment of the natural world from its place in the medieval hierarchy once the order of Christendom began to break down.

Part of the significance of the Protestant Reformation that burst forth powerfully in sixteenth-century Europe is that it challenged the way Christendom had understood the unity and diversity of God's world. On the one hand, the Reformers wanted to restore the biblical idea of the church as a community of all believers rather than as a hierarchical institution of priests and bishops who dispense God's saving grace to laypeople. The Reformers wanted to nurture the unity of the body of Christ that had been disrupted by an institutionalized hierarchy of authority that separated the clergy from laypeople. At the same time, the Reformers wanted to give greater recognition to the diversity of responsibilities that people exercised in this world and understood them all to be callings from God. The rallying cries of the Reformation that expressed these two aims were 'the priesthood of all believers' and the 'equal dignity of every

[14]See Copleston [8, pp. 192–234]. In an early work, *Summa Contra Gentiles,* Aquinas focuses on creation and the Christian confession that God is the creator of all things: Aquinas [2].

vocation'.[15] Reformed Protestants, those in the Calvinist stream, worked to articulate a more integrated view of a diversified society under the sovereignty of God. They showed greater appreciation for the multiple callings and institutional responsibilities of human life. They gave renewed attention to the Hebrew Bible—the Old Testament—and to a critical assessment of civil legal systems as well as the church as was evident in the work of Calvinist lawyer and city administrator Johannes Althusius (1563–1638) who governed in the northern European town of Emden. Althusius wrote massive tomes of political, legal, and social theory and practice. Among his achievements was a comprehensive treatise on the variety of types of human community and how, in their diversity, they could simultaneously exercise their distinctive responsibilities while also working together in harmony (*symbiosis*).[16]

However, the distinctive influence of the Protestant Reformation was not the sole force that led to a post-Christendom era. The Renaissance, which began prior to the Reformation, is equally important historically. It bred the new humanism, which became a dominant influence on the Enlightenment and the romantic idealism of the eighteenth and nineteenth centuries. The dynamism of this new humanism in the West was more than just philosophical or political in character and must be understood against the backdrop of collapsing Christendom. If the Protestant Reformers sought to recover biblical Christianity from its medieval corruptions, Renaissance scholars and artists wanted to recover the best of Greece and Rome that Christendom had obscured or discarded. Yet just as the Reformation's leaders could not entirely escape the cultural context of medieval Christendom, neither could Renaissance enthusiasts return to the classical world as it once was. The new humanistic spirit, which came to expression in Renaissance art, politics, and historical studies was not the humanism of Plato, Aristotle, and the poets and sculptors of ancient Greece and Rome. The new humanism was a creative amalgam, something we might describe as a secularized revision of the medieval, Christian-classical synthesis. It was neither classical, nor Christian, nor medieval.

The humanism of which we are speaking reached maturity in the period following the European Enlightenment of the eighteenth century and developed further with the romantic reaction to it. What emerged was more than a new approach to philosophical thought; more than a forceful rejection of authoritarian government and aristocratic privilege; more than an unprecedented push for scientific and technological control of nature; and more than creative ventures in the arts and literature. The Enlightenment gave expression to a new culture-wide, religiously deep way of life oriented toward reshaping this world. The new faith held that human beings could achieve liberation from every kind of subordination and bondage by means of autonomous rationality and free initiative. They would achieve what no philosophy or religion of the past had done. The spirit of Enlightenment and Romantic-era humanism is still very much at work today and not only in the West. It may be a stronger force than Christianity or

---

[15]On the Reformation see, for example, Hillerbrand [13], MacCulloch [19], O'Donovan and O'Donovan, *Sourcebook*, 581–694, Prestwich [23].

[16]For the best introduction to the work of Althusius see Witte [32, pp. 143–207]. See also, O'Donovan and O'Donovan, *Sourcebook*, pp. 757–770.

Islam in the wider world today, expressing itself through scientific and technological ambitions and a wide variety of nationalisms and other ideologies.[17]

In many respects, English philosopher John Locke (1632–1704) is probably the most representative transition thinker in the movement from state-established Christianity to the modern 'secular' state in the West. On the one hand, Locke wrote as a Christian with theological conviction, wanting to arrive at a broad, nonsectarian understanding of religion that could be justified rationally. This, he believed, would enable the government of England (a nationalized version of the Eastern *Caesaropapist* type, now called *Erastianism*) to establish a less imposing and less divisive religion that could unify divided England. On the other hand, Locke's broad, nonsectarian understanding of religion could be justified rationally, he believed, and could ground political authority in a social contract created by free, rational individuals. Along with Hobbes and somewhat similar to Augustine, Locke believed that politics and government are not natural to human beings. Yet he did not look to God for its ordination as a response to sin. Rather government's authority comes from those who contract to establish it. Locke believed government could thus be limited contractually to the specific task of protecting life and property and not allowed to achieve a position of omnicompetent authority over all of society.[18]

Part of the English common-law tradition that Locke took for granted was a body of civil rights and freedoms. Some of those rights and freedoms had their roots in the long historical development of private civil law going back to the Romans. The freedom of individuals to conduct their lives and to contract with one another privately on a variety of social and economic matters had been made possible, however, within the framework of a public-legal order that established some restriction on the jurisdiction of government. What Locke did was to imagine a process in reverse of that. He believed that autonomous individuals with their inherent rights and freedoms preexist society and create both society and government by means of a private contract. To put it perhaps over-simply, the contract theorists turned things upside down. Instead of seeing that a political order is necessary for the recognition and protection of civil rights and freedoms, they imagined that sovereign individuals with inherent rights created political society and sustained it by their continuing contractual commitment to the contract, which would guarantee the protection of their freedoms. This view of individual freedom lies at the heart of the Western liberal tradition (which encompasses both liberals and conservatives in the United States). One of the difficulties with that tradition is that it tends to overlook the multiple types of social institutions and organizations that are not mere creatures of the state nor reducible to private contracts between individuals.

Although most Americans think that the United States Constitution is the product of a social contract among individuals, the constitutionalizing process in the West has many roots. Some of them can be found in the biblical tradition of covenantal obligations, in particular the subordination of rulers to the law of God, and also in

[17] For an introduction to the emergence of the modern era in the West, see, for example, Willey [31], Gay [11, 12], Voegelin [30], Kolakowski [15].

[18] See Locke [16, 17].

biblical teaching that government itself must be held accountable in ways that help to restrain it from unjust practices (see for example, Deut. 17:14–20; Job 29; Prov. 8; Isa. 1:1–20; Rom. 13:1–10). Roots of constitutionalism can also be found in the emphasis on law in the Roman republican and imperial traditions, particularly in the development of the *ius gentium* and private civil law. In addition, the struggles between church and empire up to the end of Christendom pushed both sides to try to constitutionalize their institutional authority. Evidence of this is found in the Justinian law codes, the Roman Catholic Church's Canon Law, the arguments of the conciliar movement within the church, and the law systems of cities and medieval estates. In Britain particularly, the struggles of feudal lords against kings that produced the Magna Carta, the rights of Englishmen, and the development of the houses of Parliament also fed into American constitutionalism and the constitutionalizing process more broadly in the West.[19]

Although there has been no consistent and comprehensive tradition of *Christian political and legal thought*, it is possible to see some of the contours of such a perspective in biblical writings that deal with diverse human responsibilities in relation to divine covenantal law that transcends human subjectivity. The biblical tradition knows of no human authority under which every other human authority is subsumed as subordinate. God alone is the sole sovereign of human life and under divine authority humans exercise many kinds of personal, organizational, and institutional responsibility, including their role in public-legal communities. Historically speaking, we can recognize the development of an ever-increasing number of arts, sciences, and institutions, each with its distinct character, all of which manifest the complex and interdependent social life of human beings. With the differentiation of political institutions in distinction from families, schools, arts, sciences, business corporations, and multiple professions it has also become possible to develop a *science of politics*. What I mean by such a science is the study of the art of governing in conjunction with empirical comparisons of different kinds of political systems. A science of this kind cannot be built on neutral, unprejudiced ground, however, because it depends on the scientist's presuppositions about what constitutes human nature, law, political order, and the historical process of social differentiation. This is the context in which the question of *social justice* comes back into view in a more complex and diversified way. If we recognize the diversity of human responsibilities that are exercised in a wide variety of types of organizations and institutions, then we can say that justice must be done to and by the members of each association for its own good: parents and children in the home; teachers and students in a school; managers and workers in an enterprise; and similarly those involved in every other kind of organization and institution. Likewise, justice needs to be done to and within the entire diversified societies in which we live. This is typically where the questions about the order of political community come in: how is justice to be down within the public commons for the common good of all?[20] Here we arrive at the point where diversity and unity must be thought together and fit together if justice is to be done.

[19]See McIlwain [20], Tierney [28], Neumann [21], Smith [27], Lutz [18].

[20]See Skillen [24–26].

It seems to me that the challenge of developing a philosophy of social diversity and political pluralism confronts people throughout the world today at all stages of social, economic, and political development, whether from a Christian or any other standpoint.

References

1. Aquinas, T. (1948). In Anton C. Pegis (Eds.), *Introduction to Saint Thomas Aquinas*. New York: Modern Library.
2. Aquinas, T. (1956). *On the truth of the catholic faith: Creation* (Bk. Two of the *Summa Contra Gentiles*) (trans. Anderson, James F.). Garden City, NY: Doubleday Image Books.
3. Augustine. (1958). In V. J. Bourke (Ed.), *The city of God* (Abridged ed.). Garden City, NY: Doubleday Image Books.
4. Augustine. (1997). *The confessions* (trans. Maria Boulding). New York: Vintage Books.
5. Augustine. (1962). In H. Paolucci (Ed.), *The political writings of St. Augustine*. Chicago: Henry Regnery.
6. Berman, H. J. (1983). *Law and revolution: The formation of the Western legal tradition*. Cambridge: Harvard University Press.
7. Colish, M. L. (1997) *Medieval foundations of the western intellectual tradition, 400–1400*. New Haven: Yale University Press.
8. Copleston, F. C. (1955). *Aquinas*. Baltimore: Penguin Books.
9. Cranz, F. E. (1972). The development of Augustine's ideas on society before the donatist controversy. In R. A. Markus (Ed.), *Augustine: A collection of critical essays* (pp. 336–404). Garden City, NY: Doubleday Anchor Books.
10. Fox, R. L. (2015). *Augustine: Conversions to confessions*. New York: Basic Books.
11. Gay, P. (1966). *The Enlightenment: An interpretation*. New York: Random House Vintage Books.
12. Gay, P. (2008). *Modernism: The lure of heresy*. New York: W. W. Norton.
13. Hillerbrand, H. J. (2007). *The division of Christendom: Christianity in the sixteenth century. Louisville*, KY: Westminster John Knox Press.
14. Huizinga, J. (1996). *The Autumn of the middle ages* (trans: Payton Rodney, J. & Mammitzsch, U.). Chicago: University of Chicago Press, 1996.
15. Kolakowski, L. (1990). *Modernity on endless trial*. Chicago: University of Chicago Press.
16. Locke, J. (1958). In I. Ramsey (Ed.), *The reasonableness of Christianity*. Stanford: Stanford University Press.
17. Locke, J. (1973). In T. I. Cook (Ed.), *Two treatises of government*. New York: Hafner Press.
18. Lutz, D. S. (1988). *The origins of American Constitutionalism*. Baton Rouge: Louisiana State University Press.
19. MacCulloch, D. (2003). *The reformation: A history*. New York: Penguin Books.
20. McIlwain, C. H. (1940). *Constitutionalism: Ancient and modern*. Ithaca, NY: Cornell University Press.
21. Neumann, F. L. (1986). *The rule of law*. Heidelberg: Berg Publishers.
22. O'Donovan, O., & J. L. O'Donovan (Eds.), *From Irenaeus to Grotius: A sourcebook in christian political thought, 100–1625*. Grand Rapids, MI: Eerdmans.
23. Prestwich, M. (Ed.). (1985). *International calvinism 1541–1715*. Oxford: Oxford University Press.
24. Skillen, J. W. (2005). The common good as political norm. In P. D. Miller & D. P. McCann (Eds.), *In search of the common good* (PP. 256–278). New York: T&T Clark.
25. Skillen, J. W. (2014). *The good of politics: A biblical, historical, and contemporary introduction*. Grand Rapids, MI: Baker Academic.

26. Skillen, J. W., & McCarthy, R. M. (Eds.). (1991). *Political order and the plural structure of society.* In J. Witte, Jr. (Ed.), *Emory university studies in law and religion*. Atlanta: Scholars Press.
27. Smith, G. (1955). *A constitutional history of England*. New York: Scribner's.
28. Tierney, B. (1982). *Religion, law, and the growth of constitutional thought, 1150–1650*. Cambridge: Cambridge University Press.
29. Ullmann, W. (1965). *A history of political thought: The middle ages*. New York: Penguin Books.
30. Voegelin, E. (1975). In J. H. Hallowell (Ed.), *From enlightenment to revolution*. Durham, NC: Duke University Press.
31. Willey, B. (1935). *The seventeenth century background*. New York: Doubleday Anchor Books.
32. Witte, J. J. (2007). *The reformation of rights: Law, religion, and human rights in early modern Calvinism* . Cambridge: Cambridge University Press.

James W. Skillen now retired, has served as a Professor of Political Philosophy and ethics (1973–1982), and as the director of the Center for Public Justice in Washington, D.C. (1982–2009). He has lectured widely at home and in many parts of the world and continues to mentor students and practitioners on several continents. The most recent of his many books are: *The Good of Politics* (2014) and *God's Sabbath with Creation* (2019). A graduate of Wheaton College (BA, 1966), Westminster Theological Seminary (BD, 1969), and Duke University (MA and Ph.D., 1974), he also did graduate study at the Free University (VU University) of Amsterdam (1969–1970). He is a member of the Society of Christian Ethics, the Society of Biblical Literature, and the international Association of Christian Philosophy, headquartered in Amsterdam.

Chapter 10
Christianity and Social Justice: The Problem of Majoritarianism and a Search for the Common Good

Sebastian Kim

Abstract The interactions between Christian theology and wider society have been mutually beneficial but at the same time often contentious. One of the difficult issues has been the question of minorities or dissenting opinions over against the majority views in a political system with socio-cultural and economic diversities. Freedom, security, equality, and the rule of law are some of the key aspects of the responsibility of the society, which enable human community to flourish, but society must also deal with the 'problem of minorities'. This is not just a matter of tolerance, compassion or charity from the majority or from those who have authority, wealth and power but the system has to provide for the poor, marginalised and voiceless as a matter of seeking social justice for all.

Introduction

The republican political system is a form of government by representatives of the people. It is founded on the idea that sovereignty lies with the people and it is by far the most common form of government in contemporary states around the world. This political system arose in opposition to various forms of monarchy and the hallmark of this governance is identified as equality, freedom and the rule of the law. However, when it comes to forming a collective concept of the meaning of these aspects and their applications, the view of the majority is determinative, and the opinion of minority is often ignored or suppressed. Particularly during the second half of the twentieth century, wide and increasing acceptance of liberal democracy in world state politics was demonstrated by the increase in the number of nations classified as democratic,[1] and was highlighted in the much-quoted, though heavily criticised, thesis that liberal democracy is the 'end point of mankind's ideological evolution' and

[1]Editorial [10].

[2]Fukuyama [13, xi].

S. Kim (✉)
Fuller Theological Seminary, 135 North Oakland Avenue, 91182 Pasadena, USA
e-mail: sebastiankim@fuller.edu

Z. Xie et al. (eds.), *Human Dignity, Human Rights, and Social Justice*,
https://doi.org/10.1007/978-981-15-5081-2_10

the 'final form of human government'.[2] Recently the problems of democracy have become more apparent. In a feature article in *The Economist* (1st March 2014) asked 'What's gone wrong with democracy?'. The author raised a series of challenges to the 'end of history' thesis and pointed to a 'setback' in democracy developed in the west. They put forward a number of reasons for this, including the financial crisis of 2007–08 when people witnessed the incompetence of their political systems to police the workings of financial sectors and the way in which China, under the Communist Party, had achieved economic success as well as political stability. In addition, they drew attention to the serious problem of distrust towards politicians among voters in Europe and the USA. And yet, the issue concluded with some degree of optimism arguing that the most important part of the nurture and maintenance of a political system is its care for minorities:

> The most successful new democracies have all worked in large part because they avoided the temptation of majoritarianism—the notion that winning an election entitles the majority to do whatever it pleases.... the first sign that a fledgling democracy is heading for the rocks often comes when elected rulers try to erode constraints on their power—often in the name of majority rule.[3]

How then do we maintain the freedom and autonomy of individuals, groups and nations, and yet protect vulnerable minorities in a society or in a nation? The question of 'the problem of minorities', according to Jennifer Preece, is among the most contested issues in political life because of 'competing desires for freedom and belonging', especially when it comes to the issue of equality and freedom.[4] Freedom requires autonomy of action, promotes a variety of values, as well as innovation and diversity; whereas belonging requires certain constraints of freedom in order to maintain social relationships and social cohesion and preserve common identity and certain uniformity. The issue of minority rights is not only a matter of government toleration but also of positive government action to promote diversity and to 'affirm the dignity, esteem and mutual respect of all citizens whatever their religious, racial, linguistic or ethnic identities'.[5] There are some difficulties of applying rights between individual and group rights and between human rights and minority rights. The former is applied to more political, economic and social areas of life whereas the latter is more to do with the cultural sphere. Preece insists that 'what matters is not the content of the ideal but rather its ability to sustain a sense of solidarity towards other members that is not ordinarily extended to outsiders'. Typical ways to deal with the 'problem of minorities' in many societies is by means of discrimination, assimilation, persecution, or separation, but she warns that these will not solve the problem since the human diversity is 'remarkably resilient'.[6] Instead, she advocates the authority recognising diversity by setting moral and legal frameworks for it, such as the UN Declaration on the Rights of Persons Belonging to National or Ethnic, Religious and Linguistic Minorities (1992).

---

[3]Editorial, 'What's Gone Wrong....' 3.

[4]Preece [23, p. 5]. See Rawls [24, p. 277].

[5]Preece, *Minority Rights*, p. 8.

[6]Preece, *Minority Rights*, pp. 183–186.

Bhikhu Parekh discusses the difficulties of recognising and incorporating minority rights in a state. Minority groups such as gays and lesbians, women, ethnic and cultural minorities, and indigenous people demand that society should recognise their identities and take full account of these into laws and public policies, but many of these would face opposition from across the spectrum of political orientations.[7] He discusses the two distinctively different political approaches of 'redistribution' and 'recognition', and suggests that the best model for dealing with the issue should be an integral approach to the two since this is the most advantageous. In his proposal of a new theory of justice, he argues that differing views need to be acknowledged and understood and that the issues between them are not always issues of justice but rather to do with differing values and ideas. Therefore there is a need to negotiate with each other to seek a common solution.

How to deal with a minority in any society or nation is a vital part of the healthy conduct of a government, but states, whether of liberal (individualistic) or social (communal or cooperative) orientation, often fail to address the issue due to the democratic nature of majoritarianism.[8] South African theologian John de Gruchy points out that the relationship between Christianity and democracy has been ambiguous in that, although he sees that Christian faith has provided democratic values, historically Christianity has often distanced itself from the system. However, he further comments that, especially after the experience of Nazism and Stalinist totalitarianism, most churches regard democracy or republic as 'essential to [their] vision of a just world order'. De Gruchy employs Niebuhr's argument for democracy and also the way it was expressed in the perception of ecumenical Christianity.[9] Throughout Christian history, although the church has often been on the side of the state endorsing its policies, nevertheless Christians have also been among the chief critics of dominant policies, particularly on the poor and marginalised by challenging its majoritarianism. In this chapter, I shall examine Christian approaches to minorities, poor and marginalised in society by discussing three approaches: theology of the common good; liberation theology; and public theology. By way of conclusion, I will draw some findings from Chinese philosophies to enhance our search for social justice.

The Theology of the Common Good and Catholic Social Teaching

In terms of public issues of economic and political life in a national and global setting, Catholic Social Teaching (CST) has been immensely influential to Catholic communities and beyond, and the concept of the common good is at the very heart

[7]See Parekh [25].

[8]See Israel [16, pp. 1–36].

[9]de Gruchy [7, p. 9], Ibid., p. 228.

of its principles.[10] In the most comprehensive documents of CST, the *Compendium of the Social Doctrine of the Church* (2004), the Pontifical Council for Justice and Peace (PCJP) identified the common good as one of the three key principles of the church's social doctrine along with subsidiarity and solidarity.[11]

'The Common Good and the Catholic Church's Social Teaching', a document prepared by the Catholic Bishops' Conference of England and Wales in 1996, shows the close relationship between the common good and CST. In the preface, Cardinal Basil Hume asserted that 'the future of humanity does not depend on political reform, social revolution or scientific advance. Something else is needed. It starts with a true conversion of mind and heart'.[12] In the main text, the statement emphasises that Catholic social vision is based on the dignity of human beings in that all human beings are made of the image of God, Christ is present in our neighbours, especially who are suffering, and for Christians meeting our neighbour's needs is highest privilege and duty.[13] The document stresses the 'preferential option' for the poor and vulnerable. In the teaching of Jesus, Christians will be judged by their response to the 'least of these' and, as good citizens, Christians should accept their 'full share of responsibility for the welfare of society'.[14] It points out that a central concept of CST is the common good, which means 'every individual, no matter how high or low, has a duty to share in promoting the welfare of the community as well as a right to benefit from that welfare' and that 'if any section of the population is in fact excluded from participation in the life of the community, even at a minimal level, then that is a contradiction to the concept of the common good and calls for rectification, especially those that exclusion comes about from poverty.[15]

David Hollenbach, in his discussion of the common good and Christian ethics, acknowledges that there is scepticism about the compatibility of a shared vision of the good life in relation to freedom of individuals, especially in US politics. The very nature of plural society is the fact that people do not agree with each other[16] and a political arrangement of tolerance cannot handle the complexity of conflicting good and justice for each community. He also argues that, since it is a general tendency that people are safest when no one can interfere with their pursuit of their own understanding of the good,[17] there is a need for state interference to pursue shared goods such as the eradication of urban poverty. He further calls for forming a public philosophy which combines commitment to the common good with respect for the equality and freedom of all members of relevant communities.[18] He sees justice as a prerequisite for the common good in that the socio-political system cannot rely

[10]For in-depth discussion on the Catholic Social Teaching, see Curran [6], Rhonheimer [27].

[11]Pontifical Council for Justice and Peace [26, pp. 84–85].

[12]Catholic Bishops' Conference of England and Wales [4].

[13]'The Common Good…' p. 12.

[14]'The Common Good…' pp. 14–15.

[15]'The Common Good…' pp. 70–71.

[16]Hollenbach [15, pp. 20–22].

[17]Hollenbach, *The Common Good*, p. 57.

[18]Hollenbach, *The Common Good*, pp. 60–61.

on people's good will and it has to have justice with solidarity towards the poor and marginalised built in. Hollenbach argues the importance of the strengthening of 'commutative justice' (by which he means the reciprocity in exchanges among individuals, for example, wage justice, protection of contracts) but he insists that a more comprehensive system of justice is required. He argues for three types of justice: contributive (or general) justice (the contribution to the common good that justice requires from individual people—all citizens have duty to help build up these aspects of social life), distributive justice (the way members of society share in the goods that their life together makes possible), and social justice (the basic structure of society), which connects contributive and distributive justice.[19]

The CST and its emphasis on the common good have significantly shaped the political and economic aspects of the theologies of public life of Catholics and other Christians. The idea of the common good or the good society has been discussed widely among Christian communities. John de Gruchy, in his discussion on Christianity and democracy, sees the common good as binding its members together in mutual accountability and as a process rather than a static set of principles. He argues that it is a necessary vision of a just social order, which challenges individualism and promotes the welfare and fulfilment of society as a whole. He insists that the doctrine of the common good will provide an important challenge to the possessive individualism which lies at the heart of liberal democratic capitalism, and to the sacrifice of human rights by social collectivism. He points out that the relationship between power and powerlessness has always been a struggle for democratic theory and that the church's role is important in keeping those who are in power accountable and at the same time empowering those who are weak to exercise their rights for the good of the whole society.[20] He challenges the notion that a democratic system will produce morally responsible citizens as a matter of course, rather he sees that it is the morally formed and empowered who are able to make democracy work.[21]

Similarly, Robert Bellah, a sociologist of religion, in his *The Good Society*, argues that democracy requires a degree of trust and that, although freedom is the most important feature of the good society for most Americans, the meaning of freedom should be more than getting away from other people and should involve the 'right to participate in the economic and political decisions' which affect our common lives.[22] For Bellah and his colleagues, democracy means 'paying attention', employing the Zen concept of mindfulness, which they regard as a 'foretaste of religious enlightenment' and a full waking up from 'the darkness of illusion' to 'a full recognition of reality'.[23] To achieve the creation of a good society, they call for people taking responsibility to interpret the situation and take accountability by demonstrating

---

[19]Hollenbach, *The Common Good*, pp. 190–200. For discussion on the development of the concept, see McGrail & Sagovsky, 'Introduction', xxvi–xxviii. See also Rhoheimer [27], McCann and Patrick [20]. McGrail and Sagovsky [21].

[20]de Gruchy, *Christianity and Democracy*, pp. 264–267.

[21]de Gruchy, *Christianity and Democracy*, pp. 244–247.

[22]Bellah et al. [1, pp. 3–9].

[23]Bellah, et al. *The Good Society*, p. 255.

social solidarity.[24] In the same vein, Jim Wallis, a Protestant evangelical and campaigner, in his *The (Un) Common Good*, insists that the common good is a 'new ethic of civility' and a 'vision drawn from the heart of our religious traditions that allows us to make our faith public but not narrowly partisan'. For Christians, the idea of the common good derives from Jesus' commandment to love our neighbours, which he regards as 'the most transformational social ethic' and that our treatment towards the most vulnerable is the 'moral test' of any society's integrity.[25] He believes that when religion serves politics, rather than dominating it, it will provide a source of moral values and that the separation of church and state should not mean the segregation of moral values from the public life.[26] Responding to the question of how to bring prophetic values and not parochial and partisan interests into political and public life, on the basis of his understanding of the image of God as the foundation of a 'theology of democracy', he argues for two key aspects of democracy: the absolute worth of every human person and fundamental respect for every individual together with equal rights for political participation and social opportunities. Furthermore, he sees it is the relational capacity of human beings within these two aspects as what makes democracy possible.[27]

There are problems of the understanding of the common good, such as the questions of how to protect individual rights while seeking the common good; of who should define the common good within a modern plural and secular state; and who says so, on what grounds and in whose interests,[28] nevertheless, the theology of common good provides alternative approaches to the problem of minorities and makes meaningful conversation between liberal democracy and socialist democracy. The theology of the common good is based on the concept of the dignity of human beings, which is grounded in the biblical understanding of human beings as created in the image of God. In order to continue to promote this dignity, any democratic state should provide mechanisms for equality and freedom of individuals and create community for the maximum consensus for the common good. The key issue of this approach is that no one party determines what the common good is for a particular group, wider society or nation; rather, determining the common good is a process and an on-going project, which constantly seeks for the good for the majority while protecting minorities, and this has to be constantly negotiated and revised. Together with the key concepts of subsidiarity and solidarity, the theology of the common good provides some alternatives within contemporary political and economic systems, and in particular, its strength lies on its challenge to majoritarianism and the political dichotomy of liberal democracy and social democracy. The practical implementation of the common good in real politics and economics still needs to be articulated and tested. As it is, there are less robust mechanisms to counter-balance the misuse of state power or the market system that we have seen in some authoritarian community

---

[24] Bellah, et al. *The Good Society*, p. 283.

[25] Wallis [30, pp. xi–xiii].

[26] Wallis, *The (Un)Common Good*, p. 182.

[27] Wallis, *The (Un)Common Good*, pp. 183–84.

[28] D'Entreves [9, p. 225].

states and also aggressive and individualistic capitalist markets in liberal democracy. The common good could be a teaching applicable to all people of faith or rely on people's good will.

Prophetic Justice and Liberation Theology

Although CST and its teachings on the common good deal with the political and economic systems in democratic states, as we have discussed, there are still difficulties of defining and pursuing the 'common good' in a democratic society. The more recent approach of liberation theology has been more explicit in church's position on the poor and marginalised, and their theological insights are based on the prophetic tradition in the Hebrew Bible. In *Christianity and Democracy*, John de Gruchy distinguishes the democratic *system*, which is constitutional principles and procedures, and the democratic *vision*, which is the hope for society of equality, freedom and justice. In his view, the democratic *vision* originated in the message of the prophets of Israel, including that of Jesus, which is manifested in the reign of God's *shalom*:

> … western Christendom undoubtedly provided the womb within which the democratic *system*, as we now know it, gestated, and it also contributed decisively to the shaping of the democratic *vision* through its witness, albeit ambiguous and severely compromised, to the message of the Hebrew prophets.[29]

In order to establish a just world order, which he sees as an ultimate vision for Christianity, de Gruchy argues that the prophetic tradition, which is based on Israel's liberation from Egypt, provides the vision for social justice for the oppressed, poor and other victims of society so that 'all people are equally respected as bearers of God's image'.[30] The God of Israel is consistently seen as a god of justice and his people ought to be just; prophetic traditions demonstrated that justice is an '*ultimate theological* concern' and not only a '*penultimate moral* concern', as David Neville insists. He goes on to look in particular at the book of Jeremiah in which he finds justice centres around concerns for orphans, widows and resident aliens. So acting justly is not only meant for the practical activities toward the minorities in society but it is to do with knowing and relating rightly to God.[31] It is the very heart of knowing God, and since it is a relational reality and not stand-alone idea, compassion and mercy are key biblical attributes of God and his demand for his people is to practice towards the vulnerable in the society. The key issue here is that how can society provide a framework for the people to act justly and in what way the political system meets political vision, to use de Gruchy's taxonomy.

The prophetic tradition of seeking justice continues in the discussion of biblical hermeneutics in liberation theology. Peruvian priest, Gustavo Gutiérrez was the first

[29]de Gruchy, *Christianity and Democracy*, p. 8.

[30]de Gruchy, *Christianity and Democracy*, p. 11.

[31]Neville [22, pp. 1–21 at 7].

to clearly articulate 'a theology of liberation' which he defined as 'a critical reflection on Christian praxis in light of the word of God'.[32] Reading the story of the exodus from Egypt, for example, he concluded that this liberation of Israel was 'a political action', and that this is foundational to the Judeo-Christian faith.[33] This led him first to interpret Christian faith out of the suffering, struggle, and hope of the poor, and second to criticise society and the ideologies sustaining it, and also the activity and theology of the church from the angle of the poor. Gutiérrez put 'orthopraxis' alongside 'orthodoxy' (right practice as well as right doctrine) as the test of faith.[34] This revolutionary movement demanded not only a theology of liberation but also 'the liberation of theology' from being 'the erudite theology of textbooks' to 'a theology arising out of the urgent problems of real life'.[35] Constructively, liberation theology called for the reinvention and realignment of the church from an institution which supported and mirrored the unjust structures of society to communities with charismatic ministries appropriate to the context.[36] The creation of 'base (ecclesial) communities' was a way of involving the laity in ministry, as instructed by the Vatican Council, and utilized the encouragement given by the Council for lay people to read and interpret the Bible. Unlike celebration of the mass, reading the Bible was something they could do without a priest and so the communities can also be seen as a pastoral strategy to deal with the shortage of priests, and also a response to the challenge of a growing Protestant movement.

Liberation theology encouraged a hermeneutics of suspicion that raised questions of power and vested interest in theology. According to Gutiérrez, liberation theologians use four basic hermeneutical components: first, they construct a critique of framework of interpretation of the dominant traditions, whether Western, capitalist, colonial, androcentric or patriarchal. They aim to offer an alternative interpretation from their own experience and seek to expose those uses of biblical texts which serve the social interests of dominant groups. Second, and for the purpose of the first, they develop 'socio-critical' tools for hermeneutical purposes and as also to 'conscientise'. Third, they engage in intense identification of biblical texts, particularly the theme of Exodus. Fourth, they employ the language of eschatology—bringing hope—and emphasise action—praxis. Since it challenged church and state, liberation theology inevitably faced resistance from the authorities in Latin America and in Rome. Because of their work on behalf of the poor and action to reduce the power of the land-owning elite, Catholic priests, nuns and church workers suffered violent attack and persecution in the militarized societies of 1970s and 80s Latin America.

There are many examples of liberation readings in Latin America and these have been immensely influential on the rest of the world, especially in Asia and Africa where the issue of economic and political injustice has been dominant concern for the Christians. Korea also developed its own version of liberation theology called

---

[32]Gutiérrez [14, xxix].

[33]Gutiérrez, *A Theology of Liberation*, p. 88.

[34]Gutiérrez, *A Theology of Liberation*, p. 8.

[35]Segundo [28, pp. 4–5].

[36]Boff [3].

minjung theology. The obvious starting point of *minjung* theology is the distinctive concept of *minjung*—common people. Ahn Byung-Mu, one of *minjung* theology's leading exponents drew this concept from the gospel of Mark. In his study of Mark, he identified the crowd who were surrounding Jesus—*ochlos* and pointed out that this term was first used by Mark. He insisted that in comparison to the term *laos* in Luke, which means the 'people of God', *ochlos* is the common people, who belong to the 'marginalized and abandoned' group and that it is not consolidated into a concept but defined in a relational way.

> The *ochlos* are feared by the unjust and powerful, but they are not organized into a power group. Therefore, we cannot regard them as a political power bloc; rather, they should be regarded existentially as a crowd. They are minjung not because they have a common destiny, but simply because they are alienated, dispossessed, and powerless. They are never represented as a class which has a power base. They yearn for something.[37]

Ahn saw that Jesus loved the *minjung* and 'passively' stood with them as they followed him and informed them the coming of the kingdom of God.[38] This kind of identification of the people in the Bible with their own context is very common among liberation theologians, for example Dalit theologians, who represent the out-caste communities of India, have been using Isaiah 3:12–15 to show that the Lord is defender of the poor, accuser and judge of the oppressors.[39] There is strong identification with people of Israel in Exodus stories by people in a marginalized situation[40] and the church adopts the liberating role of Christ within the society. *Minjung* theologians lived out their theology in the turbulent years of military government in South Korea and were instrumental in bringing about the transition to democracy and improvements in workers' rights and conditions.

Liberation theology has certainly made clear the church's stance on the poor and marginalised and has been widely accepted by Christians, though not exclusively, in the more non-democratic situations. While they certainly share the concern for minorities and the marginalised in modern political and socio economic systems, public theology takes a different approach of challenging the monopoly of power in the public sphere. The protagonists of liberation theology took their stand with the poor and marginalised, according to their understanding of the 'option for the poor' demonstrated in the prophetic tradition in the Hebrew Bible. State and society must treat the poor and oppressed, who are victims of a competitive and aggressive market system and of politics of majoritarianism in a democracy, in a supportive and preferential way. Liberation theologians see the 'problem of minorities' in a democratic state as mainly an economic one and call for revolutionary change in the system of capitalism, but this could be seen as a major threat to the viability of liberal democracy itself. Liberation theology was formulated in the midst of abusive political power and an unjust economic system in which it made clear its stance on

---

[37] Ahn [2, pp. 150].

[38] Ibid., p. 151.

[39] Koonthanam [18, p. 107].

[40] Cyris Moon, 'A Korean Minjung Perspective: The Hebrews and the Exodus', in Sugirthrajah (ed), *Voices from the Margin*, p. 236.

the side of the poor and oppressed. It challenges the economic abuse of the liberal democracy and capitalist market and has shaped the churches, as was demonstrated in the practical implementation of base communities in Latin America and socio-political protests in South Korea. In order the achieve the goal of the common good, liberation theology challenges the status quo of economic system and calls for the necessity of change from those who hold power, prestige and wealth.

Public Theology and the Challenge Against the Monopoly of Power

The idea of public theology, though the term was not used explicitly, was present in the USA as early as the Evangelical revivals, and later in the Social Gospel movement and in Catholic social teaching. It has been prevalent in discussion of religious pluralism, and in the black and feminist theologies of recent years.[41] In particular, the publication of the two pastoral letters from the US Conference of Bishops, *The Challenge of Peace: God's Promise and Our Response* (1983) and *Economic Justice for All* (1986) triggered much discussion within the church and academy on the issues of 'civil discourse' and the ways and means to engage in public life.[42] The dominant themes of public theology in the USA in this period were the role of religion in a democratic polity, Christian social vision and political liberalism, the significance of church-related social institutions and the relationship of theological resources to the global economy.[43]

Edward Schillebeeckx, a Dutch theologian, was attentive to critical theory and he employed this in his theology. Schillebeeckx emphasised that theory and action should come together to enhance the transformation of society and that the two should mutually inform each other; as Schreiter puts it, the 'struggle for justice is not a possible consequence of reading the gospel; it is a necessary consequence of it'. For him, hermeneutics was to do with the meaning of faith in association with social and political questions, and this was influenced by Habermas' earlier works. Schillebeeckx saw that purely a theoretical and philosophical hermeneutic was untenable because understanding can be severely frustrated by social and political structures and that hermeneutics must have an emancipative, practical and critical interest that fosters human freedom and understanding. However, in doing so, Schillebeeckx maintained a firm basis in biblical studies for his critical reflections on Christian practice.[44]

The major contribution of Schillebeeckx to the articulation of public theology is their emphasis on the creation of platform where different parties can interact with one another for the pursuit of a common goal. Although, as Nancy Fraser has pointed out, the concept of the common good can be manipulated or determined by a 'strong

[41] Tipton [29, pp. 624–5].

[42] See Lindsey [19].

[43] Dean et al. [8, p. 20].

[44] Kennedy [17, p. 50 & 52].

public' and a 'weak public' could easily be marginalised,[45] there is a way to prevent this by all the parties actively engaging in the public debate so that they may be a healthy check on each other. Public theology promotes this accountability, not for the defence of religious communities or religious ideas, but for the sake of any 'weak public' being able to contribute. All publics are vital for creating and maintaining the public sphere where all the opinions are considered and acted upon appropriately. By articulation of theological thinking, participating in demonstrations or by advocacy on certain issues, public theology challenges any monopoly of a particular public body in the public sphere.

Theologians of public theology see the problem situated in the question of monopoly, particularly of the state and the market. They advocate the active public engagement of different individuals, groups and institutions to see that the welfare of the minorities is adequately addressed in a sustainable way. They are utilising philosophical and political understanding of the importance of public engagement together with a commitment to universal access and critical debates to deal with the problem of minorities. On the one hand, they call for state to acknowledge the vital importance of involving minorities in decision-making, and on the other hand, they urge religious communities to be open and active in social, political and economic issues pertaining to all and not narrowly focused on their own sectarian interests in society. By doing this public theologians try to bridge between secular and sacred understandings of contemporary issues and to bring the tradition of wisdom into society on the basis of the wisdom literature of the Hebrew Bible, which interacts with both secular and sacred resources to address issues and seeks for common solutions to strengthen the statecraft of democracy. Public theology utilises advocacy and public debate, and campaigns and works with civil societies on various issues such as the poverty and climate change. However, the difficulty of public theology is to make theological insights heard in the secular society and limited expertise of public theologians on various issues. They may end up creating 'weak public' which serves to satisfy religious communities for their social obligations, but in reality does not make any of the significant changes and transformation they seek to achieve. The key issue for public theology is its stance for minorities and bringing religious insights and resources into the public discussion without being either too exclusive or too inclusive. For those who are doing public theology, there is a clear requirement for a theological, philosophical and practical rationale and methodology for the furtherance of this approach and for the creative engagement in the public on the issue of the minorities.

[45]Fraser [11]. See also Fraser [12].

Exploration of the Chinese Philosophies of the Common Good

The three Christian theological approaches of the theology of the common good, liberation theology and public theology are the outcome of the public engagement of churches to address the problem of majoritarianism in contemporary societies. The theology of the common good provides key concepts of solidarity and subsidiarity on the basis of the dignity of human beings, while liberation theology and public theology are products of critical theory, which emphasises close interaction between theory and practice in the churches' engagement in the public sphere. Yet liberation theology and public theology take differing approaches to theological methodology: revolutionary and reforming, respectively. The former stands on the side of the poor and marginalised by protesting and bringing about radical change; while the latter challenges monopoly of any kind and brings all the voices in the common public sphere into critical inquiry and open debate. I would say that for all three theologies, achieving the common good for all the people in a society (then further extended to wider society and the global society) seems be the key aim.

By way of conclusion, I would like briefly to discuss some insights from the philosophical traditions of Confucianism and Mohism in China in order to strengthen our discussion of the common good as well as its relevance to the Chinese context. It is worth noticing that the concept of the common good is far from alien to Chinese philosophy, particularly Confucianism. Albert H.Y. Chen, in his discussion on *datong* (大同: great unity; great community; great harmony) in Confucian classics and *Datong shu* (大同 書: Book on the Great Community), written by Kang Youwei, an early twentieth century Chinese scholar, argues that the idea of the common good is close to social and political philosophy of *datong*.[46] According to Chen, *datong* in Confucian literature indicates the greater good in contrast to *xiaokang* (小康: lesser good) and that, in *datong* society, people care about all members of society and serve the common good instead of seeking primarily to benefit themselves and their family. This is a society in which the Confucian virtue of *ren* (仁: benevolence) is practiced beyond the immediate family.[47] Although Kang's suggestion to abolish the family as a social institution was radical and is in need of reinterpretation in the contemporary world, Chen sees the significance of Kang's exposition of the concept of *datong*, including that of *ren*, as realization of the common good of all, which involves 'minimization of suffering and maximization of potential happiness', as a result of the dissolution of the 'nine boundaries'.[48] Chen argues that Kang's vision of *datong* world is relevant to contemporary context of socio-economic inequality and global capitalism. It embodies a credible vision of the common good in human society. He suggests that Kang's concept of *ren* provides a persuasive and coherent

---

[46]Chen [5].

[47]Chen, 'The Concept of "Datong"…', pp. 88–89.

[48]Ibid., p. 98. Nine boundaries include the establishment of a world government, the disappearance of social classes and private property, and transfer of familial functions to publicly established institutions.

theoretical framework for contemporary society beyond Chinese society.[49] This was further elaborated by Jue Wang, who argues that *ren* is among the highest goods in human society, since mutual caring and reciprocal networks are vital for mutual flourishing, and because mutual care plays an essential role in the transformation of society. Wang further argues that through the concept of *ren* in Confucian philosophy one is, by definition, united with the situation of others; that *ren* differs from the utilitarian notion of the greatest good for the greatest number; and that it is superior to public good, which often sacrifices individuals or a totalitarian notion of good for those who hold power.[50]

Examining the texts of Mozi and Moist philosophy of the fourth and third BCE, Ellen Zhang argues that *jianai* (兼爱 inclusive care) and *jiaoli* (交利 reciprocal well-being) are key concepts in relation to the idea of the common good and provide a better understanding of the socio-political framework than Confucian philosophy.[51] For *jianai*, Zhang argues that, unlike Confucian philosophy, the Mohist approach moves from general to specific and from impartial to the partial. In Moism, the concept of community is wider and more abstract and the principle of inclusiveness is a higher and transcendent ethics than that of filial piety. Furthermore, this concept of *jianai* is closely connected to the principle of reciprocal well-being or mutual benefit, which is also closely related to *gongping* (公平 justifiable equality) or *zhengli* (正利 justifiable benefits).[52] She argues that 'benefit' was meant for common interests for all as well as *zheng* (正 rightness), *yi* (義 justice) or *gongyi* (公義 fairness). Zhang sees the key problems faced by Moism and Confucianism were the concept of commonality that defines the scope and nature of the good and also the ethical principles which could function as the basis for the orderly society. The key concept for Mozi's philosophy was inclusiveness and the common good was regarded not only as the independent good but also as an interdependent good. This common good is achieved by the power of authority through the social and intuitional contract and political authority is a necessary condition for social order. Zhang concludes that the Moist conception of the good provides a more realistic notion of social justice and fairness since it is based on rationality or principle rather than relying on relationships or personal contacts.[53]

The philosophical concepts of *datong* and *ren* of Confucianism and *jianai* and *jiaoli* of Moism do provide some conceptual and methodological insights for situations of inequality and injustice. These concepts have also close relations to the theological concepts we have discussed in the previous sections, namely, the dignity of the human being as created in the image of God; solidarity with poor and oppressed on the basis of the prophetic message of justice in the Hebrew Bible; and advocacy for critical inquiry and open debate in the public sphere by utilising wisdom traditions from both Judaism and Christianity. I envisage that there is ample scope for further

---

[49] Ibid., pp. 100–102.

[50] Wang [31, pp. 129-153 at 136–139].

[51] Zhang [32].

[52] Zhang, 'The Common Good in Moism', pp. 105–117.

[53] Ibid., pp. 117–126.

investigation of the interaction between Chinese philosophy and western theology on the issue of the common good. The three theological approaches acknowledge the strength of liberal democracy and yet realise the weaknesses of individualism and majoritarianism towards minorities, the poor, marginalised and voiceless, and therefore seek some alternative to the capitalist market model or the rigid application of the rule of law.

Freedom, equality, and the rule of law are indeed key aspirations for the modern nation-state, which enable human society to flourish, but society must also deal with the 'problem of minorities' and this is not just a matter of tolerance, compassion or charity from the majority or from those who have authority, wealth and power, but the system has to provide for the 'least of these'. As Hollenbach convincingly argues, 'the choice today is not between freedom and community, but between a society based on reciprocal respect and solidarity and a society that leaves many people behind' and this choice will have a 'powerful effect on the well-being of us all'.[54]

References

1. Bellah, R. N., Madsen, R., & Tipton, S. M. (1992). *The good society*. New York: Vintage Books.
2. Ahn, B-M. (1981). Jesus and the minjung in the gospel of mark. In Commission on Theological Concerns of the Christian Conferences of Asia (Ed.), *Minjung theology: People as the subject of history*. Maryknoll, N.Y.: Orbis Books.
3. Boff, L.(1986). *Ecclesiogenesis: The base communities reinvent the church* (trans. Barr, R.R.). London: Collins.
4. Catholic Bishops' Conference of England and Wales (1996). The common good and the Catholic Church's social teaching: A statement by the 1996. http://www.catholicsocialteaching.org.uk/wp-content/uploads/2010/10/THE-COMMON-GOOD-AND-THE-CATHOLIC-CHURCH_1996.pdf. Accessed 10 April 2015.
5. Chen, A. H. Y. (2014). The concept of Datong. In D. Solomon, P. C. Lo (Eds.), *The common good: Chinese and American perspectives*, (pp. 85–102). New York: Springer.
6. Curran, C. E. (2002). *Catholic social teaching, 1891-present: A historical, theological and ethical analysis*. Washington, D.C.: Georgetown University Press.
7. de Gruchy, J. (1995). *Christianity and democracy: A theology for a just world order*. Cambridge: CUP.
8. Dean, W., Noll, M. A., Bednarowski M.F., & Hehir, J. B. (2000). Forum: Public theology in contemporary America. *Religion and American Culture: A Journal of Cultural Interpretation, 10*(1), 1–27.
9. D'Entreves, A. P. (1967). *Notion of the state*. Oxford: Oxford University Press.
10. Editorial, (2014). Gone wrong with democracy? *The Economist*, March 1. http://www.economist.com/news/essays/21596796-democracy-was-most-successful-political-idea-20th-century-why-has-it-run-trouble-and-what-can-be-do. Accessed 10 November 2019.

[54] Hollenbach, *The Common Good*, p. 244.

11. Fraser, N. (1992). Rethinking the public sphere: A contribution to the critique of actually existing democracy. In C. Calhoun (Ed.), *Habermas and the public sphere* (pp. 109–42). Cambridge, Massachusetts: MIT Press.
12. Fraser, N. (2007). Transnationalizing the public sphere: On the ligitimacy and efficacy of public opinion in a post-westphalian word. *Theory, Culture & Society, 24*(4), 7–30.
13. Fukuyama, F. (1992). *The end of history and the last man*. London: Hamish Hamilton.
14. Gutiérrez, G. (1988). *A theology of liberation: History, politics, and salvation (rvsd edn)*. London: SCM Press.
15. Hollenbach, D. (2002). *The common good and Christian ethics*. Cambridge: CUP.
16. Israel, J. (2010). *A revolution of the mind: Radical enlightenment and intellectual origins of modern democracy*. Princeton: Princeton University Press.
17. Kennedy, P. (1993). *Schillebeeckx*. London: Geoffrey Chapman.
18. Koonthanam, G. (1995). Yahweh the defender of the dalits: A reflection on Isaiah. In R. S. Sugirthrajah (Ed.), *Voices from the margin: Interpreting the bible in the third world* (pp. 105–116). Maryknoll, NY: Orbis Books.
19. Lindsey, W. D. (1992). Public theology as civil discourse: What are we talking about? *Horizons, 19*(1), 44–69.
20. McCann, D. P., & Miller, P. D. (Eds.). (2005). *In search of the common good*. London: T&T Clark.
21. McGrail, P., & Sagovsky, N. (2015). Introduction. In N. Sagovsky, P. McGrail (Eds.), *Together for the common good: Towards a national conversation*. London: SCM.
22. Neville, D. (2014). The Bible, justice, and public theology: An introductory essay'. In D. Neville (Ed.), *The Bible, justice, and public theology* (pp. 1–21). Eugene, Oregon: Wipe & Stock.
23. Preece, J. J. (2005). *Minority rights: Between diversity and community*. Cambridge: Polity.
24. Rawls, J. (1993). *A theory of justice*. Oxford: OUP.
25. Parekh, B. (2004). Redistribution or recognition? A misguided debate. In S. May, T. Modood, & J. Squires (Eds.), *Ethnicity, nationalism and minority rights* (pp. 199–213). Cambridge: CUP.
26. Pontifical Council for Justice and Peace (2004). *Compendium of the social doctrine of the church*. London: Burns & Oates.
27. Rhoheimer, M. (Ed.). (2013). *The common good of constitutional democracy: Essays on political philosophy and on catholic social teaching*. Washington, D.C.: The Catholic University of America Press.
28. Segundo, J. L. (1976). *The Liberation of theology* (trans by John Drury; first published in 1975 in Spanish). Maryknoll, NY: Orbis.
29. Tipton, S. M. (1998). Public theology. In R. Wuthnow (ed.), *The encyclopedia of politics and religion* (624–626). Washington, DC: Congressional Quarterly, Inc.
30. Wallis, J. (2013). *The (Un)Common good: How the gospel brings hope to a world divided*. Grand Rapid: Brazos Press.
31. Wang, J. (2014). The common good and filial piety: A confucian perspective. In D. Solomon & P. C. Lo (Eds.), *The common good: Chinese and American perspectives* (pp. 129–153). New York: Springer.
32. Zhang, E. (2014). The common good in Moism: A reconstruction of Mozi's ethics of "inclusive care" and "reciprocal well-being". In D. Solomon & P. C. Lo (Eds.), *The common good: Chinese and American perspectives* (pp. 103–128). New York: Springer.

Sebastian Kim is Professor of Theology and Public Life and Assistant Provost at Fuller Theological Seminary. Kim is a Fellow of the Royal Asiatic Society and former Editor of the *International Journal of Public Theology*. Kim's research interests include public theology, world Christianity, Asian theologies, and peace building. He has authored and co-authored four books: *A History of Korean Christianity* (CUP, 2015), *Theology in the Public Sphere* (SCM, 2011), *In Search of Identity: Debates on Religious Conversion in India* (OUP, 2005), and *Christianity as a World Religion*

(2008 & 2016). Books he has edited include *A Companion to Public Theology* (Brill, 2017), *Cosmopolitanism, Religion, and the Public Sphere* (Routledge, 2014), and *Christian Theology in Asia* (CUP, 2008).

Chapter 11
Christianity and Human Rights: Foundation, Expression and Practice

Kjetil Fretheim

Abstract Although the notion of human rights has been challenged on religious, philosophical and political grounds, human rights has gained a unique and unprecedented prominence in the national and international political discourses of the post-WWII era. This development has not gone unnoticed by churches and theologians, but how human rights should be interpreted from the perspective of the Christian faith and what role they should play in the way Christianity engages with social and political issues, remains disputed. In this chapter, I will examine the foundation, expression and practice of human rights from the perspective of Christian theology.

Introduction

Although the notion of human rights has been challenged on religious, philosophical and political grounds, human rights has gained a unique and unprecedented prominence in the national and international political discourses of the post-WWII era. This development has not gone unnoticed by churches and theologians, but how human rights should be interpreted from the perspective of the Christian faith and what role they should play in the way Christianity engages with social and political issues, remains disputed. In this chapter, I will examine the foundation, expression and practice of human rights from the perspective of Christian theology.

After a review of the criticisms and limits of human rights, I will firstly discuss the relationship between religion and human rights. Secondly, I examine to what extent, and in what way, the notion of human rights should be considered a theological concept and how Christian theology can be expressed in terms of human rights. This leads to the issue of practice and, in the last section I examine how the notion of human rights has impacted Christian social practice or *diaconia*. I conclude by discussing ways that Christian actors might address political affairs.

K. Fretheim (✉)
MF Norwegian School of Theology, Religion and Society, PO BOX 5144, 0302 Majorstuen, Oslo, Norway
e-mail: kjetil.fretheim@mf.no

Z. Xie et al. (eds.), *Human Dignity, Human Rights, and Social Justice*,
https://doi.org/10.1007/978-981-15-5081-2_11

I will argue that the concept of human rights articulates important elements of the Christian faith. Christian theological discourse should, therefore, include the language of human rights. Still, human rights is not the only way of expressing the Christian faith or the concerns and arguments of the Christian tradition. Christian churches and diaconal actors need to develop and express an identity that goes beyond a mere human rights rhetoric, and that includes a wider range of Christian notions and motifs. The distinct contribution of Christian theology to the human rights discourse and public debate on social and political issues lies in the particular concepts and insights of the Christian tradition.

Critics and Culture

The prominence of human rights rhetoric in contemporary political discourse is striking. Human rights are a key reference in debates ranging from terrorism to migration and climate change. Rights, respect for rights, and the protection of human rights have become the moral language of the international community. Often expressed in a rational and secular voice, human rights have become the *lingua franca*, if not the *lingua sacra*, of our time.

However, as human rights scholar Tony Evans has pointed out, this human rights enthusiasm is matched by an equally strong scepticism or outright rejection of the whole human rights project. The resistance against universal human rights has been voiced as a defence of so-called Asian values and their "situational uniqueness", or as a form of neo-nationalism, neo-fascism or ethnic cleansing.[1] Some argue on philosophical grounds[2] while others express their scepticism on moral or social grounds, for example, as they:

> … expose how human rights legislation has functioned to protect vested power interests, to encourage litigiousness, to squeeze out consideration of the common good from public discourse, and to reduce the relationships between citizens and the state and between citizen and citizen to those of regulation by contract.[3]

A similar kind of critical attitude is reflected in contributions from scholars with an otherwise positive understanding and approach to human rights. The prolific writer on international human rights issues, Fiona Robinson, argues that the concept of rights alone is not enough to understand the ethical issues in international relations. Robinson finds that:

> Rights-based ethical theory is based on untenable assumptions about human rationality and the universality of human nature; it is an abstract, impersonal, rule-oriented morality which obfuscates the social and political dimension of global moral problems, and which can

[1]Evans [8].

[2]Rorty [18].

[3]Reed [16, p. 23].

> tell us remarkably little about who or what is responsible for ensuring that the claims of rights-holders are met.[4]

Against this background, and on a more constructive note, Robinson outlines what might be needed in addition to human rights-based ethics. She writes:

> Thinking seriously about ethics in the current era demands some exploration of the capacities involved in moral agency and responsiveness – perception, imagination, the ability to listen and to focus attention. An adequate approach to global ethics, I will argue, must not be limited to the application of rational principles, universal codes and impartiality in moral judgement; rather, it must be, at least in part, a morality of attachment and connection, which can help us to learn to respond adequately to particular others, rather than the universal, 'all others' of human rights theory.[5]

Out of similar concerns, others have argued that human rights norms simply cannot stand alone but must be combined with a culture of human rights. Lacking a human rights culture, human rights norms will not be effective. From the perspective of religion and law, John Witte Jr. and M. Christian Green write:

> Human rights norms have little salience in societies that lack constitutional processes that will give them meaning and measure. They have little value for parties who lack basic rights to security, succour, and sanctuary, or who are deprived of basic freedoms of speech, press, or association. They have little pertinence for victims who lack standing in courts and other basic procedural rights to pursue apt remedies. They have little cogency in communities that lack the ethos and ethic to render human rights violations a source of shame and regret, restraint and respect, confession and responsibility, reconciliation and restitution.[6]

This recognition of the role of culture might seem to contradict the understanding of human rights as universal norms, valid at all times, in all places and protecting each and every one of us. If culture interprets, or even defines human rights, relativism seems close. In this way, as is often the case, universalism and relativism implicitly, or explicitly, frame the discussion as contradictory positions, and we are made to choose between them.

Human rights scholar Jack Donnelly argues, however, that relativism comes in different forms with a wide spectrum between two extreme positions: radical cultural relativism and radical universalism. While the first sees culture as 'the sole source of the validity of a moral right or rule', the latter holds that 'culture is irrelevant to the validity of moral rights and rules, which are universally held'.[7] On this continuum, Donnelly further distinguishes between a strong cultural relativism that sees culture as 'the principle source of the validity of a moral right or rule' and a weak cultural relativism where cultures 'may be an important source of the validity of a moral right or rule'.[8] Donnelly argues in favour of the latter: 'a weak cultural relativist position

---

[4]Robinson [17, p. 60].

[5]Ibid., pp. 60–61.

[6]Witte and Christian Green [20, p. 5].

[7]Donnelly [7, p. 400].

[8]Ibid., p. 401.

that permits limited deviations from "universal" human rights standards primarily at the levels of form and interpretation'.[9]

Before returning to this weak cultural relativist position, I will first discuss some versions of a much stronger cultural relativism and attempts to locate the foundation of human rights in religion.

Religion and Human Rights

The authors of the United Nations' Universal Declaration of Human Rights (UDHR) avoided the question of the foundation of human rights. As one of the members of the drafting committee, the French Catholic philosopher Jacques Maritain, put it: "We agree on these rights, providing we are not asked why. With the 'why,' the dispute begins".[10] Translated into Rawlsian terminology, they avoided comprehensive doctrines and were pragmatically content with an overlapping consensus. This approach might be the clue to the exceptional success of human rights in the post-WWII era. We do not have to agree about everything. We only need to agree on this very basic set of principles. Still, despite decades of secularization in the western world, comprehensive doctrines have not disappeared and still matter in people's lives. Religion and religiosity live on in new and traditional forms, and there are even indications of a resurgence of religion.[11] Consequently, the question remains: what is the relationship between religion and human rights?

One answer to this question is dismissive and claims that religion has no place in human rights theory and practice. This position finds support among secular and religious positions alike. On the one hand there are secular voices who argue that 'religion should have no place in a modern regime of human rights' because 'by its nature, [it] is too expansionistic and monopolistic, too patriarchal and hierarchical, too antithetical to the very ideals of pluralism, toleration, and equality inherent in a human rights regime'.[12] Some religious voices see human rights as a challenge to the structure and spirit of religious bodies and argue that:

> While human rights norms teach liberty and equality, most religious bodies teach authority and hierarchy. While human rights norms encourage pluralism and diversity, many religious bodies require orthodoxy and uniformity. While human rights norms teach freedoms of speech and petition, several religions teach duties of silence and submission.[13]

Given that religion can be not only a repressive mechanism but equally, can play a liberating and constructive role, this latter argument seems hasty and based on a superficial analysis. Rather, as Witte and Green point out, what is needed in a proper

---

[9]Ibid.

[10]Bucar and Barnett [2, p. 2].

[11]Kepel [11] and Thomas [19].

[12]Witte and Green, 'Introduction', in Witte and Green, eds., *Religion and Human Right*, p. 14.

[13]Ibid., p. 17.

response to the problematic dimensions of religion is 'to cultivate the virtues of religion to confirm those religious teachings and practices that are most conducive to human rights, democracy, and rule of law'.[14] Indeed, from this perspective, and in line with the important role of a human rights culture for human rights norms to be effective, it can be argued that '[h]uman rights ultimately needs religious ideas, institutions, and rights claims to survive and thrive'.[15] Again, as Witte and Green write, 'without religion, the regime of human rights becomes infinitely expandable, [...] without religion, human rights become too captive to Western libertarian ideals [and] without religion, the State is often given an exaggerated role to play as the guarantor of human rights'.[16]

On the one hand, it seems that this is to overstate the importance of a religious foundation for human rights. On the other hand, the concern that human rights can be interpreted, and thus strengthened and made relevant from religious perspectives and with religious resources, seems highly relevant. Indeed, human rights need interpretation and religion needs to understand human rights and develop a "human rights hermeneutic". Witte and Green describe this as fourfold: a hermeneutics of (1) confession, (2) suspicion, (3) history and (4) law and religion. Confession refers here to the need for religious bodies to acknowledge their responsibilities, actions and omissions that have perpetuated violence, propagated liberty and sustained human rights violations. Suspicion, on the other hand, points to the need not to idealize recent human rights formulations or 'accept the seemingly infinite expansion of human rights discourse and demands'.[17] This points to the third dimension of a human rights hermeneutic: The hermeneutic of history that examines the genesis of contemporary human rights norms. Finally, the hermeneutic of law and religion is required to 'show that law and religion need each other and that institutions like human rights have interlocking legal and religious dimensions'.[18]

Christian Human Rights Sceptics

Moving from the broader issue of religion and human rights to the more specific issue of Christianity and human rights is not a move away from complexity. As with religion and human rights, both Christianity and human rights are interpreted in different ways. The Christian faith is expressed in different social, cultural and denominational ways and vocabularies and, consequently, the Christian understandings of human rights, are many. Not only is there a diversity of Christian theologies, but the sources drawn upon when constructing such theologies vary; they are appropriated in different ways, and some connect with human rights while others definitely do not.

[14]Ibid., p. 15.

[15]Ibid.

[16]Ibid., pp. 15–16.

[17]Ibid., p. 20.

[18]Ibid.

At one end of the spectrum, we find Christian sceptics such as the Eastern Orthodox theologian Vigen Guroian who argues that "human rights thinking is alien to his tradition".[19] Similarly, though from a very different denominational position, Stanley Hauerwas sees the notion of inalienable human rights as antithetical to the Christian faith.[20] The rationale for this kind of scepticism draws on different sources, but Nicholas P. Wolterstorff highlights two lines of thought within Christian theology that, for different reasons, have rejected human rights: *agapism* and *possessive individualism*.

Agapism refers to a line of thought that puts a strong emphasis on the role of agape in Jesus' teachings and how he was 'enjoining us to love our neighbours out of sheer gratuitous generosity, spontaneous benevolence'.[21] As God forgives the sinner out of gratuitous generosity, love supersedes justice. This line of thought has been expressed not least by Protestant theologians in the twentieth century, in particular in Swedish theologian Anders Nygren's *Agape and Eros*, but also in the writings of scholars such as Karl Barth, Reinhold Niebuhr and Paul Ramsey. Wolterstorff argues, however, that this position is incoherent and an implausible interpretation of Jesus' teachings as found in the New Testament. Here love is not indifferent or blind to justice but incorporates justice. Referring to Jesus' mission to "proclaim release to the captives and recovery of sight to the blind, to let the oppressed go free, to proclaim the year of the Lord's favour" (Luk 4.18–19) Wolterstorff finds that Jesus was anything but indifferent to justice.[22] The other line of thought—possessive individualism—does not dismiss justice, but rejects that there is any relationship between justice and natural rights. The reason is that the modern language of rights seems to be a way of asserting one's claims and entitlements against others. Wolterstorff acknowledges how this kind of understanding has emerged, but simply dismisses it as an expression of "cultural amnesia".[23]

Christian Human Rights Enthusiasts

This scepticism should, of course, not be too easily dismissed. As the Christian ethicist Esther D. Reed argues:

> … there are good reasons for wariness in the Christian community with respect to overt Christian engagement with human rights agendas – not least because the new human rights culture is inherently individualistic and can encourage an aggressive, protectionist, and/or acquisitive mind-set. Moreover, there is no denying that human rights are often construed as an ethic independent of theology, based on the human body alone.[24]

---

[19] Esther D. Reed, *The Ethics of Human Rights*, p. 8.

[20] Ibid., p. 13.

[21] Wolterstorff [23, p. 46].

[22] Ibid., p. 47.

[23] Ibid., p. 49.

[24] Reed, *The Ethics of Human Rights*, p. 16.

The question remains, however, if it is not possible to offer a more positive interpretation of human rights from the perspective of Christian theology. After having rejected both agapism and possessive individualism, this is what Woltersdorff does. He shows how natural human rights were taken for granted, not only by church fathers such as Ambrose, Basil of Caesarea and John Chrysostom but also in the Old and New Testaments. In the Christian Scripture the issue of rights first appears as God's rights. God is worthy of respect. But also, human rights are implied in the Biblical narratives. Wolterstorff points to the Second Table of the Ten commandments where it becomes quite explicit how people have natural obligations toward each other.[25] Further, both the notion of the image of God (Gen 2, 5 and 9; and Psalm 8) and Paul's emphasis on God's impartiality and that God's justification is offered to everyone, both Jews and Gentiles (Rom 2), express a universal perspective in the Christian Scripture.[26]

It seems fair to conclude that there is an integral connection between Christianity and human rights. Although we cannot find natural human rights explicitly conceptualized in Scripture, the idea is implied. Indeed, as Wolterstorff points out, 'one does not have to conceptualize something in order to take its existence for granted or to imply it'.[27]

From these Biblical resources, and with the aid of the Christian tradition, reason and human experience, a number of Christian theologies of human rights have emerged.[28] In *Rights and Christian Ethics* (1992) Jesuit scholar Kieran Cronin developed a covenantal approach to human rights.[29] Twenty years later, David Hollenbach developed a theological understanding of human rights based on the natural law-tradition.[30] Jean Porter followed a similar strategy and emphasis in *Nature as Reason: A Thomistic Theory of the Natural Law*.[31] With a stronger practical focus the World Council of Churches (WCC) has actively voiced its affirmation of human rights, as have for example the Lutheran World Federation, the World Alliance of Reformed Churches and others. Indeed, a number of Christians of various denominations contributed to the formulation of the declaration of human rights in 1948.[32]

To summarize, human rights can be considered a theological concept and Christian theology can be expressed in terms of human rights. The discussion above has also shown how this can be expressed in different ways using different parts of the Christian narrative and terminology. Still, this is not all that can or should be said

---

[25] Wolterstorff [23, p. 52].

[26] See also Adeney [1].

[27] Wolterstorff, 'Christianity and Human Rights', in Witte and Green, eds., *Religion and Human Rights*, p. 53.

[28] Reed, *The Ethics of Human Rights*, pp. 6–7.

[29] Cronin [6].

[30] Hollenbach [10].

[31] Porter [15].

[32] Nurser [14].

about Christianity and human rights. Religion is not defined purely in terms of doctrine or narratives and Christian faith; theology and ethics should not be reduced to human rights language. As Reed argues, Christian theology needs to:

> … seek a route between, on the one hand, the kind of reconciliation with the world that risks abandonment or compromise of substantive theological doctrines in favor of secularist modes of rationality and, on the other, the kind of ecclesiasticism that leaves church members ill equipped to be active citizens who can engage critically with human rights instruments and institutions for the practical benefits that they might achieve.[33]

Indeed, in her own work, Reed has shown 'that there is no essential reason why the evangelical command to love must be expressed in the language of rights',[34] and that there is a need to specify, in practical terms, how a Christian theology of human rights makes a difference to how Christians engage with social and political issues.[35] This brings us to the issue of Christian social practice—*diaconia*—and human rights.

The History of Diaconia

The Norwegian theologian and scholar of diaconal studies Kjell Nordstokke traces the roots of the modern diaconal movement to Pietism and the revivalist movement in Germany in the mid-19th century. More specifically it is closely linked to the work of the German pastors Theodor Fliedner (1800–1864) and Johan Hinrich Wichern (1808–1881). At that time, and in their work, diaconia was understood as individual piety and humble service. The individual emphasis did not, however, prevent, but rather inspired, the establishment of a wide range of diaconal institutions with a clear Christian identity—so-called motherhouses—where deacons and deaconesses would work as health and social workers for the sick, orphaned or those otherwise in need. Fliedner opened a refuge for discharged female convicts, a hospital and a deaconess training centre. Wichern established a home and training institution for poor children and for training of deacons.

To some extent these individualistic and institutional features separated the diaconal movement from the life of local congregations and the established church. Nordstokke argues that these diaconal institutions 'developed as rather independent structures, eventually with more affinity to the health and social services of the government'[36] and also made the dedicated deacons and deaconesses pioneers in professional health and social work.

The understanding of diaconia as a humble service drew on a specific interpretation of the Greek word *diakonia* and the way it is used in the New Testament. As Nordstokke points out:

---

[33]Reed, *The Ethics of Human Rights*, p. 17.

[34]Ibid., p. 40.

[35]Ibid., p. 42.

[36]Nordstokke [13, p. 42].

> The early German pastors of the motherhouse tradition constantly reminded the deaconesses of the origin of their name and calling by drawing upon gospel teachings like the parable of the Judgement of the Nations in Matthew 25, upon the sayings of Jesus such as, "I am among you as one who serves" (Luke 22:27), and upon the story in Acts 6 of the choosing of seven men to "serve at tables". These and similar passages in the New Testament provide instances of the Greek daikon-words which also lay behind the title of the deacon (*diakonos*).[37]

In addition to these passages, the early diaconal movement drew on passages where the *diakon*-words are not used, for example Jesus washing the feet of his disciples (John 13) and Jesus "made himself nothing by taking the very nature of a servant" (Philippians 2:7). This indicates how this understanding of diaconia not simply relies on a translation of from the Greek, but also on a specific notion of what Christian social practice is and how it should be performed.

Later studies have shown how this notion of diaconia as humble service is based on a misunderstanding. Convincingly, the Australian scholar John N. Collins has shown that diaconia does not relate to charity work at all, but is rather used for a 'person who has received a mandate to deliver a message or to perform a task for a person or for a community'.[38] In fact, deacons in the early church were not primarily involved in charity work, but rather to the assistance and administrative work of the bishop.

Against this background, Nordstokke argues that we should understand diaconia 'not as a humble self-effacing and silent service in the tradition of pietistic lifestyle, but as conscious intervention representing God's active love for creation and his project of salvation as revealed in Jesus Christ'[39] or as 'active expression of Christian witness in response to the needs and challenges of the community in which Christians and the churches live'.[40] It is in line with this kind of interpretation that the concept of diaconia has remained a label for the social work of Christian churches, in particular in the Protestant, Northern European context.

This also reflects how, over the years, this kind of diaconia has widened its scope from individual, charitable acts to an increased concern with welfare, employment and other policy matters. Issues that were previously considered and dealt with primarily as challenges facing individuals or local communities, are now increasingly seen in the wider context of national policies or global structures. In the field of international diaconia, a focus on emergency or humanitarian aid has been supplemented with long-term development aid and advocacy work. The number of topics of concern has come to include economic injustice, political oppression and stewardship for the creation. This is articulated for example in the Church of Norway's (CoN) definition of diakonia as 'the caring ministry of the Church [...] expressed through

[37] Ibid..

[38] Collins and Nordstokke [4].

[39] Nordstokke, *Liberating Diakonia*, p. 37.

[40] Ibid., p.18.

loving your neighbour, creating inclusive communities, caring for creation and struggling for justice'.[41] Similarly, the Lutheran World Federation (LWF) highlights two assumptions in its understanding of diaconia:

> One is that diakonia is a theological concept that points to the very identity and mission of the Church. Another is its practical implication in the sense that diakonia is a call to action, as a response to challenges of human suffering, injustice and care for creation.[42]

Note how justice is a key concept in both of these cases—as a response to injustice (LWF) and a struggle for justice (CoN). This mirrors how diaconia has moved from a primary focus on piety and humble service—individually and institutionally—to include a concern for justice in a local, national and global context.

Christian Social Practice and Human Rights

Several actors in the field of Christian social practice have not only come to focus on advocacy and social justice but have also adopted the human rights rhetoric. Deacons, diaconal organisations and institutions describe their work as rights-based, and it can be argued that this focus on human rights has changed the practice of these diaconal actors and (re)shaped their self-understandings. Accordingly, although diaconia traditionally was described and understood in terms of compassion, benevolence and/or love, it is today increasingly interpreted in terms of values or principles such as dignity, non-discrimination, accountability, rule of law, transparency, participation and empowerment.[43] Diaconia scholar Hans Morten Haugen refers to these as '*human rights principles*, understood as basic norms specifying minimum standards of conduct'[44] and then lists key elements of a human-rights based approach:

> First, there must be an adequate analysis of the relevant context, identifying the most vulnerable and marginalized, and those seeking to prevent changes from taking place. Second, there must be an understanding of capacities and other resources of both right-holders and duty-bearers. Third, participatory processes are important for achieving good outcomes. Fourth, human rights provide and objective standard upon which states and companies' conduct can be assessed – and criticized. Fifth, the human rights system has produced guidelines and tools that give additional assistance.[45]

To examine to what extent, and in what way, diaconal actors have adopted or implemented this kind of human rights-based approach in their work, Haugen analyses strategic documents and reports from two diaconal organisations: Eurodiaconia and the Norwegian Church Aid (NCA). He finds that NCA has three rights-based working methods (long-term development aid, emergency response and advocacy)

---

[41] Church of Norway Council [3, p. 5].

[42] Lutheran World Federation [12, p. 8].

[43] Hans Morten Haugen [9].

[44] Ibid., p. 124 (original emphasis).

[45] Ibid., p. 136.

and that all aspects of NCA's operative work are defined as being rights-based. NCA's work is guided by five values: the integrity of creation, human dignity, global justice, inclusive communities and compassion. Eurodiaconia, on the other hand, claims that there are five necessary elements in diaconal work: creation, fellowship, justice, care and praise. All but "praise", come close to the values of NCA.[46] Haugen concludes that '*there are no contradictions between human rights principles and diaconal principles*'.[47]

In Haugen's analysis, the distinction between Christian social practice and human rights based practice thus seems to largely be lost. What his discussion does show, however, is that a Christian theology of human rights can become, or be expressed as, a Christian social practice of human rights. Indeed, in this way diaconia can move from being a compassion driven concern for the well-being of others to becoming a practical expression of Christian theology, human dignity and respect for rights, political participation, citizenship etc.

The human rights language among diaconal actors is, seen from this perspective, a positive contribution. It is a language that communicates key concerns in Christian theology and ethics both within the Christian churches and to a wide range of other audiences. By using this kind of language, Christians can interpret the key concerns of their religious tradition and thus facilitate an important discussion in the public sphere. It is also a language that can be operationalized as a human rights approach that might help and challenge Christian groups, organisations and institutions in their diaconal work. Indeed, the human rights language might have an important function in critically broadening our perspective on the moral dimensions of any social practice, diaconia included. As Wolterstorff writes:

> The moral order has two fundamental dimensions, the agent-dimension and the recipient dimension (patient-dimension). With the language of duty, responsibility, love, benevolence and the like we bring the agent-dimension to speech; with the language of rights we bring the recipient-dimension to speech. Guilt pertains to what I did; being wronged pertains to what was done to me. It's because rights-talk brings speech to the moral condition of the victims – they were wronged – that it has proved so powerful in protest movements.[48]

It is through this recipient dimension that the notion of human rights can also help us assess theologies: To what extent can the way we think, speak and act be justified in a human rights perspective? In what ways do—or do not—our theologies support and promote universal human rights?

Christian Identity and Human Rights Politics

The roots of human rights can be traced back to a number of traditions, cultures, religions and philosophies, and the United Nations' Universal Declaration Human

[46]Ibid., p. 130.

[47]Ibid., p. 132.

[48]Wolterstorff [21–23].

Rights (UDHR) can be justified and supported on the basis of very different comprehensive doctrines. The discussion above started with the critics of human rights, examined the relationship between religion and human rights, and has focussed on Christian approaches and adoptions of human rights in practical terms.

I have argued that there is a close relationship between Christianity and human rights. Human rights can find its foundation in Christian theology, and key elements of the Christian faith can be expressed in the language of human rights. Christianity can also be seen as the foundation for human rights in the sense that Christian individuals, congregations and churches contribute to the culture of human rights. Christianity interprets human rights and supplements them with a thicker description of what they are and what they require. This is possible because Christian thought stretches beyond rights and entitlements, duties and demands—and speaks of sin, guilt, responsibilities, reconciliation etc. When this happens, a public theology of human rights emerges on the basis of an implicit weak cultural relativism that interprets the practical, political and normative implications of universal human rights standards.

While the language of Christian theology can articulate a human rights ethics, Christian social practice does the same through a form of lived religion. This practical expression of Christian faith or the practice of Christian theology should therefore not simply be seen as an afterthought that follows doctrinal discussions or the theo-philosophical deliberations in confessional statements. Rather, I suggest, diaconal practice can be seen as a foundation and expression of human rights. Indeed, as we have seen, the foundation of human rights can be found in several places in religion and in Christianity. Human rights are grounded in key theological ideas such as the *Imago Dei* and the dignity of every human being. But equally, it can be seen as being grounded in the social practice that promotes this dignity. In important ways, practice precedes theory and diaconal practice facilitates, incorporates and interprets human rights.

To sum up, Christian thought and practice both interpret and interrupt human rights talk. By offering a broader language, new concepts and narratives, Christian theology challenges the rational, secular, thin description of human rights. Christian contributions broaden our imagination as to what human rights means, and, at their best, they facilitate the kind of innovation that is needed in the search for new, better and more efficient ways of promoting and protecting the human rights of every human being. It is in this way that human rights take us to the core of Christian identity, both in theory and in practice. The Christian identity is a call to Christians and non-Christians alike to defend and promote human rights for everyone—in all spheres of life, in national and international politics, today and tomorrow.

References

1. Adeney, F. S. (2007). Human rights and responsibilities: Christian perspectives. In F. S. Frances, & A. Sharma (Eds.), *Christianity and human rights: Influences and issues* (pp. 19–39). New

York: State University of New York Press.
2. Bucar, Elisabeth M., & Barnett, Barbra. (2005). Introduction: The "why" of human rights. In Elisabeth M. Bucar & Barbra Barnett (Eds.), *Does human rights need God?* (pp. 1–21). Grand Rapids, MI: Eerdmans.
3. Church of Norway Council. (2009). *Church of Norway plan for diakonia*, Oslo: Church of Norway, National Council.
4. Collins, John N. (1990). *Diakonia: Re-interpreting the ancient resources, New York*. NY: Oxford University Press.
5. Collins, J. N. and Nordstokke, K. (2011). Diakonia—theory and praxis. In K. Nordstokke (Ed.), *Liberating diakonia* (pp. 41–47). Trondheim: Tapir akademisk forlag.
6. Cronin, K. (1992). *Rights and Christian ethics*. New Studies in Christian Ethics. Vol. 1, Cambridge: Cambridge University Press.
7. Donnelly, Jack. (1984). Cultural relativism and universal human rights. *Human rights quarterly, 6*(4), 400–419.
8. Evans, T. (1998). Introduction: Power, hegemony and universalization of human rights. In T. Evans (Ed.), *Human rights fifty years on: A reappraisal* (pp. 1–23). Manchester: Manchester University Press.
9. Haugen, H. M. (2014). Diakonia as rights-based practice. In S. Dietrich, K. Jorgensen, K. K. Korslien & K. Nordstokke (Eds.), *Diakonia as social practice: An introduction* (pp. 123–38). Oxford: Regnum.
10. Hollenbach, D. (2003). *The global face of public faith: Politics, human rights, and Christian ethics*. Washington, DC: Gorgetown University Press.
11. Kepel, G. (1994). *The revenge of God: The resurgence of Islam, Christianity and Judaism in the modern world*. Cambridge: Polity Press.
12. Lutheran World Federation. (2009). *Diakonia in context: Transformation, reconciliation, empowerment*. Geneva: The Lutheran World Federation.
13. Nordstokke, Liberating. (2011). *Diakonia*. Trondheim: Tapir akademisk forlag.
14. Nurser, J. (2005). *For all peoples and all nations: The ecumenical church and human rights*. Washington, D.C.: Georgetown University Press.
15. Porter, Jean. (2005). *Nature as reason: A thomistic theory of the natural law*. Cambridge: Eerdmans.
16. Reed, Esther D. *The ethics of human rights: Contested doctrinal and moral issues*. Waco, Tex: Baylor University Press, 2007.
17. Robinson, F. (1998). The limits of a rights-based approach to international Ethics. In T. Evans (Ed.), *Human rights fifty years on: A reappraisal* (pp. 58–76). Manchester: Manchester University Press.
18. Rorty, Richard. (1993). Human rights, rationality and sentimentality. In Stephen Shute & Susan Hurley (Eds.), *On human rights*. New York: Basic Boocs.
19. Thomas, S. M. (2003). Taking religious and cultural pluralism seriously: The global resurgence of religion and the transformation of international society. In P. Hatzopoulos & F. Petito (Eds.), *Religion in international relations: The return from exile* (pp. 21–53). New York: Palgrave Macmillan.
20. Witte, J. Jr., & Christian Green, M. (2012). Introduction. In J. Witte Jr. & M. Christian Green (Eds.), *Religion and human rights: An introduction* (pp. 3–24). Oxford: Oxford University Press.
21. Wolterstorff, Nicholas. (2008). *Justice: Rights and wrongs*. Princeton, N.J: Princeton University Press.
22. Wolterstorff, Nicholas. (2011). *Justice in love*. Grand Rapids, MI: Eerdmans.
23. Wolterstorff, N. (2012). Christianity and human rights. In J. Witte Jr. & M. Christian Green (Eds.), *Religion and human rights* (pp. 42–55). Oxford: Oxford University Press.

Kjetil Fretheim is Prorector and Professor of Ethics and Diaconal Studies at MF Norwegian School of Theology, Religion and Society in Oslo, Norway. He is the author of *Rights and Riches. Exploring the Moral Discourse of Norwegian Development Aid* (Peter Lang, 2008) and *Interruption and Imagination Public Theology in Times of Crisis* (Pickwick, 2016). He has edited and co-edited books on human rights, intercultural communication and church research, and published peer-reviewed articles on public theology, diaconia, development ethics, religion and development, and ecumenism. His articles have appeared in journals such as *International Journal of Public Theology, Journal of Intercultural Communication, Studia Theologica, Dialog* and *Journal of Global Ethics*.

Chapter 12
Being Responsible in the Public Domain

Clive Pearson

Abstract The call to be responsible in the public domain is addressed here through a particular rendering of the discipline of a public theology. It is assumed that the intention of such a theology is to nurture the common good, a civil society, the flourishing of all. The Christian faith is thus placed among a 'company of strangers' and a relative reliance upon middle axioms like justice, dignity and responsibility as it seeks to engage with contemporary issues—such as (a). what constitutes climate justice? (b). what kind of tensions must a culturally diversifying democracy negotiate for the sake of an agreed basis for dignity and justice? These two concerns are discrete; at face value they are not intimately inter-related. They are being situated in this argument alongside the rhetoric of call and responsibility due to the self-understanding of a denominational church and how it engages with the nation in which it finds itself. The praxis of the Uniting Church in Australia is informed by a *Statement to the Nation* that was made public at its inception in 1977. That *Statement* was built upon a belief in a "Christian responsibility for society being regarded as fundamental to the mission of the church".

Introduction

The themes of human rights, dignity and morality are often explored via abstraction. They are played out, nevertheless, in concrete contexts in the lives of human agents. In terms of theological practice, they are immersed in the confessional claims and deeds of particular churches. In this instance the church is an ecumenically born and bred Uniting Church in Australia. Its practice is explored in the light of a public theology and its pursuit of the common good and the flourishing of all. In recent years the Uniting Church has made free use of this rhetoric and has bound that aspirational vision to its understanding of the gospel being the equivalent of the reconciliation of all things in Christ.

C. Pearson (✉)
Public and Contextual Theology Research Centre, Charles Sturt University, 16 Masons Drive, North Parramatta, NSW 2151, Australia
e-mail: cpearson@csu.edu.au

Z. Xie et al. (eds.), *Human Dignity, Human Rights, and Social Justice*,
https://doi.org/10.1007/978-981-15-5081-2_12

This church has not been overly concerned with the confusions and lack of clarity regarding the niceties of definition, purpose and intended audience identified by Harold Breitenberg.[1] It is doubtful whether its ecclesial agencies have been able to negotiate the distinction between working with a model of a civil religion over and against a public theology. The specific problem arising out of this seemingly niggardly judgement lies in whether the Uniting Church has practised a sufficiently robust bilinguality. Breitenberg has argued that a public theology is 'a religiously informed discourse that intends to be convincing to adherents within its own religious tradition while at the same time being comprehensible and possibly persuasive to those outside it'.[2] Elaine Graham is among those practitioners who term this vocation as one of being bilingual. In order to establish a bridge between the symbolic nature and resources of the church and its engagement with the world the tendency is to make use of middle axioms.[3] The critical step is not to detach the practice of a public theology from its beliefs about the being and purpose of God. The risk intrinsic to the use of middle axioms is how they can lose touch with their life and practice in the church. They no longer then possess the power to inspire allegiance. The life of discipleship is easily separated from the call to be a responsible citizen.

This emphasis on bilinguality lends itself to a public theology being interdisciplinary. It anticipates activism and 'doing'. The awkward legacy of such is for the discourse of responsibility to fasten upon the many good works performed and policy-making at the potential expense of a divine initiative. There is a critical question that needs to be posed: does the shift focus too much on 'what we do' for the sake of a civil society to the exclusion of an 'us' that is being responsive to a transcendent God? Here is a need for a further distinction. The nature of public theology is not identical with that of its close relative—political theology. The quest for the common good itself happens within a diversity of spheres. It is made up of an ever-changing raft of presenting issues, stages, influences, power plays and actors. It is not fulfilled through the successful resolution of an individual piece of legislation or lobbying. How well a church negotiates these tensions determines the quality of it being a designated a public church.

The Ecclesial Setting

The Uniting Church in Australia came into existence on 22 July 1977. After many years of discussion the Presbyterian, Methodist and Congregational Churches agreed to form a new 'indigenous' church in Australia. At the inaugural service the necessary instruments of faith and order were expressed through the foundational document of the church *The Basis of Union*. It was accompanied by a *Statement to the Nation*.[4]

[1] Breitenberg [1].

[2] Breitenberg, 'To Tell the Truth', pp. 65–66.

[3] Elaine Graham [7, pp. 99–100].

[4] Uniting Church in Australia [34].

The explicit purpose of the latter was to introduce the new church while setting out what is a manifesto of intent. The *Statement* declared how this particular movement of a pilgrim people 'on the way' would relate to the public domain at home and beyond.

Through ensuing decades the *Statement* has assumed an iconic status: it is invoked in various actions and declarations. It set the basis for a further *Statement to the Nation* in 1988.[5] The prologue of the 'Submission to the White Paper on Foreign Policy' made to the Federal Government by the Social Justice Forum of the Synod of New South Wales-ACT (Australian Capital Territory) drew upon the original in order to explain 'our social concern'. This White Paper advised the relevant government department of how 'Uniting for the common good' was currently the Synod's theme and then drew upon the *Statement* to justify the church's 'Christian responsibility to society' as being 'fundamental to the mission of the Church'.[6] That rationale led into an outline of 'the issues we consider most important'.

This first *Statement* was addressed to the nation rather than the government. It conceived its purpose in terms of social character rather than politics per se. Its rhetoric of responsibilities gave rise to a long list of affirmations, pledges, urgings and concerns. Some of those identified had to do with the very substance of a democratic civil society. It declared the need for integrity in public life and a commitment to a civil discourse that was established in the desire to proclaim truth and justice. Its concern for the well-being of society was played out in two ways. The first was a call to act against injustice, discrimination and greed and work towards the eradication of poverty and racism. It sought to overcome as such the tendency to disregard the need of others. The second way lay more ostensibly within the right to participate in the public domain and thus be a responsible democratic agent. Its advocacy for each citizen's right to participate in decision-making in the community was complemented by several core human rights: the right to equal educational opportunities, adequate health care, and freedom of speech.

The *Statement* concluded with an intimation of the kind of concerns that Rachel Muers and Willis Jenkins[7] would much later make with reference to a future ethics: what sort of world might we bequeath to children yet unborn (Muers) and, in the case of Jenkins, for the intersection of sustainability, social justice and religious creativity. The Uniting Church found itself committed to the basic human rights of future generations, the wise use of energy and the protection of the environment.

The ecumenical impulse at work in the new church further played itself out in a dialectic between catholicity and particularity. Its sensitivity towards the whole inhabited earth was expressed *via* an intention to work for the welfare of the human race. The *Statement*'s sense of being part of a much larger whole was mediated through a realistic invocation of the principle of contextuality. The call to work for the welfare of the whole human race was set within a particular theological setting that was geographic. The newly established church was situated in Australia: its

[5]Uniting Church in Australia [35].

[6]Social Justice Forum [32].

[7]Muers [23] and Jenkins [12].

horizons of interests were deemed to lie within Australia, south-east Asia and the Pacific Islands.

Through time the Uniting Church has striven to honour its *Statement* of intentions in diverse modes. Through its agencies of care, it has sought to ensure the dignity of the elderly, the frail, the abused, the homeless and the vulnerable child. It has done so at a time when federal and state government has sought to service these needs through voluntary agencies. The Uniting Church is the largest provider of these services. It has also been willing to initiate new ventures in the interests of the protection and improvement of life itself—most notably, accepting responsibility for the setting up the country's first medical injecting centre. Of all the churches in Australia, the Uniting Church has been the ecclesial body most likely to air the debate and act upon LGTBIQ issues in a reasonably pro-active and supportive way with the exception of the Metropolitan Church. Through its assembly and synodal offices it has developed the art of understanding the policy-making process and lobbying. Through its agency, Uniting World, it has brokered a programme-based policy of development with ecumenical partners in the region identified by the *Statement.*

The strength of the church's intentions is evident at election time. Its relevant agencies and councils have made the case for what it means to be a Christian citizen in a democratic society. It has advised members to exercise their right to vote and identified a number of 'hot issues' that have included the following: the constitutional recognition of first peoples, income support, early childhood education and support, climate change, energy affordability, disability, multiculturalism, gambling, people trafficking, asylum seekers and offshore processing, children in immigration detention and alcohol misuse.

Its members have collaborated with trade unions, networks of non-governmental organisations and other faiths in alliances designed to improve the quality of life in cities. Its Presidents have made public stands on detention centres for 'illegal migrants' or 'boat people' and workplace agreements that diminished the protection for employees. Under the leadership of Elenie Poulos, the former Director of Uniting Justice, its assembly has produced reports and declarations that merged incisive comment on matters to do with various issues and rights with a functional and appropriate theological reflection and warrant. This work has included documents and booklets such as *Dignity in Humanity: Recognising Christ in Every Person* (2006), *For the Sake of the Planet and All its People: A Uniting Church Statement on Climate Change* (2006), and *An Economy of Life: Re-Imagining Human Progress for a Flourishing World* (2009).

The Uniting Church has become the denomination most often associated with social justice. The inaugural *Statement* has inspired a living tradition. It has imagined a continuing involvement in 'social and national affairs' as part of the church's faithful response to the gospel. This vocation was established in a primary allegiance to the reconciling work of God. From the outset it was recognized that stands made on behalf of various rights can create a degree of distance from popular opinion and government. The *Statement* foresaw how this allegiance 'may bring us into conflict with the rulers of the day'.

The common reflective practice has been to emphasize the dignity of all people through recurring biblical and theological themes. The most prominent ones are the confession that all are made in the image of God and the call to love one's neighbour as oneself. Those themes do not stand on their own. There is a clear recognition of sin and of living in an imperfect world. The *Statement* of 1988 was indeed confessional in tone at points where past injustices and the denial of dignity to the indigenous peoples were acknowledged. It was recognized that 'we' are the 'beneficiaries of injustice'. The image of God itself is understood in the light of a perichoretic rendering of the triune God. The implicit anthropology surfaces on occasion in a way that situates humankind alongside the rest of creaturely existence in a manner that is inter-relational; it is mindful of the intrinsic worth of God's good creation upon which we depend. The tendency is to view the Uniting Church as a pilgrim people on the way to a promised End. The soteriological dimension of belief in and about Christ privileges the language of reconciliation which is bound to a missional imperative.

And yet there has not been much work done on prying open the textual support for declarations by way of a more rigorous academic exegesis. There is no equivalent to that undertaken by Cynthia Moe-Lobeda who constructed a theology of being a public church for the Evangelical Lutheran Church of the United States.[8] Nor has there been an equivalent to the study document produced by the Lutheran World Federation on being *The Church in the Public Space*.[9]

The Anatomy of Responsibility

The various stands made by the Uniting Church flow from the rhetoric of responsibility that permeate the *Statement*. The way in which the term has been put to use is to create a cumulative effect; there has been no sustained discussion on what being responsible means. How helpful is that lack of theological precision is a moot point. There has been no apparent need to consider what other disciplines—as well as theology—might have to say about its particular anatomy.

The democratic virtue of responsibility has been described as a 'background social good' that 'directs the distribution of other social goods'.[10] It requires a kind of citizenship (and discipleship) that is willing to own and operate that act of distribution and to do so in a manner that is accountable. To whom, and to what (and why) is that accountability directed requires specificity. Being responsible is not an abstract virtue. It exists within a 'messy', 'complicated', 'thick context' of appropriated and/or legislated duties.

For Tisha Rajendra responsibilities are 'distributed by means of social narratives that map responsibilities onto various kinds of relationships'. They provide the glue

---

[8]Cynthia Moe-Lobeda [22].

[9]Junge [13].

[10]Rajendra [27, p. 115].

that 'bind[s] people to each other'—we are 'moral agents'. Those narratives further furnish the link between commonly accepted universals—like justice—to particular situations. The very nature of responsibility is such that its practice must then 'bridge' and 'navigate' that territory. It must do so for the sake of an equitable and just relationship.[11]

The manner in which the relational nature of responsibility and its status as a middle axiom is captured by Richard Niebuhr: he envisaged the responsible self in terms of 'a Christian who seeks to understand the mode of his existence and that of his fellow beings as human agents'.[12] The relatively open-ended nature of responsiveness lent itself to 'an ethic of appropriateness of fitting response' to 'the created worth of others'.[13] The semantics expect dialogue. Niebuhr believed that persons are best defined by their capacity for responsiveness: 'we answer to and with others'. The attraction of the language of responsibility is that it shifts the moral claim away from the individual autonomous self who may or may not act; it presupposes relationality, intersubjectivity and intercommunality. We exist in communities and in relationships. The strength of this call to responsibility lies in the claims the other makes upon us as individuals and collectives.

The way in which the case for responsibility plays itself out leads to the Uniting Church being an actor in any one of several social narratives. This focus on agency and response becomes pivotal. The obvious question becomes: accountable and responsible to whom—and in what ways? Here Gerald McKenny has identified three types: imputability, responsibility and liability.[14] In terms of its history the strong social justice impulse within the Uniting Church and its commitment to care is likely to respond to those most in need, the frail, and those at risk of war, violence, and now shifts in climate. The bilingual task of a public theology, nevertheless, remains. On what basis is such responsibility exercised?

Of particular importance is the place in which this self-confessed responsible church claims to occupy within the fabric of society. The *Statement* reckoned that this new church saw itself as an 'institution' within the nation. Exactly what this might mean in terms of an ecclesiastical polity and its relationship to the public domain of Australia is not clear, however, there is no established church in the country; the Constitution does not allow for the privileging of one faith or one denomination over another. The *modus vivendi* is thus *ad hoc*.

In terms of its own self-understanding a prophetic necessity remains, irrespective of institutional status. The importance of such has indeed been made obvious in recent national life. During the course of her tenure as President of the Australian Human Rights Commission (2012–2017), Gillian Triggs was subject to much adverse political and media pressure in the prosecution of her brief.[15] According to statute,

---

[11]Rajendra, *Migrants and Citizens*, pp. 114–15.

[12]Niebuhr [25, p. 42].

[13]William Schweiker, 'Foreword', in Niebuhr, *The Responsible Self*, p. xi; McKenny [18, p. 240].

[14]McKenny, 'Responsibility', in Meliaender and Werpehowski, eds, *The Oxford Handbook*, pp. 242–251.

[15]Kenny [14] and Simon [30].

her role imposed upon her the imperative of speaking out 'if particular acts are contrary to Australia's obligations under international law … [and] drawing attention to government actions that were inconsistent with international treaties covering human rights'. The Forgotten Children's Report deemed that 116 children of asylum-seekers detained on the remote island of Nauru to be suffering from 'extreme levels of physical, emotional and psychological distress'. Their condition of being amounted to 'multiple breaches of the Conventions of the Right of the Child' while the Federal Government pursued an unyielding policy of border protection.[16] Triggs was also embroiled in the controversy surrounding section 18C of the Racial Discrimination Act where pressure was being exerted in favour of changes that would allow it to be lawful to offend, insult and intimidate on the basis of race. Such attacks demonstrate how vulnerable human rights can be to waves of populism in well-established liberal western democracies. There are risks if the responsible self and the moral order are neglected. Triggs expressed her gratitude for support from Poulos, in particular, and the Uniting Church in general.[17]

Who Is the 'We'?

This invocation of responsibility at its inception sets in place a notable distinguishing feature of the Uniting Church. The language of responsibility would gradually dissipate and give way to the talk of social justice, uniting care and the more frequent employment of rights-based discourse. The irony behind this masking of responsibility is that these alternatives all seem to reside under that initial urge to be responsible.

There is a dilemma here, however. There is an inherent risk in being responsible. It has to do with a matter of agency. It has to do with that 'we' found in the original *Statement*. The complaint can be made against responsibility that it 'has the power to impose on others a way of "making claims about human life" that really reflects the power and status of those seeking to be responsible'. William Schweiker notes that 'those seeking' may be 'say, modern western males'. There is then a potential for a clash of category between 'the rhetoric of particularity and identity'.[18] The claim to act responsibly should attract hermeneutic of suspicion. It needs to be addressed lest a tacit kyriarchy simply assumes power and the right to be responsible on behalf of everyone else.

This risk that Schweiker named is strategically critical to the life and witness of the Uniting Church. The *Statement* was issued at a particular point in time that represented the coming together of three denominations that were Anglo-Celtic in origin. Through changes to the law overseeing migration the Uniting Church has become culturally and linguistically diverse to a degree that the first *Statement* could

[16] Gordon [6].

[17] Mulvey [24] and Uniting Church [36].

[18] Schweiker, 'Foreword', in Niebuhr, *The Responsible Self*, p. x.

not have imagined. In 1985 the Uniting Church declared itself to be a multicultural church, little realizing at the time how problematic that naming might be. In terms of the ontology of the church the claim has proved to be more aspirational than realized.

This shift in demography has coincided with a deepening awareness of the multiple and systemic injustices suffered by indigenous peoples. The bicentennial *Statement* of 1988 lamented 'what was done to them in colonisation' and continues. The pursuit of social justice, human rights and the dignity of all is now carried out against a background of following Jesus Christ in invaded space.[19] It coincides with a distinction made between first (indigenous) peoples and second peoples (all others).[20] The church that now inhabits this tradition of being an institution committed to social justice for the sake of the gospel is not the same as it was when the *Statement* was formulated. Its acknowledgement of the indignities suffered by indigenous as well as more recent migrants to Australia adds a self-reflexive dimension to the invitation to responsibility.

Being Just

The issues embedded in the changing nature of this 'we' are not slight. The theme of human rights and dignity presupposes some degree of consensus over what constitutes justice. The *Statement* was built upon an architecture of truth and justice. What might seem self-evident in a more homogeneous church and culture may not be so obvious in the highly globalized world in which that language of responsibility now performs. The work of the political philosopher David Miller who poses two inter-related questions can be of help here: what constitutes justice in a multicultural society? can it be implemented?

Miller argues that social justice comprises a number of 'primary goods' and 'steps'. Those goods which go into the making of the common good have to do with rights and liberties, opportunities and power, and wealth and income. The most obvious strategy for the realization of social justice is the distribution of resources and benefits that fulfil these goods on the basis of need and equity. From empirical research Miller insists that such a conclusion is not straightforward. In the first instance the composition of social justice is itself more complex. In order to illustrate this assertion Miller identifies several steps which intersect with one another in various ways. Those steps embrace a concern for rights (or equality or desert), scope (to whom is justice owed), context (in what circumstances does any particular principle apply) and application (which practices and policies are mandated by justice). Miller is effectively defining social justice not merely in terms of principles but also by its practice of distribution. The very idea of social justice, of course, presupposes the coming together of these two otherwise discrete component parts.

---

[19]Budden [3].

[20]The Revised Preamble [33].

Miller's interest lies in the sociology that accompanies the quest for social justice. The very nature of a multicultural society is one where 'citizens belong to a number of distinct ethical and religious groups that constitute an 'important source for personal identity' and which also compete for loyalty. What happens in a 'social union' where a compelling allegiance is given to a minority culture rather than to the democratic citizenship of the larger society? What happens when the dominant majority is deaf to the cries of those who are disadvantaged by race or the status and history of their citizenship? Miller is addressing the question whether there are different understandings of justice held 'by cultural groups within the same political community'.

For a true social justice Miller argues there must be agreement on the principles of what is just. In a society made up of people who hold different religious, moral and philosophical beliefs there is need for 'an overlapping consensus'. Miller is not convinced that this implicit sociology actually exists in the 'real world' of multiculturalism as distinct from its 'text-book' rendering. It cannot be assumed; it is entirely possible that a culture is willing to exercise justice towards its own insiders but not to outsiders.[21]

Miller has recognized that multiculturalism possesses the potential for disruption of a national social imaginary; the possible consequences for a distributive justice can be far-reaching. On the basis of his empirical research Miller concluded that there was more or less agreement on what constitutes the principle of justice—but that was not the problem solved. There are potential differences to be found in the application of the various steps.

The kind of research Miller has done should be heeded by those who demonstrate a concern for a public theology addressing matters arising out of minority, diasporic and cross-cultural experience. Some careful definitions and theoretical work needs to be done due to the axiomatic role that justice plays in such a theology and conceptions of the common good—not to mention responsibility and the risk of kyriarchy. The same is true with how discourses related to human rights and dignity operate between and across different societies. Miller knows that some cultures privilege the moral autonomy of the individual while others are more self-consciously collectivist in outlook.[22] This distinction Miller observes mirrors the differences which tend to exist between western and non-western cultures in liberal democracies which are multicultural in character. Such a conclusion should not be too surprising—but the implications for the call to be responsible, truthful, and just should not be ignored. It matters whether a culture's self-understanding is established on an instrumental view of inter-personal relationships or one which seeks to maintain the inner strength and harmony of a discrete community.

The comparison can be made with minority and diasporic cultures, which are non-western. The basic distinction between the individualistic and communal frameworks makes itself felt in the way in which largely agreed upon principles of justice are applied. So much depends on whether the underlying sociology nurtures alienation,

---

[21]Miller [21, pp. 70–74].

[22]Miller, *Justice for Earthlings*, pp. 74–84.

segregation or some form of integration. In terms of a coherent and comprehensive understanding of social justice Miller argues that the role of trust is pivotal.[23] He has no illusions: there are 'different levels of trust' ranging from the inter-personal through to trust in government via a 'generalized trust in one's fellow citizens' and a 'willingness to support socially just policies'.

Life in the Anthropocene

Miller was addressing these matters within a wider concern for what he described as justice for earthlings. That theme has a deepening urgency now that humankind appears to be taking leave of the Holocene and entering the Anthropocene. For a church that urges responsibility for the well-being of God's good creation the prospects are daunting. They are so on several grounds.

The very idea of responsibility carries with it an expectation that beneficial courses of action can be pursued. At the very least, the *Statement*'s declared ecological concern for the wise use of energy resources represents a significant advance on mechanisms of climate denial. The call to be responsible aligns well with Pope Francis' recognition that climate is a common good[24] and that we ought to care for our common home. Being responsible for such is not simple, however.

The first of two critical issues at stake has nothing to do with 'our' complicity in the problem. It can be safely assumed that 'we' have benefited from and contributed to the 'Great Acceleration', which is arguably the beginning point of the Anthropocene.[25] Nor is the immediate issue of how we support and negotiate 'our' way through policies of mitigation and adaptation. There is a much more deep-seated dilemma that deals with acting justly in the Anthropocene and thus with how we frame human rights, dignity and being responsible. Is it (already) too late?

The philosopher Clive Hamilton has insisted upon a worrying prognosis. The Earth system has been radically compromised. Humankind has become a 'geologic agent' and, as such, a 'telluric force'.[26] We now find ourselves called to be responsible in a time and place for which there are no precedents. It is too late for some things to be reversed. The created order in which we pursue responsibility has become one characterized by radical uncertainty. The epoch into which we are moving (and which will be home to future generations) is not the same as the one in which cultures, civilisations and religions flourished. Intimations of such are mediated through discourses of energy security, militarisation of the environment[27] and ecology and war.[28]

---

[23] Ibid., pp. 84–92.

[24] Pope Francis [26], Paragraph 23.

[25] McNeill and Engelke [20].

[26] Hamilton et al. [9].

[27] Marzec [15].

[28] Elvey et al. [4].

Hamilton distances himself from those who argue in favour of 'the good Anthropocene'. Responsibility here would accept the benefits of climate engineering and technological innovation on the back of the belief that human mastery over nature should be welcomed. From this vantage point the potential loss of biodiversity and the risk to particular human cultures becomes collateral damage.[29] The advocates for this position thus assume a level of injustice and a denial of basic rights and dignity. Hamilton thinks the scenario in which those future generations will find themselves is more likely to be bad. That belief is consistent with the recent release of a statement made by 15,000 concerned scientists.[30] Such statements can be aligned alongside health considerations.[31] In a way that could never have been envisaged by those who framed the *Statement* back in 1977, this call to be responsible has become much more demanding. Humankind is now faced with a perfect 'moral storm' and 'an ethical tragedy'.[32]

This grim rendering of the place of *homo sapiens* in the Anthropocene lends itself to a further dimension of Miller's justice for earthlings. In the light of the deepening threat of the super-wicked problem of climate change the 'we' has become generic referring to the human species in general. It does so at the potential expense of the particular and the specifics of those most vulnerable. There are two threats to human rights and dignity that can become apparent at this point: what constitutes climate justice and how that might be observed? and, how might the rights and dignity of 'climate refugees' be preserved?

The implications of the Anthropocene for climate justice are far-reaching. Its advent intensifies some of the points of tension Henry Shue had identified in his work *Climate Justice*.[33] Writing from a practical philosophical perspective Shue is adamant that the issue of justice is unavoidable. There is a radical imbalance between nations over questions of responsibility for emissions—and thus culpability, as well as matters of who benefits most and then the inequity of power relationships when it comes to negotiating a way ahead. The first of these imbalances is captured in the distinction he makes between luxury and subsistence emissions. There is also the absence of future generations from the bargaining table at which the probability of 'bequeathing hazards' and 'surprises' will unfold.[34] There is a delicate balance to be achieved between acting in a way that does not do further injustice to the current most vulnerable while seeking to act in the interests of the future's most vulnerable.

This debate takes place within a most intractable problem. Shue's overriding concern is that the notion of climate justice brings into play two discrete agendas that cannot always be superimposed on one another. 'The central question' for him is 'how can we limit the dangers from climate change without driving hundreds of

[29]Hamilton [10]

[30]Ripple [28].

[31]McMichael [19].

[32]Gardiner [5].

[33]Shue [29].

[34]Shue, *Climate Justice,* pp. 162–79, pp. 208–43.

millions of people into poverty'?[35] Such descent would most likely imperil human rights and personal and communal worth in general. Shue is painfully aware of historic grievances to do with how many cultures have been exploited by colonial powers in the past; for the sake of mapping the legacy of that initial violation he draws upon the idea of a compound injustice.

The coming of the Anthropocene has sharpened the problem. Shue had imagined that there would need to be a planetary wide 'pre-arrangement on how equity was to be determined and understood'. It is unlikely that the planet itself could sustain a 'pure equity'. There would need to be 'a unique sacrifice'.[36] There is a niggling question pervading his work: is there a need to attend first to matters pertaining to the phenomenon of climate change and mitigating its effect irrespective of historical grievances?

Without using such terminology Shue was effectively identifying the liability side of responsibility. What Shue did not have to consider directly was the possibility of loss of lands, culture and sovereignty—and thus an escalation of compound injustice. It is clear that climate justice must also engage with the 'pre-legal' experience of being a climate-displaced person. This is the likely fate of citizens of small island states—Tuvalu, Kiribati, the Maldives—and then the densely populated delta lands like parts of Bangladesh. This is the region to which the Uniting Church declared itself to be responsible while it itself is located in a country noted for its fossil fuel emissions.

Being responsible in the Anthropocene is going to be very different from being responsible in the Holocene. What can be said and done to protect the rights of those living in low-lying islands when there is no international legislation that recognises the existence of climate refugees, let alone protects their interests and rights?[37] From a legal perspective how is a knot of abstract issues that manifest themselves in the lives of the vulnerable to be worked through? Can the declaration on refugees and asylum seekers be extended to those who are forced to migrate due to the effects of climate? What happens to sovereignty if the land has been invaded by the sea? How can such a displacing of peoples be managed? How can the right to life, food, shelter be ensured? How can culture be preserved if the dignity and well-being of a people is bound to ancestral lands that are no more?

This summons to responsibility looks like a task beyond the capacity of any denomination. It is not simply a matter of limited resources and energy. Moving into the Anthropocene the very conditions of life upon which human flourishing, rights and a bestowal of dignity depend are becoming more unstable and difficult to predict. One possible way ahead for a would-be responsible church is to heed Stefan Skrimshire's invitation to enter into the deep realism of a 'penultimate ending'. Facing the possibility 'we' have already passed over the threshold of no return he turns to a reading of a Christian eschatology for the sake of moral purpose. That eschatology endeavours to 'remain faithful to two features of the Christian faith': (i)

[35]Ibid., pp. 4, 47–67.

[36]Ibid., pp. 142–61.

[37]McAdam [16, 17].

there are grounds for hoping in a future that is given by God; (ii) God's presence in the world makes possible good action—ethics—in the interim before the end. In the Anthropocene the natural world (as we know it) may well now be beyond repair. To what extent can a Christian eschatology transform the ethical life from one of 'mere waiting' as opposed to that of 'transforming the present' and doing so mindful of competing human rights and the dignity of all. Skrimshire reminds us that eschatology is not just about endings. It is intimately bound to how 'we act in the time we have at our disposal in the full knowledge of an end being likely'.[38] Being responsible becomes an interim ethic expressed in the shadow of the eschaton—'the promised End' signified in *The Basis of Union*.

Being Responsible in a Public Theology

Skrimshire is effectively asking us to do 'good to all' (Galatians 6:10) in the presence of that ending. It is time to revisit the bilingual task of a public theology and its sometimes-obscured sensitivity to the role of transcendence and providence in the call to be responsible. There is an awkward dilemma noted by Gerald McKenny: 'the concept of responsibility coincides with the modern withdrawal of God from the world'. It represents as such a consequence of the expansion and intensification of the role of the human subject. It carries with it a dimension of 'it's up to us'. This state of affairs has arisen due to the increasing strength of human freedom and power.[39]

If McKenny is right, then there is need to be wary. The temptation is to emphasize the activism of the church that can nurture an imbalance between care and social justice, on the one hand, and worship and spirituality, on the other. If McKenny, and also Schweiker, is right, then the dawning of the Anthropocene requires a responsible anthropology that is mindful of our ever-increasing sense of power and freedom while the 'defiant earth' imposes fresh constraints.[40]

It is at this point that the bilingual nature of a public theology comes back into view. The case for a Christian responsibility ought to be made in the first language of faith itself and not simply through a United Nations declaration or list of universal values. The complexity of the issues demanding responsibility requires a thickening biblical and theological discourse as an accompaniment. That call is consistent with the original *Statement*'s understanding of its concerns being a response to the gospel. The ever-present risk in a social justice forum or a discussion on climate change is to assume transcendence and God-talk—and, then, 'it's up to us'.

James Gustafson has suggested that there is always a prior question. It is not 'What are we to do?' It is rather 'what's going on?', 'What is God doing?'[41] What

---

[38]Skrimshire [31].

[39]McKenny, 'Responsibility', in Meliaender and Werpehowski, eds, *The Oxford Handbook*, p. 237.

[40]Hamilton [11].

[41]Gustafson, 'Introduction', in Niebuhr, *The Responsible Self*, pp. 6–41 at p. 14.

Gustafson is raising in a modest way is an uneasiness with regards to how the field of responsibility can be limited to the immanental at the expense of the transcendent. Writing on Karl Barth's ethics McKenny identified how responsibility begins with God and is woven into a rhetoric of command and covenant. It is God who first exercises responsibility by assuming responsibility for us. Our responsibility comes from 'God who makes us responsible by His (*sic*) command'.[42] It can be so easy for the prior responsibility of God to be left unnoticed in the passion 'to do something' for social activism.

How should such then play itself out in talk of human rights and dignity? Is it time for the Uniting Church to revisit its default understanding of 'all being made in the image of God'—so often the rationale for responsibility towards the other? Is it time to clarify how this well-used organizing text actually has a built-in transcendence: it presupposes the existence and otherness of God in whose image all are made. Faced with the prospect of life in the Anthropocene the responsible church will need to clarify its understanding of the relationship between the divine initiative and human freedom.

References

1. Breitenberg, E., & Harold Jr. (2003). To tell the truth: will the real public theology please stand up! *Journal of the Society of Christian Ethics, 23*(2), 55–96 (Fall/Winter 2003).
2. Brown, D. A. (2012). *Climate change ethics: Navigating the perfect moral storm.* Abingdon and New York: Routledge.
3. Budden, C. (2011). *Following Jesus in invaded space: Doing theology on aboriginal land.* Cambridge: James Clarke and Co.
4. Elvey, A., Dyer, K., & Guess, D. (Eds.). (2017). *Ecological aspects of war: Engagements with biblical texts.* London: T & T Clark.
5. Gardiner, S. (2011). *A perfect moral storm: The ethical tragedy of climate change.* Oxford: Oxford University Press.
6. Gordon, M. (2017). Lauded and vilified: Gillian Triggs, Australian human rights commission president. *Sydney Morning Herald*, June 16, 2017.
7. Graham, E. (2013). *Between a rock and a hard place: Public theology in a post-secular age.* London: SCM Press.
8. Gustafson, J. M. (1968). *On being responsible: Issues in personal ethics.* New York: Harper & Row.
9. Hamilton, C., Bonneuil, C., & Gemenne, F. (Eds.). (2015). *The anthropocene and the global environmental crisis: Rethinking modernity in a new epoch.* Abingdon and New York: Routledge.
10. Hamilton, C. (2015). The theodicy of the 'good anthropocene'. *Environmental Humanities, 7,* 233–238.
11. Hamilton, C. (2017). *Defiant earth: The fate of humans in the anthropocene.* Cambridge: Polity Press.
12. Jenkins, W. (2014). *The future of ethics: social justice, sustainability and religious creativity.* Washington: Georgetown University Press.

[42]Gerald McKenny, 'Responsibility in Karl Barth and Modern Ethics', Religion and Ethics Workshop, University of Chicago Divinity School, March 1, 2012.

13. Junge, M. (preface). *The church in the public space*. Lutheran World Federation, 2016. Accessed November 1, 2017. https://www.lutheranworld.org/sites/default/files/exhibit_9.3_the_church_in_the_public_space_-_a_study_document_of_the_lwf_0.pdf.
14. Kenny, C. (2017). Gillian Triggs leaves inglorious legacy. *The Australian*, July 26, 2017.
15. Marzec, R. P. (2015). *Militarizing the environment: Climate change and the security state*. Minneapolis: University of Minnesota Press.
16. McAdam, J. (Ed.). (2010). *Climate change and displacement: Multidisciplinary perspectives*. Oxford: Hart Publishing.
17. McAdam, J. (2012). *Climate change, forced migration and international law*. Oxford: Oxford University Press.
18. McKenny, G. (2005). Responsibility. In G. Meliaender & W. Werpehowski (Eds.), *The Oxford handbook of theological ethics* (pp. 237–253). Oxford and New York: Oxford University Press.
19. McMichael, A. J. (2016). Woodward, Alistair, and Muir, Cameron. *Climate change and the health of nations: Famines, fevers, and the fate of populations*. New York: Oxford University.
20. McNeill. J. B., & Engelke, (2016). Peter. *The great acceleration: An environmental history of the Anthropocene since 1945*. Cambridge: Belknap Press.
21. Miller, D. (2013). *Justice for earthlings: Essays in political philosophy*. Cambridge: Cambridge University Press.
22. Moe-Lobeda, C. (2004). *Public church: For the life of the world*. Minneapolis: Augsburg Fortress Press.
23. Muers, R. (2008). *Living for the future: Theological ethics for coming generations*. London and New York: T. & T. Clark.
24. Mulvey, P. (2015). Exclusive interview with Gillian Triggs. *Crosslight*, August 20, 2015.
25. Niebuhr, H. Richard. *The responsible self: An essay in Christian morality* (1963). Louisville: Westminster John Knox Press, 1999.
26. Pope Francis. *Laudato Si': On care for our common home*. Vatican 2015.
27. Rajendra, T. (2017). *Migrants and citizens: Justice and responsibility in the ethics of immigration*. Grand Rapids: Eerdmans.
28. Ripple, W. J., et al. (2017). World scientists' warning to humanity: A second notice. *BioScience*, November 13, 2017. Accessed November 22, 2017. https://doi.org/10.1093/biosci/bix125.
29. Shue, H. (2014). *Climate justice: Vulnerability and protection*. Oxford: Oxford University Press.
30. Simon, M. (2018). When the politics got personal: Gillian Triggs' culture shock. *The Monthly*, December 2017-January 2018.
31. Skrimshire, S. (2014). Eschatology. In M. S. Northcott & P. M. Scott (Eds.), *Systematic theology and climate change: Ecumenical perspectives* (pp. 157–174). Abingdon and New York: Routledge.
32. Social Justice Forum. Submission to the White Paper on Foreign Policy: February, 2017. Accessed November 22, 2017. http://dfat.gov.au/whitepaper/submissions/documents/170302-553-Uniting-Church-Social-Justice-Forum.PDF.
33. The Revised Preamble. (2012). Accessed November 22, 2017. https://assembly.uca.org.au/resources/covenanting/item/668-the-revised-preamble.
34. Uniting Church in Australia. *Statement to the nation, 1977*. Accessed November 22, 2017. https://assembly.uca.org.au/resources/introduction/item/134-statement-to-the-nation-inaugural-assembly-june-1977.
35. Uniting Church in Australia. *Statement to the nation, Australian Bicentennial Year, 1988*. Accessed November 22, 2017. https://assembly.uca.org.au/resources/introdcution/item/133-statement-to-the-nation-australian-bicentennial-year-1988.
36. Uniting Church. (2017). Champion of justice: Elenie Poulos. Accessed November 22, 2017. https://assembly.uca.org.au/news/item/2570-champion-of-justice-elenie-poulos.

Clive Pearson is a Senior Research Fellow of the Research Centre for Public and Contextual Theology at Charles Sturt University, Australia. He is the Editor-in-Chief of the *International Journal of Public Theology*. He has published widely in the fields of public theology, ecological theology, responding to Islamophobia and cross-cultural/diasporic theologies. Among his most recent anthologies are *Imagining a Way: Exploring Reformed Practical Theology and Ethics* (ed) (2017), published by Westminster John Knox Press and *Enacting a Public Theology* (ed) (2019), published by AFRICAN SUN MeDIA, Stellenbosch.

Chapter 13
Inequality in Urban America and Clergy Advocacy on Economic Restructuring

R. Drew Smith

Abstract Clergy responses to economic formation and de-formation within American 'Rust Belt' cities such as Pittsburgh and Detroit are examined in the light of conceptions of civic and Christian 'community' as drawn from select sources in ethics and political philosophy. The relative absence of clergy from urban economic restructuring efforts within these contexts is noted in the essay, while also paying attention to several notable clergy exceptions to this pattern who provided important critiques of corporate sector economic predations and of clergy moral indifference or active complicity.

Introduction

Severe socio-economic disparities, imbalances, and conflicts within urban America make clear the urgent need for rethinking preconditions and prospects for vibrant and sustainable communities. Mediating competing interests within 21st century social contexts where diversities have both increased and become more insistent cannot take place effectively without attention to structural conditions that give rise to those competing interests. Nor can effective mediation take place without attention to moral frameworks that situate competing interests within conceptions of a broad public good. Christian thought leaders in the U.S. have been inclined more toward the moral than the structural framings of these dilemmas, and only rarely have pointed to intersections between those two dimensions.

One of the 20th century's leading theologians, Reinhold Niebuhr, served as pastor of a congregation in Detroit from 1915 to 1928, at a time when the auto industry's influence was widely encompassing. In Niebuhr's public theological praxis

This chapter is a revised version of the original article "Higher ground: The elusive church consensus on equality, empowerment, and community in urban America" appeared in *Pittsburgh Theological Journal* 2014: 25–39.

R. Drew Smith (✉)
Pittsburgh Theological Seminary, 616 North Highland Avenue, Pittsburgh, PA 15206, USA
e-mail: rsmith@pts.edu

Z. Xie et al. (eds.), *Human Dignity, Human Rights, and Social Justice*,
https://doi.org/10.1007/978-981-15-5081-2_13

during his Detroit pastorate, and more explicitly in his writings about that experience, Niebuhr challenged social imbalances of power and divergences of perspective between "aristocratic" auto industry executives and Detroit's laboring classes, juxtaposing the political, economic, and moral self-certainties of auto industry movers and shakers with the day-to-day uncertainties and increasing misgivings of underpaid semi-skilled laborers. Niebuhr objected to the indifference demonstrated toward the struggles of workers by persons in the power structure and by community constituencies actively or passively aligned with persons in power (including clergy) and made clear that an appropriate response to these community-threatening dichotomizations and imbalances was unionism.

For Niebuhr, unionism was the best available strategy at the time and deserved broad support among community leaders entrusted with community interests. He therefore applauds the handful of clergy leaders in Detroit who supported unionization, even in the face of the Detroit power structure's systematic capacity for reprisal against pro-union community leaders, and he strongly criticizes clergy 'who talked endlessly about love and brotherhood but [whose] preachments had little relevance to the problems … of adjudicating interests and balancing power'.[1] Niebuhr addressed similar concerns in a published collection of reflections on his Detroit pastorate, entitled *Leaves from the Notebook of a Tamed Cynic.* In *Leaves*, Niebuhr assails the social inequalities, economic disparities, and racism evident within the Detroit context, he rejects prevailing rationalizations of Detroit's growing inequalities as inevitable and acceptable costs of economic progress, and he challenges church conformity to these rationales and the failure of church leaders to draw connections between the spiritual and social aspects of their faith. In these various Detroit reflections and involvements, Niebuhr's intersecting theological and sociological positioning allowed him to bring into view essential contradictions between economically-defined panaceas of human fulfillment and the realities of social disparity and inequality characteristic of industrializing Detroit—while also disabusing the church sector of notions of neutrality on these issues.[2]

Conflicting ideas within 20th- and 21st-century Detroit (and across urban America) about what it means to be 'in community' and what it means to operate in a community's 'best interest' make clear the ongoing need for moral leadership in arbitrating conflicting interests and promoting common cause. Given the ubiquitousness of church institutions across urban landscapes and the moral capital these institutions collectively embody, clergy possess a credible platform from which to contest economic inequalities existing in sharp relief within urban contexts. Despite the fact that clergy rarely have actualized their collective potential as urban economic restructuring advocates, the essay discusses several notable clergy exceptions to this pattern within the Detroit and Pittsburgh contexts, where individual or small groups of clergypersons emerged as critics of corporate sector economic predations and of moral indifference or active complicity on the part of fellow clergy.

---

[1]Niebuhr [12].

[2]Niebuhr [11, pp. 47–48, 83–84, 113–119, 132–135, 160].

Also, after itemizing urban depopulation and disinvestment dynamics that have eroded urban communities, the essay also appeals for conceptions of urban community and 'peoplehood' (along lines identified by political scientist Rogers Smith) operative at the sometimes egalitarian intersections between competing traditions of American civic ideals. A sub-text of the present essay (and frequently of American civic traditions) is that a concern for neighbor and a commitment to community well-being are divinely-instilled within humanity, but find fulfillment only though intentional, sacrificial action. Christian teachings challenge us to seek this higher ground, and the growing disparities, imbalances, and conflicts within our urban contexts signal a new urgency for us to do so.

Resource Retractions, Relocations, and Mobility

In 1915, the year Niebuhr arrived in Detroit, the American auto industry was experiencing rapid growth, including a manufacturing infrastructure concentrated in metropolitan Detroit producing an enormous number of Ford, Chrysler, and General Motors vehicles. The explosive early-20th century growth of Detroit's auto industry generated a large influx of whites from nearby rural areas and African Americans from the South seeking employment within Detroit's mass-assembly auto plants. When Niebuhr began his pastorate in Detroit the city's population was roughly a half million people, but by the time Niebuhr departed from Detroit in 1928 to begin teaching at Union Theological Seminary in New York, Detroit's population had increased by another million. Detroit's population would peak at 1.9 million in 1950, which was also about the time its economic fortunes peaked.

Detroit's *municipal* fortunes began shifting dramatically during the 1950s, with the big automakers building plants in Detroit's suburbs and pulling residents out of the city, and with the ongoing black influx into Detroit from the South eventually producing a tipping point in white perceptions and experiencing of the city and pushing them toward the suburbs in ever greater numbers. In 1910, there were less than 6,000 blacks in Detroit, comprising less than 2% of Detroit's overall population. In 1930, there were 149,000 blacks, which constituted 9% of Detroit's population. By 1950, blacks numbered more than 300,000 in Detroit, which was 16% of the population. At that point, the black percentage of Detroit's population increased even more rapidly, not due to population influxes, but due to white exodus. Detroit's population went from 83% white, 16% black in 1950, to 70% white, 29% black in 1960, to 55% white, 44% black in 1970. By 1980, blacks were in the majority at 63% compared to 34% white population, and that eroding white percentage would continue apace over the next few decades. By 2010, Detroit's overall population had declined to 713,000 persons, 10% of which were white and 82% of which were black.[3]

---

[3]Detroit Free Press [4, pp. 107, 110, 114, 622].

Coinciding with the exodus of Detroit's white population was a significant exodus of resources. Between 1947 and 1955, Ford, Chrysler, and General Motors decentralized their Detroit operations and built 20 new plants in suburban Detroit. This auto industry decentralization contributed to a loss of manufacturing jobs in Detroit, with Detroit's percentage of manufacturing jobs within the metropolitan area declining from 60% in 1948 to 53% in 1954. Manufacturing jobs continued declining in Detroit, with the number of manufacturing jobs falling from 145,200 to 141, 400 between 1958 and 1963, and decreasing another 15% between 1972 and 1977. By 1982, the city of Detroit accounted for only 25% of manufacturing jobs within the metropolitan area. Retail jobs were also becoming more concentrated in suburban Detroit by the 1950s, with Detroit's share of retail jobs within the metropolitan area decreasing from 72% in 1948, to 63% in 1954, to 15% in 1982. Emblematic of the sharp decline of retail jobs in Detroit is the absence of a real shopping mall within Detroit's city limits (with the exception of a modest mall in Detroit's downtown Renaissance Center. One other important indicator of Detroit's declining resource base is that between 1958 and 1977, 'metropolitan industrial development targeted to Detroit fell from 44% … to 22%—a decline of 50% in just two decades'.[4] The degree of depopulation and disinvestment that has occurred in Detroit over the last 60 years has been unmatched by any major U.S. city—and it has eventuated in an even more ignominious precedent for Detroit.

The historical context of Niebuhr's Detroit activism and analysis was the early-20th century, but Detroit (and America) has since undergone dramatic changes that are accounted for, perhaps, only partly by Niebuhr's framework. The contexts of early-industrialization and urban concentrations of people and capital addressed by Niebuhr gave way by the mid-20th century to nascent de-industrialization and urban disinvestment and depopulation. This was true of Detroit, but this was also true of other U.S. cities, especially throughout the Rust Belt. Cleveland's population peaked at 914,000 persons in 1950, but by 2010 its population had declined to 396,000 and it was designated as the poorest city in the U.S. based upon per capita income (the second poorest city being Detroit).[5] Similarly, Buffalo reached the height of its population in 1950, when it numbered 580,000 people, but by 2010 its population had fallen to 261,000 people, 27% of its population was classified as living in poverty, and its median family income (at $33,000) was 40% below the national average.[6] Each of these contexts of early-20th century industrial promise fell victim to a mid-20th century de-industrialization, depopulation, and disinvestment, and then to a 21st century despair.

Pittsburgh has fared somewhat better than its Rust Belt neighbors, at least as it relates to a 21st century recovery. Nevertheless, its social low points have stood out for their severity, dating back to the hostile and sometimes violent labor relations of the late-19th century, and later including the precipitous 20th century decline of a steel

---

[4] Darden [2, p. 24].

[5] World Population Review.Com [19].

[6] World Population Review.Com [18].

sector that was once one of the top steel producing sectors in the country, with a mid-20th century employee base of 90,000 Pittsburgh-area workers. By 2009, Pittsburgh's steel sector employed only 6,900 workers, with much of its steel mill activity long since shut down in response to stiff competition from other parts of the U.S. and from overseas. Pittsburgh's population suffered similarly stark numerical decline, peaking in 1 950 when it numbered 677,000 residents, but dropping to 307,000 by 2010.[7] Where Pittsburgh has achieved greater success than several of its neighboring Rust Belt cities, however, has been the diversification of its post-industrial economy during the latter-20th and early-21st century. The largest employer in Pittsburgh is now the University of Pittsburgh Medical Center (UPMC), which had more than 87,000 employees in 2018 and revenues in excess of $18 billion.[8]

UPMC's considerable impact within metro-Pittsburg has been fervently celebrated as well as criticized (much like the steel industry which preceded it within Pittsburgh, and the automobile industry in Detroit). These major industries have provided the economic life blood within their respective urban contexts but, in important respects, with noticeable costs to the social and moral fabric that binds communities together. One of Niebuhr's concerns about industrialization was that it magnified the economic basis of social organization and relationships and conferred upon corporate executives (guided by financial or technological considerations more than by community impact) the ability to become 'arbiters over the lives and fortunes' of masses of people.[9] Niebuhr did not discount the possibility of industry moguls pursuing a public good broader than the financial interests of their corporation. He did, however, sharply criticize the inordinate influence of industry leaders and the unacceptable extent to which the normative trajectories of civic leaders and church leaders of his day took their cues from industry logic and leaders—a deference Niebuhr regarded as a broader cultural deference to power.[10] Niebuhr's critique of the power of industry executives (who during his Detroit pastorate received an average compensation approaching 40 times that of an average worker's pay) possesses even greater relevance for today's context, where the compensation of corporate executives reached 360 times the pay of an average worker in 2018, and where corporate executives could preside over a corporation potentially possessing more wealth than a number of the world's individual nations.[11] This is a troubling concentration of power in the hands of persons not subject to validation by a democratic electorate nor to any broadly public process whereby a commitment to a robust definition of the common good could be assessed. That is why Niebuhr and many others have viewed unions as one way of insuring a systematically negotiated interaction between corporate leaders and the people over which they exercise power.

UPMC has been at the center of contestations within Pittsburgh (and, in some ways, nationally) over the unionization of workers. Workers at the lower end of

[7]Haler [5, pp. 9–10] and World Population Review [20].

[8]UPMC [16].

[9]Niebuhr, *Leaves*, p. 123.

[10]Niebuhr, "Lessons of the Detroit Experience', p. 487.

[11]Hembree [6].

UPMC's pay scale have expressed concerns about their financial insecurity and about the need for collective representation, and have been exploring becoming part of the Service Employees International Union, a union to which many hospital workers around the country belong. UPMC management feels they are on good footing with their employees, paying service workers a starting wage of $11 per hour, providing good benefits for service workers, and maintaining an open communication process between workers and management that allows for dialogue when issues arise. The dispute has been ongoing for two years, with UPMC management accused by pro-union activists (and by the National Labor Relations Board in a case that stuck) of union-busting activities, and UPMC countering by pointing to the existence of unionization among various professional sectors of UPMC's workforce.[12] The ongoing tensions manifested in fairly large street protests by service workers and their allies outside UPMC's downtown Pittsburgh headquarters in March 2014 and a few weeks earlier 10 clergy affiliated with Pittsburgh Interfaith Impact Network were arrested for blocking an entrance to UPMC headquarters after being refused an audience with the CEO of the company. The clergy said their purpose was 'to see UPMC offer employees a more friendly work environment free of intimidation and to be able to earn a honest living wage to afford premiums of their healthcare'.[13] Roughly 90 years after the pro-union stance by Niebuhr and a remnant of Detroit clergy, a remnant of Pittsburgh clergy saw the need for what continues to be a risky and unpopular stance.

Even where cities and neighborhoods have begun to reverse the outward flow of resources and population, the poor are still losing out as a result of displacement by corporate sector development agendas and by gentrification. As corporations and wealthier residents move into what had become impoverished urban core neighborhoods, low-income residents may end up dispersed to even poorer central city neighborhoods or to outer ring neighborhoods where they become cut off from social networks upon which they had come to depend. This was seen in mid-20th century Pittsburgh's decision to build a civic center in its downtown area, acquiring a significant portion of the historic African American Hill neighborhood through eminent domain in order to do so. The encroachment upon the Hill District neighborhood resulted in the displacement of 8,000 residents and 400 businesses from the Hill neighborhood while providing little compensation to the displaced in the process. Many of the more than 1,800 displaced black families ended up dispersed across town to low-income housing largely in Pittsburgh's East Liberty neighborhood. By the 1980s and 1990s, the East Liberty neighborhood would itself become a target of major corporate speculation and development, displacing many of the low-income black residents that had concentrated in that neighborhood, pushing them out into the even poorer adjacent neighborhood of Homewood.

Whether or not the arrival of corporations in urban neighborhoods is objected to by local leaders or residents for its displacement effects, it may be viewed as imposing its will on communities in other ways that overrule or undermine stated or agreed-upon local community development objectives or policy priorities. An interesting

[12]Belser [1], Jamieson [7], Zullo Balingit [21].

[13]Marsico [9].

example of this took place recently in Washington, D.C., where local leaders pushed back against an agreement between Wal-Mart and the city government for Wal-Mart to introduce six stores into the District. Although there was general support (if not enthusiasm) for Wal-Mart's soon-to-come presence in the District, a number of local leaders felt Wal-Mart had the capacity and the obligation to pay livable wages to the workers in these new locations, and City Council leaders approved a bill requiring 'retailers with corporate sales of $1 billion or more and operating in spaces 75,000 square feet or larger to pay persons working in their District stores a minimum of $12.50 an hour,' rather than the official local minimum of $8.25 an hour.[14] In response, Wal-Mart indicated that if the bill was signed into law by the mayor, the company would not pursue construction of three of the stores at all and might hold off completing construction of the three stores where construction was already underway. This left local leaders, including the mayor, with a choice between standing for job-creation (within a city where jobs were desperately needed) or wage fairness (in a national context where too many Americans find themselves working jobs that do not pay livable wages). In the end, the mayor vetoed the bill, so Wal-Mart will eventually provide the District with approximately 1,800 new jobs—most of which paying what many do not consider to be a livable wage.[15]

As evident in these various examples, the corporate sector wields enormous power in the shaping of priorities within their organizations and within the communities and municipalities in which they operate. They make decisions bearing on the financial prospects, working conditions, and advancement possibilities of large populations of workers, as well as on the developmental trajectories, cultural milieus, and policy dynamics within their community contexts. But they are able to wield this kind of power because they are vital to the well-being of the community contexts in which they operate. They make jobs available to large population of workers, they facilitate working contexts for these workers that generally are safe and conducive to worker productivity and advancement, and they enhance communities through the products they generate, through the catalyzing of secondary economies, through direct and indirect infrastructural development, and through donations of human, financial, and material resources. But with this kind of power and influence come obligations to the communities and people affected by the exercise of that power and influence—at the very least through effective mechanisms and processes for negotiating conflicting interests between corporations and communities and between the executives and the rank-and-file within corporations.

"Who Is My Neighbor?" Variations on a Biblical Theme

American social divisions have been of a kind more or less pronounced from one time or place to another. Although current urban social divisions along lines of race,

[14]DeBonis [3].

[15]Ibid.

ethnicity, income, and ideology are of crisis proportions in many contexts, the crises have not escalated to the red hot levels of the urban riots that broke out in many cities during the late-1960s, including in Detroit, Buffalo, Cleveland, and Pittsburgh (or even the much earlier 1877 riot in Pittsburgh connected to labor disputes). These 'civil disorders' (as they are euphemistically referred to at times) represented breaking points in a fragile co-existence between various groups, where conflicting interests escalated into warring interests and community fragmentation hastened toward community dissolution.

The 1967 riot in Detroit was one of the deadliest and most destructive riots in U.S. history and in response President Lyndon Johnson appointed a commission to investigate the causes of the riots. Referred to as the Kerner Commission (after its chair, Governor Otto Kerner, Jr. of Illinois), the commission issued a report in 1968 that included the now often cited conclusion that 'America is moving toward two societies—black and white, separate and unequal.'[16] Almost 50 years has passed since the commission issued its report, and its sobering conclusion remains relevant to our current context given the country's enormous economic disparities and the continued racial dimensions of that economic stratification. According to 2010 U.S. Census data, 20.5 million Americans, or 6.7% of the U.S. population in deep poverty, defined as 50% or less of the official poverty level.[17] In actual income terms, people living in deep poverty had an income of $5,570 or less for an individual and $11,157 for a family of four. What is also noteworthy is that the percentage of persons living in deep poverty in the U.S. is higher than at any point in the 35 years that the Census Bureau has kept track of these figures. In addition, there continue to be troubling income and wealth disparities between whites and people of color. In 1963, black families earned 55 cents for every dollar earned by whites and only 66 cents for every dollar earned by whites in 2011. The wealth gap is far worse than the income gap, with blacks possessing 6 cents and Latinos 7 cents for every dollar possessed by whites. Meanwhile, a figure that communicates the stark wealth disparities more than these comparative racial figures is the share of income going to the top 10% of U.S. earners, which rose from 33% in 1950 to 43% in 2002 and to just over 50% in 2012.[18]

These kinds of resource disparities are clearly not in the best interest of urban community-building, national cohesion, or a democratic system of governance, and they certainly run counter to a Biblical ethic of loving our neighbors as ourselves. Yet these disparities are maintained and advanced through social policies, economic policies, and personal and collective practices that have received surprisingly little pushback from the American public—including the church sector. There are certainly democratic, pragmatic, humanitarian, and theo-ethical instincts within American social culture that would seem capable of producing a greater sense of outrage over the social injustice or illogic of these social imbalances and greater concern over their dire individual and social consequences. Within the contemporary American context,

[16]United States [15].

[17]U.S. Census Bureau [17].

[18]Douglas Massey [10].

however, public outrage and concern too often has been less about our growing social imbalances than about our growing governmental budgetary imbalances, and less about what is happening to our neighbors than about who qualifies as our neighbor. As communications, media, and transportation technologies have made us more proximate to persons outside our homes, neighborhoods, cities, and country, our concepts of community have in some ways contracted rather than expanded; and as social inequities have multiplied, a growing number of Americans are contending governmental and corporate sectors should do less rather than more to address these inequities.

What all of this suggests, perhaps, is that a sense of social obligation is in critically short supply within the American context. That is not to say that policies and approaches by the American governmental and corporate sectors in pursuit of collective well-being have not been socially generous in many respects. But the generosity in both instances has tended more toward charity and relief than toward empowerment. Americans with great individual wealth also have operated with a similar generosity in the form of charity rather than empowerment. The empowerment of socially less-advantaged populations is what is most needed, and what has been most desired by less-advantaged populations themselves. For example, the pursuit of employment-related opportunity in the form of job security, job benefits, job advancement, institutional leadership and voice, job creation, personal entrepreneurialism and business development—these bear on empowerment, and much of this agenda has been at the heart of unionism (though not only unionism, and not always effectively within unionism). Nevertheless, the resistance to unionism cannot help but be seen as resistance to the empowerment of less-advantaged populations—unless corporations choose independently of unions to effectively implement power-sharing and resource-sharing measures that satisfy expressed empowerment concerns and needs of less-advantaged workers.

Similarly, community empowerment concerns (both with respect to process, and economic and social prospects for the community) have animated activists who object to the community impact of corporations that push in or pull out of neighborhoods without properly consulting or showing consideration for local residents. The movement of corporations away from American cities into suburban or overseas contexts, and the devastating impact on the urban contexts and communities these corporations leave behind (as in the Detroit case) has been clearly a sore point in this regard. Also objected to has been the kind of corporate (and governmental) disregard for community costs of grand development schemes, as in the case of the mid-20th century maneuverings related to the Civic Center project in Pittsburgh or the contested impact Wal-Mart's current entrance into Washington, D.C. will have on local labor relations and workforce culture.

The extent to which the corporate sector has facilitated public input, approaches that advance and safeguard short-term and long-term community interests, or internal power-sharing and resource-sharing procedures across their workforce are matters that are subject to debate. Equally debatable may be the extent to which collective attempts to reorient corporate practices (through unionism or otherwise) have operated at cross-purposes with economically rational outcomes for workers or for the geographical contexts they inhabit. Nevertheless, it is fairly evident that prevailing policies and practices on the part of the corporate and governmental sectors in response to the nation's crisis-level social imbalances have been inadequate and, any steps toward diminishing rather than broadening conceptions of mutual social obligation, inappropriate.

Responses by church leaders to these social imbalances have also been inadequate, although there have been some trajectories of engagement that have demonstrated the strategic and unique role church leaders can play in response to these urgencies. Pope Francis and many Catholic bishops have taken especially strong and clear positions in recent months against poverty. In January 2014, the U.S. Conference of Catholic Bishops called on the U.S. Senate to take steps against inequality in America, including raising the federal minimum wage to livable levels. This call was echoed by Catholic bishops at state levels across the country who advocated that their state legislative bodies pass comparable state legislation. While Catholics have had a strong anti-poverty focus since at least Vatican II, that focus has become even more strongly stated since the 2013 election of Pope Francis, who has referred to poverty as a "scandal" and has openly criticized cultural orientations and social structures that perpetuate inequality, as he does in the following statement: 'A way has to be found to enable everyone to benefit from the fruits of the earth, and not simply to close the gap between the affluent and those who must be satisfied with the crumbs falling from the table, but above all to satisfy the demands of justice, fairness and respect for every human being'.[19] Protestant leaders, especially through the National Council of Churches of Christ, USA and the World Council of Churches, have also waged systematic campaigns in recent years, challenging economic inequality and promoting livable wages. Important anti-poverty critiques emanating more centrally from within black church leadership circles have included community hearings convened in various cities by the Samuel DeWitt Proctor Conference (a network of social just-oriented church leaders) to examine the national response to poverty as reflected in the crisis endured by black residents left behind in New Orleans during and after Hurricane Katrina and as reflected in structural and policy components of black mass incarceration. These anti-poverty and anti-inequality campaigns waged at high levels of Catholic and Protestant leadership are certainly encouraging but, unfortunately, the views promoted at these levels are not widely-enough embraced among their church constituencies or within society more broadly.

In fact, there is far more clash than consensus with respect to the frameworks of social philosophy and tradition out of which Americans form their understandings of community and social obligation. An influential book on American civil ideals written by political scientist, Rogers Smith, draws attention to what have been viewed historically as two competing civic outlooks within American socio-political culture: one that is more 'individualistic and property oriented', and another that is more 'democratic, public-spirited, and community-oriented.' In this view, says

[19]Pope Francis [13].

Smith, conflicts occur 'between those benefitting from ... property rights, and majorities suffering from them'.[20] Smith actually takes issue with this historical rendering of American civic culture, and argues for a more complex integration and overlap between the two trajectories in which the two trajectories need not be mutually exclusive. The key, for Smith, is that either of the tracks, or combinations thereof, proceed from a sense of shared citizenship and peoplehood from which to respond to inequities (built into any social arrangement), but with a sense of cross-cutting interests and memberships (as opposed to more particularistic and compartmentalized constructs of community). At the heart of any such vision of citizenship and peoplehood, says Smith, must be a shared commitment to 'protect and enhance all persons' capacities for personal and collective self-governance'.[21]

Applied to the very real conflicts seen in Detroit, Pittsburgh, and elsewhere between a free-wheeling corporate culture, on the one hand, and the communities being pushed and pulled by corporate decision-making and actions, on the other, Smith's argument would first reinforce the need to work to transcend "ascriptive mythologies" that compartmentalize group interests and particularities rather than build consensus across often complex and conflicting social positionings. Consensus, however, is very difficult across conflicts that are very real—and that is certainly the case in the deeply embedded conflicts of race, class, and social and physical geographies at stake in the demographic and economic reconfigurations of metro-Detroit and metro-Pittsburgh over the past century. It will certainly take more than a consensualizing narrative to bridge the structural divide between urban and suburban or between corporate executives, laborers, and local communities within these contexts. But what Smith pushes for is the ability to envision a shared stake—without which, actions toward structuring shared interests likely will not happen. For example, the likelihood of resource-sharing and problem-solving taking place across urban-suburban or neighborhood boundaries is less likely in metro contexts where all residents within such a context do not identify as a singular, connected "people" or where corporate commitments to a metro area are not sufficiently deep, wide, or enduring. The momentum over the past few decades toward distinctive neighborhood or township demarcations, identities, and renaming does not contribute favorably to prospects of constructing or reinforcing metropolitan area identities—nor does corporate willingness to move assets and operations from one community context to another, including off-shore, without sufficient regard for the impact of such actions on the various communities in question. Whole communities cannot be seen as expendable, nor can individual sub-groups within those communities—such as low-income residents who are displaced by urban renewal agendas or low-wage workers whose needs for fair wages, benefits, and voice are resisted by the power structure.

Capital and populations are mobile within free societies, and their movements may be driven by numerous factors related to reconfigurations of social landscapes and opportunities and shifts in economic markets and trends. Dynamic, competitive

[20] Smith [14], pp. 8–9.

[21] Ibid., p. 449.

processes such as these will inevitably prove favorable for some communities and populations and unfavorable for others. But when a process is framed in a way that gives clear advantage to one side over another, it is more adversarial than competitive, and when resulting in the kinds of socio-economic disparities and imbalances being witnessed within American society (and elsewhere), it is a process that is unacceptable and unsustainable. In the face of the rapid urbanization of the American population, disengagement in any form from urban and metropolitan community building solutions is not an option. Ultimately, more effective and creative approaches to the sharing of resources and opportunities across geographic and social boundaries must be advanced—through both corporate and governmental backing and leadership—and more robust conceptions of community and social obligation must be cultivated from all directions—including from within the church sector. In a 1964 sermon, Martin Luther King, Jr. placed before us a critical challenge facing that period, and ours. He stated: 'We must learn to live together as brothers [and sisters] or perish together as fools'.[22]

References

1. Belser, A. (2014). Union Sees National Focus in UPMC organizing effort. *Pittsburgh Post-Gazette*, March 9, 2014.
2. Darden, J. T. (1990). *Detroit: Race and uneven development*. Philadelphia: Temple University Press.
3. DeBonis, M. (2013). Wal-Mart says it will pull out of D.C. plans should city Mandate 'Living Wage'. *Washington Post,* July 9, 2013.
4. Detroit Free Press. (2001). *The Detroit Almanac*. Detroit: Detroit Free Press.
5. Haler, W. (2005). Industrial restructuring and urban change in the Pittsburgh region. *Ecology and Society*, *10*(1).
6. Hembree, D. (2015). CEO pay skyrockets to 361 times that of the average worker. *Forbes Magazine,* May 22, 2018. Retrieved 10, Sep 2018, from https://www.forbes.com/sites/dianahembree/2018/05/22/ceo-pay-skyrockets-to-361-times-that-of-the-average-worker/#334ddcad776d.
7. Jamieson, D. (2014). Pittsburgh largest employer draws hundreds of protesters over 'Poverty' wages. *Huffington Post*, March 3, 2014.
8. King, M. L. Jr. (1965). Remaining awake through a great revolution. Oberlin, OH: Oberlin College, June 1965. Retrieved March 5, 2018, from http://www2.oberlin.edu/external/EOG/BlackHistoryMonth/MLK/CommAddress.html.
9. Marsico, A. (2014). 10 clergy members arrested during UPMC protest. *Pittsburgh Post-Gazette*, February 27, 2014.
10. Massey, D. (2007). *Categorically unequal: The American stratification system*. New York: Russel Sage Foundation.
11. Niebuhr, R. (1929). *Leaves from the notebook of a tamed cynic*. New York: Harper & Row.
12. Niebuhr, R. (1965). Lessons of the Detroit Experience. *Christian Century*, April 21, 1965.
13. Pope Francis. (2013). Address to Participants in the 38th Conference of the Food and Agriculture Organization of the United Nations. June 20, 2013. Retrieved September 20, 2015, from http://w2.vatican.va/content/francesco/en/speeches/2013/june/documents/papa-francesco_20130620_38-sessione-fao.html.

[22] Martin [8].

14. Smith, R. M. (1997). *Civic ideals: Conflicting visions of citizenship in U.S. history*. New Haven: Yale University Press.
15. United States *Kerner Commission Report of the National Advisory Commission on Civil Disorders*. Washington: U.S. Government Printing Office, 1968.
16. UPMC "UPMC Fast Facts" *World Population Review,* 2018. Retrieved 5 March 2018, from https://www.upmc.com/-/media/upmc/about/facts/documents/fast-facts.pdf.
17. U.S. Census Bureau (2010).
18. World Population Review.Com, 'Buffalo, New York Population' (2017). Retrieved March 5, 2018, from http://worldpopulationreview.com/us-cities/buffalo-population/.
19. World Population Review.Com, 'Cleveland, Ohio Population' (2017). Retrieved March 5, 2018, from http://worldpopulationreview.com/us-cities/cleveland-population/.
20. World Population Review.Com, 'Pittsburgh, Pennsylvania Population' (2017). Retrieved March 5, 2018, from http://worldpopulationreview.com/us-cities/pittsburgh-population/.
21. Zullo, R., & Balingit, M. (2014). Hundreds protest UPMC over wages for service employees. *Pittsburgh Post-Gazette*, March 3, 2014.

R. Drew Smith is Professor of Urban Ministry at Pittsburgh Theological Seminary. He also serves as Co-Convener of the Transatlantic Roundtable on Religion and Race, a transnational network of scholars, religious leaders, and activists concerned with intersections of religion, race, class, and social identity. He has published widely on religion and public life, including nine edited or co-edited books, four edited journal collections, and a forthcoming monograph on black clergy activism. He has also published more than 70 articles and essays in academic journals and mass media platforms. He received a Ph.D. in political science and a Master of Divinity degree from Yale University.

Chapter 14
On Human Dignity and Rights: The Dialectics of Religious and Secular Law in Israel

Pauline Kollontai

Abstract Throughout the history of Judaism some Jews have defended human rights and dignity while other Jews have sought to deny these especially to those who are perceived either to endanger Israel's existence, Jewish continuity, or Jewish control of the land. In the 1948 Declaration of the Founding of the State of Israel (thereafter known as the Declaration of Independence) the values of justice, freedom and peace are identified as being rooted in the traditions of the Hebrew Prophets, and a commitment to the practice of these by the State of Israel is given to ensure complete equality of social and political rights to all its inhabitants irrespective of religion, race, or sex. Based on this clearly articulated commitment one would assume therefore that the principles of human rights and dignity for all those living within Israel was afforded full constitutional status. However, as this discussion shows there is a clash between religious and secular law regarding gender quality and the role and status of women.

Introduction

Throughout the history of Judaism some Jews have defended human rights and dignity while other Jews have sought to deny these especially to those who are perceived either to endanger Israel's existence, Jewish continuity, or Jewish control of the land. In the 1948 Declaration of the Founding of the State of Israel (thereafter known as the Declaration of Independence) the values of justice, freedom and peace are identified as being rooted in the traditions of the Hebrew Prophets, and a commitment to the practice of these by the State of Israel is given with the aim of providing equality of social and political rights to all Israeli citizens irrespective.

In this chapter, I will explore how the core theological affirmations of Judaism express the values and ideas which constitute the contemporary concept of human rights both as ethical and legal systems of thought and practice. The next stage in the discussion will be to examine the political reasons for the adoption of the 1992 Basic Laws and the nature of the opposition to these from Jewish communities and

P. Kollontai (✉)
School of Humanities, York St John University, Lord Mayor's Walk, York YO31 7EX, UK
e-mail: p.kollontai@yorksj.ac.uk

Z. Xie et al. (eds.), *Human Dignity, Human Rights, and Social Justice*,
https://doi.org/10.1007/978-981-15-5081-2_14

organisations. Then using some current examples, the clash between religious and secular law regarding gender equality and the role and status of women will be discussed. The overall aim of the paper is to consider two key issues: How do we manage the contradiction between basic human rights and religious rights which when practised can be an infringement of the Universal principles of human rights? Is there a place for religious courts in any democratic state?

Theological Affirmation of Human Rights and Dignity in the Jewish Tradition

In the Jewish tradition, there exists a set of ethical values concerning human rights and dignity *(kvod habriot)* which is primarily a result of the Torah teaching that human beings are created in the image of God. Respect for this divine image in each person is an essential aspect of preserving and protecting human dignity. Over the centuries there has evolved a legal code intended to enable the practice of these values. The key underpinning principles are justice, peace and compassion. The essentiality of human rights and dignity to Jewish belief and life is expressed in Deuteronomy with an exhortation to, 'Observe them carefully, for this will show your wisdom and understanding to the nations, who will hear about all these decrees and say, 'Surely this great nation is a wise and understanding people' (Deut. 4:6). Jacobs argues that these values are 'deeply rooted in the Jewish consciousness' which are embedded in the daily life of Jews who, he argues, need to recognise, 'the particular difficulties of the modern man trying to live by these values'.[1] These difficulties can be overcome by favouring one ancient interpretation rather than another and by recognising that the application of these values may require a new interpretation:

> There is no monolithic system of Jewish values but a series of complex applications of Jewish truth in which the more subtle distinctions and shades of meaning were debated at length by the best Jewish intellects. Some selective process is necessary because there are in the traditions many contradictory ideas as well as conceptions which have their origins in conditions no longer obtaining.[2]

Jacobs is recognising that the practice of such values has at times been distorted or undermined by religious and political elites throughout the history of biblical and contemporary Israel. Or sometimes the apparent abuse of human dignity and rights has been justified based on Jewish teaching when an individual is considered to have insulted God. Accordingly, if God's honour is desecrated then the individuals who do this are not to be afforded rights and their dignity can be infringed. Here arises a perennial problem with the oxymoronic character of religious teachings which can result in a purely subjective biased interpretation of a given situation and may indeed result in the unjustified violation of an individual's rights and dignity. There is a

---

[1] Jacobs [14, p. 8–9].

[2] Jacobs, *Jewish Values*, p. 9.

significant body of teaching within Judaism to support dignity and rights of all—Jew and non-Jew alike. This centres on the ethical values and legal code enshrined in the command regarding treatment of the neighbour and stranger. The duty to care for and love the stranger is an important aspect of Jewish behaviour, and it is spoken of about thirty-six times in the Hebrew Scriptures. Probably the best known of these teachings is in the Book of Leviticus:

> When a stranger resides with you in your land, you shall not wrong him. The stranger who resides with you shall be to as one of your citizens; you shall love him as yourself, for you were strangers in the land of Egypt: I the Lord am your God (Lev. 19:33–34).

These verses in Leviticus follow on from sections that present fundamental ways of living together, teaching general moral principles about duties the Israelites should have towards others in terms of social and economic responsibilities. Alongside this is the prohibition of hatred and vengeance and the promotion of love of each other. The point where these teachings appear in the Book of Leviticus is important to note. They are located in the teaching about the imitation of God's holiness. A dimension of God's holiness is that is 'stands for the fullness of God's ethical qualities' and therefore the Israelites' treatment of another person with respect and love, is regarded as an expression of how the Israelites imitate God's holiness.[3] These requirements are not meant to be merely of the mind but also embedded within the human heart to produce right action. The underpinning principle is about rights and justice and as Hertz points out, 'The tremendous seriousness with which justice to the stranger is inculcated is seen from the fact, that among the covenant admonitions at Mount Ebal, we read, "Cursed is the man that perverted the justice of the stranger".[4] The importance of not oppressing the stranger and practising justice towards them also appears in several places in the Book of Deuteronomy.

Overall, there are numerous teachings in the Hebrew scriptures of both a legal, ethical, and moral nature aimed at providing a code of behaviour covering all aspects of relations between people. These teachings are encapsulated in the command, 'Thou shalt love thy neighbour as thyself' (Lev. 19:18). The interpretation of this teaching in second century rabbinic thought is given as a warning which if ignored could have serious consequences, 'With a solemn warning was the declaration made, 'Thou shalt love thy neighbour as thyself'. I (God) created him: and if you love him, I am faithful to replay you a good reward; but if you do not love him, I am the Judge to exact a penalty'.[5] Both Rabbi Hillel (110BCE–10CE) and Rabbi Akiba (40–137CE) taught that the fundamental principle of the Torah is the Leviticus commandment, 'Thou shalt love thy neighbour as thyself', known as the Reciprocity Rule.[6] Ben Azzai, a student of Rabbi Akiba, commented on the same commandment and the inherent principle of the reciprocity rule, emphasising the importance of love for all humankind because, 'all human beings are descended from Adam, a common

[3]Cohen [5, p. 223].

[4]Hertz [12, p. 208].

[5]Babylonian Talmud [1].

[6]Finkelstein [8, p. 210].

ancestor which means being bound together by the kinship of a common origin.[7] Azzai's perspective teaches about the importance of love in human relations, the importance of rights and dignity and in accentuating the principle of Divine equality. The reciprocity rule is applied in various ways in Talmudic literature from a general appeal of not being the oppressor to a responsibility of protecting the honour and reputation of others. The command to love your neighbour should be applied across all levels of society, from the individual to the collective, in the public, religious and political spheres in ways that nurture, reflect and respect policies and actions designed to contribute to the well-being of all citizens. It is evident therefore that within Jewish theology and its accompanying *Halakha* (religious law) the recognition of the need to respect rights and treat others with dignity is evident. However, there are times when these teachings in Biblical Israel have been interpreted in ways which result in these principles and values being either totally ignored or in some way violated. In contemporary Israel, identified as a Jewish and democratic state there are areas of society where the rule of traditional patriarchal *Halakha* takes precedence and has authority over and above secular law, concerning personal status, family matters and religious observance, which can result in the violation of dignity and rights particularly in terms of gender and sexual orientation.

The Shaping of Israeli Secular Law on Human Rights

The historical development of secular law in contemporary Israel emerges from a historical and socio-political context in which the three major religious communities (Judaism, Christianity and Islam), in what was known as Palestine until 1948, had autonomy over matters of personal status and family law. This was known as the Ottoman Millett System, implemented during the Ottoman rule of Palestine. Following the British overthrow of the Ottomans in 1917 and its acquiring of the Mandate on Palestine, it was decided to allow the Millett System to continue.[8] In 1948 the leaders of the new state of Israel faced significant disagreement from the Jewish population over what was meant by the Jewish nature of the state, 'whether its identity is and was religious of necessity, or whether it has a non-religious, historic, cultural and political identity'.[9] Regarding the status of religious law Israel's political leaders decided keeping the Millett System to allow Jewish religious law and values to have a presence in both the political and judicial spheres. The result of this decision is that an attitude of deference to *Halakha* has been created in the legal, political spheres and public consciousness concerning issues of personal status and family law. Orthodox Judaism has the dominate role in applying *Halakha* to these areas of everyday life by the *Beth Dins* whose consist only of Orthodox representatives. Non-Orthodox Judaism (Reform, Liberal and Progressive) are not officially recognised

[7] Cohen, *Everyman's Talmud*, p. 225.
[8] Robson [24, pp. 44–74].
[9] Frances [23, p. 195].

in Israel, therefore members of their communities cannot participate in *Beth Dins.* But it appears that the influence of the non-Orthodox Jewish communities, although small in numbers has had some impact as Israeli governments have developed some policies and laws applicable primarily to all other areas of life, except personal status and family law, which have been intended to reflect the secular and democratic nature of the Israeli state and its commitment to rights, and dignity. Since the late 1990s certain aspects of these policies and laws have slowly begun to be used more overtly to try and influence and on occasions challenge decisions of *Beth Dins*.

Enhancing and elevating the status of laws appertaining to human dignity and rights began in the 1980s in the Knesset through work on new legislation dealing with Human Rights. Four Basic Laws were presented, but only two were eventually accepted in 1992. This was *The Basic Law on Freedom and Occupation,* which unfortunately in 1994, 'was drastically amended in favour of the religious parties; and the other was *The Basic Law on Human Dignity and Liberty'*.[10] The passing of the 1992 *Basic Law: Human Dignity and Liberty* was not without its opponents from the Ultra-orthodox and Orthodox Jewish leaders and their communities. This opposition to a comprehensive Bill of Rights, 'is motivated by the persistent fear that the unqualified recognition of fundamental rights to all citizens will seriously affect the Jewish character of the state'.[11]

The overall aim of the *Basic Law: Human Dignity and Liberty* is stated in Sect. 1 as being, 'to protect human dignity and liberty, to establish in Basic Law, the values of the State of Israel as a Jewish and democratic state,' this Law applies to all citizens of Israel, Jews and non-Jews.[12] Despite the failure of passing the other two laws, which most certainly would have had a serious impact on the *Beth Dins,* Judge Aharon Barak, President of the Israeli Supreme Court, commented that the passing of the *Basic Law on Human Dignity and Liberty* in particular was a constitutional revolution, 'Not everyone knows this, but recently a revolution has occurred in Israel. I am speaking of a constitutional revolution, in which the Knesset, as the constitutive branch, enacted *Basic Law: Human Dignity and Freedom,* and *Basic Law: Freedom of Occupation*'.[13] Although Barak and others claimed that a constitutional revolution had occurred, this was only in secular law, not religious law. In his speech Barak points out that:

> The revolution is not one of content so much as of force. From now on, they (*Basic Laws)* bind not only the citizens and residents, and not only the administrative authorities, such as the government and the local authorities. From now on, they bind the Knesset itself as the legislative branch. A Knesset law many no longer infringe the basic rights mentioned, unless it is enacted for a worthy purpose, even then only to the extent necessary, and it fits the values of the state of Israel as a Jewish, democratic state.[14]

[10]Goldberg [10, p. 216].

[11]Englard [7, p. 1927].

[12]Knesset [17, Sect. 1].

[13]Barak [2, p. 83].

[14]Barak, 'A Constitutional Revolution', p. 83.

Note however in Barak's statement the total absence of any reference to these laws being binding on *Beth Dins*. All Jewish residents continue to be subject to mandatory jurisdiction of rabbinical courts in regards to family law and matters of personal status.

It was not only internal pressures which led to the adoption of the Basic Laws in 1992. There was also the international arena where Israel continued to be challenged over aspects of its policies towards Palestinians, Israeli Arabs and Bedouin and was accused of contravene aspects of international human rights law and brought into question whether Israel could be considered a democratic state. In 1991 the Israeli government ratified five major international conventions concerned with various elements of human rights: the 1966 *Covenant on Civil and Political Rights*; the 1966 *Covenant on Economic and Social Rights*; the 1979 *Convention on the Elimination of Discrimination against Women*; and the 1984 *Convention Against Torture and the Convention on the Rights of the Child*. The influence of international human rights was identified by Barak, 'We must draw inspiration from the universal human rights accepted by modern democracies'.[15] Barak argues that if Israel is a signatory of these international agreements then this allows Israel to become more aligned with being a modern democracy. Some members of the Judiciary and Knesset also recognised that, 'the international standards on human rights can also help in interpreting Israel's two Basic Laws concerning human rights,' in effect it could be said that the 1992 Basic Laws, 'had been enacted in fulfilment of the duty under Article 2 (2) of the 1966 international Covenants'.[16] However, it continues to be difficult for aspects of human rights as expressed in international law and reflected in the 1992 Basic Laws to be evidenced in the decisions of *Beth Dins* with regard to women and gender issues in particular.

The Sacrifice of Gender Equality: Religious Law Rules!

According to Raday, despite the fact that providing equality to all Israeli citizens is prominent in the Declaration of the Establishment of the State of Israel, 'The principle of equality has been a withered branch of Israeli law,' and the main reason for this is because there is too much deference in the Israeli legal system to religious values as represented in *Halakha*.[17] A Women's Equal Rights Law was passed in 1951 but two inherent problems exist with this Law. First, this was an ordinary statute which could had no effect on the decisions of *Beth Dins*. Second, the content of the law had been constructed in such a way as not to give equality to women especially on marriage and divorce, 'The Law expressly excluded marriage and divorce laws from the scope of its guarantee of equal treatment of women'.[18] As mentioned above, until 1992

[15]Ibid., p. 84.
[16]Benvenisti [3, p. 148].
[17]Raday, 'Religion, Multi-culturalism and Equality', p. 193.
[18]Ibid., p. 211.

there were no Basic Laws that dealt with the issue of human rights and dignity for all. Of course, these principles existed in the Israeli legal system but their enactment was based on ordinary legislation and case law. With the passing of the 1992 Basic Laws these principles were afforded 'constitutional' status having been passed by the highest Israeli political body: the Knesset. The adoption of two basic laws in 1992: (i) Freedom of Occupation and (ii) Human Dignity and Freedom has been important in raising the profile and importance of human rights to be acknowledged and adhered to. But specific areas of Israeli Jewish life (such as marriage, divorce, status and roles of women in the private and public spheres), referred to as personal and family law, remain with *Beth Dins* who continue to have primary jurisdiction on these areas using a traditional interpretation of *Halakha.* With the passing of the two 1992 Basic Laws the Israeli Supreme Court has had a stronger platform to challenge, but not overturn, *Beth Din* decisions which are generally in opposition to the principles and values of the 1992 Basic Laws. A key area of conflict between these two legal systems revolves around the issues of gender equality with regards to the status, role, and rights of women in both the public and private spheres. This conflict arises because most *Beth Dins* represent interpretations of *Halakha* that reflect a patriarchal hierarchy in which *Halakha* has been historically formed, whereas the secular courts aim to implement a legal system that reflects the State of Israel's commitment to being a democracy but at the same time, a Jewish state.

In Sect. 2 of the *Basic Law: Human Dignity and Liberty* it states, 'There shall be no violation of the life, body or dignity of any person as such'.[19] It is the implementation of this aspect of the Law however that is normally a problem when put alongside *Halakhic* principles and rulings made by *Beth Dins* on matters that deal with the role and status of Jewish women both in the public and private spheres. Sections 8 and 11 of this Law seems to perpetuate this difficult situation because it states, 'There shall be no violation of rights under this Basic Law except by a law befitting the values of the State of Israel, enacted for a proper purpose, and to an extent no greater than is required; All government authorities are bound to respect the rights under the Basic Law'.[20] The reference in Sect. 8 that only a law which befits values of the Israeli State can violate any of the rights identified in the Basic Law would appear to have provided a compromise with the decisions and rulings of the *Beth Dins,* because for traditional observant Jewish leaders and their communities, the strict application of *Halakha* is key to maintaining the Jewish nature of Israel and ensure the survival and continuity of the Jewish people. The fact that it is only government and secular authorities are 'bound to respect the rights under this Basic Law,' but *Beth Dins* and their Rabbinic judges are above aspects of this law when applied to certain areas of personal status and family law. To illustrate this point two examples will be discussed to demonstrate the nature of the violations, the reasoning for such judgements, and the extent to which traditional patriarchal use and interpretation

[19]Israeli Knesset, *Basic Law: Human Dignity and Liberty*, Sect.2.

[20]Israeli Knesset, *Basic Law: Human Dignity and Liberty,* Sects. 8 and 11.

of *Halakha* contradicts the basic and fundamental values of Judaism, which Justice Aharon Barak speaking referred to as, '…the values of love of humanity, sanctity of life, social justice, doing what is good and just, protecting human dignity'.[21]

Religious Patriarchy and the Slowness of Reform

According to an Israeli government report submitted to the United Nations in 2015 on gender equality opportunities it showed that the number of women in key roles in political, economic and social spheres has risen. For example: '50% of Israeli judges are women; 25% of Supreme Court judges are women, more women are in the Knesset, but the number of female ministers is still inadequate'.[22] A more critical review of the same government report appeared in the *Times of Israel* which described the report as showing 'much talk, but little progress', had been made, 'Despite initiatives to promote gender equality, Israeli women still face discrimination in nearly every aspect of life'.[23] This is despite over fifty initiatives passed by the Knesset between 2010 and 2014 intended to promote gender equality and empower women in areas of education and employment. Although progress remains slow as regards closing the opportunity gap for women in certain levels of employment and equality in salaries there has been a concerted effort by government and the judiciary since the latter part of the 20th century to rectify this. A judicial principle of equality has been developed by the High Court of Justice, and according to Raday there has been a definite lessening of the impact and influence of religious norms in the public sphere but the clash with religious personal law continues in the private sphere particularly in the lives of religious observant Orthodox and Ultra-Orthodox Jewish women.[24] The two examples which follow show the continuing influence and power of traditional Jewish legal norms as regards rights and dignity for women.

Example 1: Controlling women in marital and sexual relations

The infringement of gender equality within the family sphere centres around the issues of marriage and divorce. There is no civil marriage available in Israel. Therefore, to marry in Israel and have it recognised by the dominant Orthodox religious establishment means it must be a religious ceremony. Marriage between a Jew and a non-Jew cannot take place under religious law and gay people cannot marry. There is also no civil divorce available, the only option available is to apply to the *Beth Dins* for a *Get* (Bill of Divorce). This often causes significant difficulty for many women as under religious law a *Get* can only be legally initiated and given by a man. Sometimes a husband will demand a large financial package from his wife before agreeing to a divorce. There are cases in Israel of this practice which can be termed

[21] Barak, 'A Constitutional Revolution', p. 84.

[22] Eichner [6].

[23] Prince [21].

[24] Raday [22, p. 23].

none other than financial blackmail. One recent example is of a woman's parents who paid $1000,000 to their son-in-law for him to agree to issue a *Get*.[25] In cases where a man refuses his wife a divorce the woman either must continue in the marriage or she becomes *'agunah'* a chained woman, she and her husband no longer live together.

The status of *'agunah'* means that a woman is unable to remarry or have a sexual relationship with another man, such relationships are classed as adulterous and any children born from such a relationship are considered *mamzer* (bastard) who are not recognised by the Jewish authorities as being Jewish. But the husband who refuses a *Get* can have sexual relationships and this is not consider adulterous. Also, if a woman refuses a divorce from her husband then this refusal can be overturned by the *Beth Dins*. However, *Beth Dins* also have the ability to impose sanctions on a man who refuses to issue a *Get* but, 'they are generally reluctant to do so'.[26] These sanctions date back to the 12th century, developed by Rabbi Yaakov Ben Meir Tam and are known as 'Rabeinum Tam's Distancing Rules'. In brief, these sanctions centre on the distancing of the husband from his community. This can include not having any financial or business dealings with him, not providing him with hospitality, not paying him a visit if he is sick, not allowing him to be called to read the Torah in synagogue, and not allowing him to say the Mourner's Kaddish. On occasions where women experiencing protracted divorce proceedings have taken their cases to the secular courts because *Beth Dins* appear reluctant or unable to apply or enforce sanctions, then Israel's Supreme Court (ISC) have ruled in some cases, 'that the Rabbinical courts in Israel should act in light of the constitutional principles in the 1992 *Basic Law: Human Dignity and Freedom'*, thereby urging sanctions to be applied.[27] An example occurred in February 2017, where seven members of the ISC, considered two cases whereby two husbands had refused to issue a *Gett* for over five years and had left Israel. The cases had come to the ISC because both husbands were challenging the sanctions decided by the *Beth Dins*, on grounds that the Medieval Jewish code of sanctions, '…are not explicitly authorized under Israeli law and are not enforceable by state authorities, therefore these could not be recommended by *Beth Dins* as a way to influence Jewish husbands to comply with divorce decisions'.[28] In a five-to-two decision the ISC ruled, 'The rabbinical courts were authorized to recommend application of the RTDR in response to the unlawful behaviour of the petitioners and their refusal to give their wives a *Get* in violation of the judicial decisions requiring them to do so'.[29] The court's decision received significant media coverage, and on the surface it would seem that this example shows that there is some evidence of a growing awareness and dialogue on the plight of *agunot*. Justice Rubenstein noted in his ruling decision that more needed to be done to help such women. However, he also points out, '…although the RTDR are unenforceable, there

[25]Fournier [9, p. 346].

[26]Kaplan [15, p. 1].

[27]Kaplan, 'Enforcement of Divorce Judgments in Jewish Courts in Israel', p. 4.

[28]Ruth [20, p. 3].

[29]Levush, *Israel: Extrajudicial Sanctions against Husbands*, p. 8.

is no reason why rabbinical courts should not recommend that they be applied'.[30] The key word here is 'unenforceable' because the successful implementation of these sanctions is dependent on the grass-roots Jewish community in complying with the sanctions request.

Looking for an alternative way to deal with the *agunot* phenomena has led some like Susan Weiss, Founder and Director of the Women's Centre for Justice, established in 2004 in Jerusalem, to campaign for civil marriage and divorce in Israel. Writing in 2014 Weiss identifies areas of Israeli society where the fault for the continuing of the *agunot* phenomena lay. First, she criticises *Beth Dins* as being staffed by 'indifferent and inflexible rabbis'. Her solution in this sphere is that, 'Rabbinic courts need to be better able to interpret *Halakha* in a flexible manner in accordance with true Torah values', and if this reform cannot happen in the state-backed *Beth Dins* then she proposes that private courts be set up that are staffed by rabbis who can apply flexible interpretations of *Halakha*.[31] Weiss's second criticism is of the Knesset who she describes as 'indifferent' to the plight of chained women and this should be rectified with the passing of laws which help rabbis to apply more pressure on husbands. But having made criticisms of these two establishments Weiss turns her attention to Israeli citizens who she argues are also to blame, and that the solution is within their hands:

> We have not sufficiently challenged and demanded that our Jewish and democratic state cease coercing all of us to marry in accordance with our respective religious communities in ways that entrap us all in our respective failed patriarchal bargains. This means that we must demand that the state not only allow, but mandate civil marriage and divorce for all its citizens. A democratic state, by definition, cannot coerce religious acts.[32]

Having more 'flexible interpretations' of *Halakha* and the state legislating to allow civil marriage and divorce are yet to be manifest. And whilst there appear to be attempts by some members of judiciary and government who recognise the need for change in trying to influence the decisions of *Beth Dins,* the reality is that some women continue to have the *agunah* status and numbers are not declining.

Example 2: Controlling the presence of women in public places and spaces

In the 1990s religious leaders of the *Haredi* (Ultra-Orthodox) community began pressurising Israel's main bus company to run segregated buses through areas of cities and towns predominantly populated by Ultra-Orthodox Jews. These buses, also known as 'Modesty Buses', require women to sit or stand at the rear of the bus, thereby allowing men to sit at the front and not have any contact with a woman. 'Modesty Bus' supporters of both sexes argue that this is in keeping with Jewish modesty laws. One woman in her 60s expressed her support for these buses, 'I wish all lines were like this. This is about modesty and ideally how things should work in the Land of Israel. Chaos follows when men and women sit near one another'.[33] This is the

---

[30]Rubenstein [26, p. 11].

[31]Weiss[28, p. 1].

[32]Weiss, 'Civil Marriage for the Sake of the Agunot', p. 1.

[33]Kraft [18, p. 1].

view of a very orthodox understanding and interpretation of Jewish teachings which is from an era past, where the dominant mode of teaching, thinking and operating was one where women and men are considered to be equal in the sight of God, but both have different roles and responsibilities in public and private life which is where gender inequality has developed. On this reasoning has been constructed both religious, political and legal paradigms which have violated the rights and dignity of women. Whilst people have a right to hold such opinions, such views are seriously problematic when these are the rule of law for people who would not support these opinions or practice these expressions of Judaism.

From 1994–2011 over one hundred and fifty gender segregated buses ran in various parts of Israel. There are instances where women who refused to observe such segregation, both orthodox and non-orthodox Jewish women, faced verbal and physical violence from male passengers. Two examples illustrate this, one which took place on a non-segregated bus. First is the example in July 2004 of an American-Israeli novelist Naomi Ragen who, 'unintentionally boarded a mehadrin bus toward her home in Ramot and was physically threatened for refusing to give up her seat and move to the back of the bus'.[34] The second example occurred in 2006 on a non-segregated bus where an American Jewish woman, Miriam Shear, was on her way to pray at the Western Wall in Jerusalem when she was verbally and physically attacked by a group of ultra-Orthodox men for sitting at the front of the bus and refusing to go to the back.[35]

Lobbying of the Israeli judiciary and the government by groups and individuals has taken place since the mid-1990s over such incidents. In 2008 the Orthodox American-Israeli novelist Naomi Ragen and the Reform Jewish Israel Religious Action Center, brought a petition to the High Court of Justice to at least reduce the number of segregated buses and prevent men and women from being forced to sit separately. The initial response to this Petition led Israel's High Court of Justice (IHCJ) to set up the Langer Committee in 2009 to make a detailed investigation. The Langer Committee recommendations proposed that all signs outside and inside buses declaring that they were gender-segregated should be removed and that drivers did not have the right to tell women where to sit, and women who choose to sit at the back of the bus would do this voluntary. The recommendations were accepted by the IHCJ in 2011, and a ruling was issued that gender-segregated buses were unlawful, they could only be operated on a voluntary basis.[36] Justices Rubenstein, Joubran and Dangzier stated in their decision, 'Coercing segregation arrangements against women's will and often with verbal violence and beyond is a severe violation of equality and dignity that cannot be permitted, including on the criminal law level'.[37] However, the ruling did not include stopping the practice that women still had to enter via the back door of the bus.

---

[34] Yoaz [29, p. 1].

[35] Berman [4, p. 1].

[36] Izenberg and Mandel [13, p. 1].

[37] Rubenstein, et al., [25, p. 30].

Following the court's decision buses were no longer marked as gender-segregated but reports of verbal and physical abuse continued of women who tried to sit at the front of buses. Tensions within Israeli society spilled over into demonstrations and protests in some Israeli towns and cities during 2011. The issue of segregated buses became a springboard for protests over other areas of gender segregation present in society, such as in schools and for public prayers at the Western Wall in Jerusalem. Concern over these tensions led a prominent Orthodox leader, Rabbi Eliezer Melamed, Head of the Yeshivat Har Bracha, to publicly condemn gender segregation on public buses saying that such policies, '...destroy the foundations of the Torah', pointing out that gender segregation is only appropriate when performing 'public acts' and he considered riding a bus was a 'private act'.[38] His reasoning centres on the interpretation of Jewish law and he saw no need to create new modesty laws. The IHCJ reviewed voluntary gender-segregation on buses again in 2012 and decided to extend this for a further year. By 2013 public pressure on the government against this voluntary segregation and over other areas of public life where orthodox religious beliefs were dominating and undermining women's dignity and equality, led the Justice Minister, Tzipi Livni, to announce that a law would be passed making discrimination against women in public places and public services illegal.[39] One of the key players in pushing for such a law to be passed was the attorney general, Yehuda Weinstein, who called on public agencies to, 'act fast, efficiently and decisively in applying the law....the continuance of behavior which prevents women from receiving public services with equal conditions should be subject to criminal prosecution'.[40] An assessment of the extent of the impact of this law is yet to be fully done across the various areas of public life. On the positive side there is the fact that gender-segregated buses can no longer officially run, of course this does not mean that some women will continue to adhere to the demands of some orthodox men either because they agree with this or because they are fearful. The government continues to rule against segregation of women. In 2016, after decades of campaigning by various groups, the government ruled that a space would be allocated at the Western Wall where both men and women can pray together. This is in addition to the traditional spaces of gender separation at the wall. In this new space women will be allowed to pray aloud, wear a *tallit* (prayer shawl) and use a Torah scroll. But progress on this is not without its problems as incidents have occurred when groups of Orthodox men and women try to disrupt worship of women even in this new space for prayer. But one of the areas which has not been affected at all by the anti-segregation law is state-run religious schools which continue to segregate boys and girls.

[38]Levinson [19, p. 1].

[39]Heller [11, p. 1].

[40]Rudoren[27, p. 1].

Conclusion

The interplay between religious law and the principle of rights and dignity as understood in secular terms is complex and fraught with sensitivities and difficulties. How can a balance be achieved between religious law, as prescribed and interpreted based on a legal set of norms which originated in a predominantly patriarchal culture, and the norms and values of dignity and equality which has evolved as part of the character of a modern democratic state?

In Israel the Jewish voices of opposition are present but their numerical presence in society and in the political sphere are small compared with the Orthodox Jewish community's presence. However, in the last decade certainly the voices of opposition appear to be having some impact as seen in the example of recent laws passed regarding the outlawing of segregation of women in public places and spaces. This would suggest that there is a way in which religious law can have a role to play in Israel if the interpretation of that law is contextualised in the secular notion of dignity and rights, which in essence was partly shaped by religious values and principles. Whilst the reform of *Beth Dins* might seem a solution, this will be very problematic, and it could result in the state being accused of denying religious freedom for those citizens who live according to Orthodox values. Instead perhaps it is the promotion of the importance of having 'critical legal pluralism,' which according to Kleinhans and Macdonald, '…imagines legal subjects as "law inventing" and not merely "law abiding". Any re-conception of law within a framework of critical legal pluralism is a form of emancipatory prescription'.[41] This would require allowing secular courts to also deal with personal status and family law which would include the introduction of civil marriage and divorce. Overall, the key issue is about providing Israeli citizens with choice. Those aspects of *Halakha* which are interpreted in ways that mitigate against contemporary understanding and practice of rights and dignity need to be clearly shown in public, political, legal and religious discourses as a contradiction and violation of essential Jewish teachings about love and care of each other and more generally disregards the wider issue of social justice for all. So, what is to be done? There is no simple, quick-fit answer to this and changes will require ongoing pressure from Israeli citizens and the wider Jewish diaspora on the government, secular judiciary and Orthodox religious leaders and their communities. But the only way that religious law can exist alongside secular law in a democracy is that all spheres of life are also under the jurisdiction of the secular courts, and a benefit would be that the Orthodox *Beth Dins* undertake enlightened theological reflection and study of perhaps the most essential Jewish teaching: 'Love the neighbour and the stranger as yourself', which in the context of a democratic state includes respecting the dignity and rights of others irrespective of gender.

[41] Kleinhans and Macdonald [16, p. 26].

References

1. Babylonian Talmud. (1981). Book 5: *Tractate Aboth, Derech Eretz-Rabba, Eretz-Zuta, and Baba Kama (First Gate)*, Chapter 5 (L. Michael & Rodkinson, Trans.). http://www.sacred-texts.com/jud/t05/ere04.htm.
2. Barak, A. (1993). *A constitutional revolution: Israel's basic laws*. Yale Faculty Scholarship Series Paper 3697, 1993. Retrieved August 9, 2017, from http://digitalcommons.law.yale.edu/fss_papers/3697.
3. Benvenisti, E. (1994). The influence of international human rights law on the Israeli legal system: Present and future. *Israel Law Review, 28*(1), 136–153.
4. Berman, D. (2006, December 15) Woman beaten on J'lem bus for refusing to move to rear seat. *Haaretz*. Retrieved September 24, 2017, from https://www.haaretz.com/woman-beaten-on-j-lem-bus-for-refusing-to-move-to-rear-seat-1.207251.
5. Cohen, A. (2008). *Everyman's Talmud: The teachings of the Rabbinic Sages*. Hawthorne, CA: BN Publishing.
6. Eichner, I. (2015, March 11). Israel report to UN on gender equality shows progress and deficiencies. *Y Net News*. Retrieved July 7, 2017, from https://www.ynetnews.com/articles/0,7340,L-4635728,00.html.
7. Englard, Izhak. (1999). Human dignity: From antiquity to modern Israel's constitutional framework. *Cardozo Law Review, 21,* 1903–1927.
8. Finkelstein, L. (1969). *Sifrei on deuteronomy*. New York: Jewish Theological Seminary.
9. Fournier, P., McDougal, P., & Lichtsztral, Merissa. (2012). Secular rights and religious wrongs? Family law, religion and women in Israel. *William and Mary Journal of Women and the Law, 18*(2), 333–362.
10. Goldberg, G. (1998). Religious zionism and the framing of a constitution for Israel. *Israel Studies, 3*(1), 211–220.
11. Heller, J. (2013, September 5). Israel to ban gender segregation on public transportation. *Huffington Post*. Retrieved September 8, 2017, from https://www.huffingtonpost.com/2013/05/09/israel-ban-gender-segregation_n_3243781.html.
12. Hertz, J. H. (1936) *Leviticus*. London: Oxford University Press.
13. Izenberg, D., & Mandel, J. (2011, November 6) Court scraps 'Mehadrin' buses. *Jerusalem Post*. Retrieved September 23, 2017 from http://www.jpost.com/National-News/Court-scraps-mehadrin-buses.
14. Jacobs, L. (1960). *Jewish values*. Eugene, OR: Wipf & Stock.
15. Kaplan, Y. S. (2012). Enforcement of divorce judgments in Jewish courts in Israel: The interaction between religious and constitutional law. *Middle East Law and Governance 4*(2012), 1–68.
16. Kleinhans, M.-M., & Macdonald, R. (2014). What is a critical legal pluralism? *Canadian Journal of Law and Society, 12,* 25–46.
17. Knesset.(1992). *Basic Law: Human dignity and liberty*. Retrieved May 20, 2016, from http://www.knesset.gov.il/laws/special/eng/basic3_eng.htm.
18. Kraft, D. (2011, November 13). Growing gender segregation among Israeli haredim seen as repressing women. *Jewish Telegraphic Agency*. Retrieved September 20, 2017 from https://www.jta.org/2011/11/13/news-opinion/israel-middle-east/growing-gender-segregation-among-israeli-haredim-seen-as-repressing-women.
19. Levinson, C. (2011, December 28). Top Israeli rabbi: Gender segregated buses go against Jewish law. *Haaretz*. Retrieved October 2, 2017, from https://www.haaretz.com/israel-news/top-israeli-rabbi-gender-segregated-buses-go-against-jewsih-law-1.404200.
20. Levush, R. (2017, May). Israel: Extrajudicial sanctions against husbands noncompliant with rabbinical divorce rulings. *Report of the global legal research centre*, Washington D. C. Retrieved September 24, 2017, from https://www.loc.gov/law/help/divorce-rulings/israel-divorce-rulings.pdf.

21. Prince, C. J. (2015, March 19). Israel's report to UN on women shows much talk, little progress. *Times of Israel*. Retrieved September 10, 2017, from https://www.timesofisrael.com/israels-report-to-un-on-women-shows-much-talk-little-progress/.
22. Raday, F. (2005). A free people in our land: Gender equality in a Jewish state. In *Free People in Our Land: Israeli Democracy and Pluralism*, edited by Yuval Karniel, Israeli Ministry of Foreign Affairs Report. Retrieved August 21, 2017, from http://www.mfa.gov.il/MFA_Graphics/MFA%20Gallery/Documents/A%20Free%20People%20in%20our%20Land.pdf.
23. Raday, F. (1996). Religion, multi-culturalism and equality: The Israeli case. In D. Yoram & T. Mala (Eds.), *Israel yearbook on human rights* (Vol. 25, pp.193–241). Netherlands: Brill.
24. Robson, L. (2011). *Colonialism and Christianity in mandate Palestine*. Austin: University of Texas Press.
25. Rubenstein, E., Jouban, S. & Danziger, Y. (2011, January 6). *Ragen v Ministry Transport*, Verdict of the High Court of Justice, HCJ 746/07, (in Hebrew only).Retrieved October 4, 2017 from http://elyon1.court.gov.il/files/07/460/007/t38/07007460.t38.pdf.
26. Rubenstein, E.(2017, February 28). *Anonymous and Gez v. Great Rabbinical Court in Jerusalem*, HCJ 5185/13. Verdict of High Court of Justice. Retrieved August 2, 2017, from http://elyon1.court.gov.il/files/13/850/051/t36/13051850.t36.pdf.
27. Rudoren, J. (2013, May 8). Israel moves to end gender segregation in public spaces. *New York Times*. Retrieved October 12, 2017, from http://www.nytimes.com/2013/05/09/world/middleeast/israel-moves-to-end-gender-segregation-in-public-spaces.html.
28. Weiss, S. (2014, March 12). Civil marriage for the sake of the agunot. *The Jerusalem Post*. Retrieved August 2, 2017, from http://www.jpost.com/Opinion/Op-Ed-Contributors/Civil-marriage-for-the-sake-of-agunot-345204.
29. Yoaz, Y. (2008, January 14). Court to hear petition against segregation of sexes on buses. *Haaretz*. Retrieved September 30, 2017, from https://www.haaretz.com/news/court-to-hear-petition-against-segregation-of-sexes-on-buses-1.237185.

Pauline Kollontai is Professor of Higher Education in Theology and Religious Studies in the School of Humanities at York St John University, UK. She has published in journals and been invited to contribute chapters for several edited books. She has co-edited a number of books, which include: *Peace and Reconciliation: In Search of a Shared Identity* (Ashgate, 2008); *Religion Creating Cultures of Peace*, Vols. II & III (Nanumsa, 2012); and *Mediating Peace: Reconciliation through Visual Art, Music and Film* (Cambridge Scholars Press, 2015); and *The Role of Religion in Peacebuilding: Crossing the Boundaries of Prejudice and Distrust* (Jessica Kingsley Publishers 2018). She is one of three series editors for a new book series published by Routledge: *Religion Matters: On the Significance of Religion in Global Issues*. In 2019 she was appointed as a resident member of the 2019 International Spring Seminar on Religion and Violence at the Centre of Theological Inquiry, Princeton, USA.

Concluding Remarks: Continuing Global Dialogue

The theme of human dignity, human rights and social justice has been a major concern for the scholars of various disciplines especially in the context of secularism, changing socio-political and economic dynamics, and the rise of religious fundamentalisms in various parts of the world. In recent years, Chinese and Confucian concepts of social justice have been extensively discussed both in academia and in the context of socio-political practical arrangements. The distinctive approach of this volume is the conversation between Chinese scholars and western theologians on the topic of human dignity, human rights and social justice in the public sphere. Scholars of Confucianism, religious studies, theology, political science, international politics, and sociology from China and the West have contributed to this volume. Many of the scholars have an academic background from more than one discipline, and some of them are interested in religious issues even though their research areas are within branches of the social sciences. This creates a dynamic and on-going conversation between Chinese and western contexts and also between various academic disciplines. The volume covers some critical aspects of the main topic from both Chinese and western perspectives and also by interacting between the two socio-cultural and religious traditions. The critical aspects include: the philosophical, religious, political resources of human dignity, human rights and social justice; some case studies on the issues of patriotism, the problem of majoritarianism, sexual violence in the Chinese and other contexts in light of Christian, Confucian and other resources; and religious engagements in relation to matters of human dignity, human rights and social justice.

By way of concluding this volume, we would like to contribute some reflections on human dignity, human rights, and social justice by addressing the following question: How can we pursue the common good while, on the one hand, maintaining the freedom and autonomy of individuals, groups and nations, and on the other, protecting vulnerable minorities and the marginalized in a society or nation? We will touch on Western, Hindu, Chinese, and Judeo-Christian thought.

First articulated in the western philosophy as early as Aristotle in his *Politics*, the concept of the common good (or common interest) has been an important concern for western philosophers and political scientists since it provides a framework for the

Z. Xie et al. (eds.), *Human Dignity, Human Rights, and Social Justice*,
https://doi.org/10.1007/978-981-15-5081-2

relationship between the interests of individual and of community.[1] The contribution of John Rawls on the issue of justice and the common good is his challenge to John Stuart Mill's use of a utilitarian concept of justice in which the common good was what suited the majority of the members of a society. Rawls saw "justice as fairness", which was derived by rational choice of individuals in a fair setting resulting in a distributive principle which benefits the less advantaged. His theory is based on two aims: maximizing of the liberty of the individual (provided it does not impinge on others' freedom) and providing disadvantaged people in the society with the best opportunities possible.[2] Rawls made a significant contribution in showing the vital importance of justice as what holds together a decent society. He also affirmed both human equality and diversities, being concerned for the least advantaged. His key argument of fairness as a central component is sharper than notions of righteousness or equality. And with respect to the tensions between freedom and equality, his approach stressed fair process, rather than only the result, which encourages the participation of all individuals and groups in society.

In responding to Rawls, Michael Sandel continues his theme of justice, for which he defines the key issues as maximizing welfare, respecting freedom, and promoting virtue.[3] However, Sandel also insists that a just society should seek and promote the virtue of its citizens. He further argues that moral reflection is not a solitary pursuit but a public endeavor as he sees that we cannot discover the meaning of justice by introspection alone.[4] In support of Alasdair MacIntyre's virtue ethics[5] and in his own pursuit of the "communitarian" concept of justice, Sandel asks how is it possible to acknowledge the moral weight of community while still giving scope to human freedom? He answers this by stressing the vital importance of seeking justice in the light of the common good.[6] The key factor in Sandel's argument for our discussion of social justice and the common good is the inclusion of personal morality, which opens the possibility that religion can play a key role in relation to the building of a good society. The problem of injustice requires not only just social structures but also a change of hearts and change of minds. Sandel asks: "Why should we not bring our moral and religious convictions to bear in public discourse about justice and rights? Why should we separate our identity as citizens from our identity as moral persons more broadly conceived"?[7] He further argues that since moral questions are not separate from the questions of justice and rights, a just society cannot be achieved simply by maximizing utility or by securing freedom of choice. To achieve a just society, we have to reason together about the meaning of the good life to create a public culture hospitable to the disagreements that will inevitably arise not only

[1] Smith [1] and Diggs [2].

[2] Rawls [3].

[3] Sandel [4].

[4] Sandel, *Justice*, pp. 9, 28–29.

[5] MacIntyre [5].

[6] Sandel, *Justice*, p. 220.

[7] Sandel, *Justice*, pp. 244–248.

about the right way to distribute things but about the right way to value things.[8] Sandel's argument that as well as the theoretical pursuit of the concepts of justice and the common good, there must be a moral, ethical, and practical framework for the actualization of these ideals in a contemporary society is important for our discussion.

While western discussion on the concept of the common good focuses on the political systems and theoretical concepts of justice, Indian thinkers have thought more in terms of "tolerance" to accommodate the different communities of India, many of which are defined by faith. Tolerance involves a measure of respect and recognition of the other group.[9] Such respect involves restraint but does not result in "any weakening of certainty, confidence, or commitment to our own beliefs and values".[10] In the early twentieth century, S. Radhakrishnan, the prominent Indian philosopher, challenged Western societies when he portrayed tolerance as a hallmark of Hinduism and a sign of maturity, and insisted that it should be adopted "not as a matter of policy or expediency but as a principle of spiritual life" and a "duty" rather than a "concession". He saw tolerance as based on the belief that "every community has inalienable rights which others should respect", which should result in "equal treatment for others' views."[11] In Indian politics, tolerance has been well described as "at once a pragmatic concept of living together and a philosophic concept of finding truth and goodness in every religion".[12] Radhakrishnan's argument was not only influential at a cultural level, it also contributed to the adoption in independent India of a form of secularism in the context of multi-cultural and multi-religious society where the state is called on to ensure the equal treatment of various different communities.

As we have seen through the discussion of human dignity, human rights and social justice in this volume, in Chinese academia, the search for social justice or social harmony has been examined through a number of disciplines including philosophy, law, political science and sociology. These deal with the problems of poverty, unemployment, inequality, oppression, violence, racism, classism, sexism, and ageism, and particularly in the areas of judicial (criminal justice), education, medicine, and employment. Yet to date there has not been much interaction between scholars of religion and scholars from these other disciplines. Chinese religious traditions provide rich insights to deal with the issue of social justice. It is worth noting that the concept of the common good is far from alien to Chinese philosophy, particularly Confucianism. In particular, Confucian concern regarding the people's socio-economic situation has been expressed in the form of benevolent rule. This does not necessarily provide a framework of social justice as it is understood in modern western political philosophy, but rather the emphasis lies on the sense of the political community as a moral community shown in community bonds and care. In this volume, it is argued that the Confucian concept of justice is mainly focused on socio-economic justice,

---

[8]Sandel, *Justice*, pp. 251–261.

[9]Williams [6].

[10]David Heyd, "Introduction" in Heyd (ed.), *Toleration*, pp. 11–7.

[11]Radhakrishnan [7]; Hinduism and Basham [8]; *Eastern Religions and Western Thought* 2nd edn (Oxford: Oxford University Press, 1940), pp. 313–7.

[12]President's address on the eve of Republic Day, *The Hindu*, 26 Jan 1999.

but that nevertheless, Confucianism provides a "thin concept" of human rights and makes an in-depth reflection on human dignity, which is a foundational concept of human rights.

In Judeo-Christian traditions, the concepts of human dignity, human rights, and social justice are the outcome of the public engagement of religious communities with the problem of social injustice in contemporary societies in light of the tradition. As a result, they have close relations to theological concepts: namely, the dignity of the human being as created in the image of God; solidarity with poor and oppressed on the basis of the prophetic message of justice in the Hebrew Bible; and advocacy for critical inquiry and open debate in the public sphere by utilising wisdom traditions from both Judaism and Christianity. In Christian tradition, the theology of the common good provides key concepts of solidarity and subsidiarity in society to support the dignity of human beings. A number of theological and religious concepts have been discussed in the volume, for example, how the biblical concept of *diakonia* could be utilised to deal with relieving the pain of others, fighting poverty, and promoting equal opportunities, human rights and justice for all. Furthermore, the biblical tradition integrates concepts which in the west are often divided such as love and justice,[13] justice and peace,[14] and justice and righteousness.[15]

This volume contains valuable materials on the topic of human dignity, human rights, and social justice in the form of Chinese and western conversations involving various academic disciplines and religious traditions. As the critical theory of Frankfurt School has challenged us, the understandings of each of these concepts should be translated into the positive transformation of socio-economic systems as well as individuals in both Chinese and western societies. A further challenge will be on-going and in-depth conversations between scholars and practitioners, and also with scholars of Africa, Asia, and Latin America.

References

1. Smith, T. W. (1999). Aristotle on the condition for and limits of the common good. *American Political Science Review, 93*(3), 296–306.
2. Diggs, B. J. (1973). The common good as reason for political action. *Ethics, 83*(4), 283–293.
3. Rawls, J. (1979). *A theory of justice* (pp. 3–19). Oxford: OUP.
4. Sandel, M. (2009). *Justice: What's the right thing to do?* (pp. 6, 19). New York: Farrar, Straus and Giroux.
5. MacIntyre, Alasdair. (2007). *After virtue*. Chicago: University of Notre Dame Press.
6. Williams, Bernard. (1996). Toleration: An impossible virtue? In David Heyd (Ed.), *Toleration: An elusive virtue* (pp. 18–27). Princeton: Princeton University Press.
7. Radhakrishnan, S. (1927). *The Hindu view of life* (pp. 21–36). New Delhi: Harper Collins.
8. "Hinduism", Basham, A. L. (ed.), *A cultural history of India* (pp. 70–72). Delhi: Oxford University Press

[13]Hosea 12:6.

[14]Psalm 85:10.

[15]Psalm 89:14.

The manufacturer's authorised representative in the EU is Springer Nature Customer Service Centre GmbH, Europaplatz 3, 69115 Heidelberg, Germany. If you have any concerns regarding our products, please contact ProductSafety@springernature.com

Printed and bound by CPI Group (UK) Ltd, Croydon, CR0 4YY
30/09/2026
02225503-0002